HOW TO
AUDITION

Table of Contents

v

ACKNOWLEDGEMENTS

A word of thanks to
Rita Chambers, Linda Francis and Jane Hunt
for their invaluable help in preparing this book.

This book is for:
Jane
Colleen
and
Helen
and
Liz

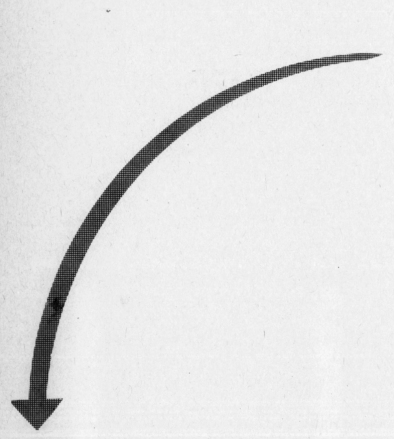

"Amateur or professional, dilettante or devoted disciple of drama, they one and all have a desire to stand up in front of their fellow human beings and attempt to portray something above, beyond, or just plain different from ordinary day to day communications."

Auditioning

You are sitting on a hard metal chair in some hallway or waiting room. Your palms sweat. Your heartbeat has increased by a third. Pangs of fear dit-dat across your chest, down to your stomach and back up to the chest again. Your mouth is dry. Your hands shake, and when you stand your knees tremble. Breath is short. You sweat. Your mind clouds over. For all you know or care, your life could end at that moment, and no one, especially you, would mind too much. As a matter of fact, death might be a blessed relief.

The above is not a Prisoner of War about to undergo interrogation or a patient waiting for a life or death diagnosis or a convict about to be sentenced for a capital crime.

It's you...to a greater or lesser degree...it is you, the actor, or actress... about to go through that agonizing life or death process known as the audition.

You are waiting in the anteroom of a little theatre in Albuquerque. It's eight at night, you've worked all day, raced home, prettied yourself up, dressed in your best looking dress, gulped a hamburger and rushed down to the auditions for the local production of NEVER TOO LATE.

Or maybe you are backstage at the 46th Street Theatre, half a block west of Broadway. Your agent has called. You have an appointment to audition for a new Broadway musical at 2:00. It's now 3:30. You are supposed to go out there and sing a song you've sung a hundred times and suddenly you can't remember a word.

Or, your high school is doing a production of BYE BYE BIRDIE and

1

you are the only one in the world who is just right to play Kim. You've memorized the part, you've practiced a song and even created some dance steps for this audition. So when they call you and you try to walk out on stage, it seems strange to you that your own name which was right on the tip of your tongue a moment ago, suddenly eludes you. Not only that, somehow, both your feet suddenly seem to be left ones.

Or, you are outside a T.V. producer's office at ABC in Hollywood. You've been through three interviews, four readings, God knows how many others have been eliminated along the way, but there, sitting across the office, is one other guy, the only other contender for the lead in this T.V. pilot. Why does he look so tall? And why does he look so much like Cary Grant? And why are you so little and ugly and insignificant and worthless?

Or, you're a seasoned veteran of 23 years "in the business". You're used to your agent setting a deal and giving you the time, place and money, and reporting to work. But suddenly a big one comes along. A juicy part in a major motion picture. "Oh, just one thing," says the boy-genius director as he hands you a script. "You want to look this over a couple of minutes? Then we'll read a little." All your instruments go dead.

Why? Why does any human being submit himself to tortures like those described above?

For money? Yes, that's part of it. For fame? That's part of it too. But basically it is because they want to perform. Amateur or professional, dilettante or devoted disciple of the drama, they one and all have a desire to stand up in front of their fellow human beings and attempt to portray or communicate something above, beyond, or just plain different from ordinary day to day communications.

Why do some people have a desire to do this? The reasons are as varied as the number of people who do it. One actor I know has an almost violent need to be rejected, and so will constantly audition, with just enough of a chip on his shoulder so that, though we like his work, we don't want to have him around. Another—a well-known comedienne from T.V. and the theatre, told me that she underwent years of therapy and finally found that the only praise she got from daddy was when she did a little dance, or sang a little song, and for years and years and years after that she tried to relive those brief shining moments. One actor I know, a very successful one, does it because "it's easier than stealing." Another, "because it's a good way to meet girls." An actress, "because it's a good way to meet boys".

But whatever your reasons seem to be on the surface, I have a feeling there are more basic, more fundamental reasons why people want to go through the kind of agonizingly blissful torture known as acting (a term I'll use at least for now as synonymous with performing). Viola Spolin in her marvelous, invaluable book, *Improvisations for the Theatre*, talks about intuition, and at the same time, gives what I consider to be one of the primary reasons people want to act: "Intuition is often thought to be an endowment or a mystical force enjoyed by the gifted alone. Yet all of us have known moments when the right answer 'just came' or we did 'exactly the right thing without thinking'. Sometimes at such moments usually precipitated by crises, danger or shock, the 'average' person has been known to transcend the limitation of the familiar, courageously enter the arena of the unknown, and release momentary genius within himself." That's not a bad description of what happens to an actor when all systems are go...and not a bad reason to want to act.

Actor, T.V. executive, teacher Darryl Hickman has explored with his students what he calls "energies" which pervade the atmosphere when people interrelate. For example, those energies which fill a room when a potentially violent person bursts in. Or those different energies when a joyous, free individual comes in. Or those energies when an actor and an audience share together one electric moment.

Hickman tells of the vast untapped resources of the mind—energies which have yet to be measured, forces which have yet to be harnessed; powers of thought and feeling which have been investigated only on the very thinnest of surface levels. Witness the interest in ESP, psychic healing, and psychic phenomena in general. The exploration, use and expression of these extraordinary forces is another reason people want to act.

In thinking over this question as to why people want to act—along with the obvious desires for fame and fortune, which can be realized much more easily in other areas of endeavor—something occurs to me which has to do with what Spolin, Hickman, and others, have to say. It occurs to me that we human beings have within us a strong, strong drive to open ourselves up—to be a free and open channel for creative thoughts, ideas and feelings which come from we know not where. Think about the really "good days" you have had when "nothing could go wrong." Know the feeling? I call it the Safeway syndrome, named for a supermarket chain whose stores all feature big sliding glass doors which silently part as you approach, leaving you a clear, unobstructed path to walk through, so you can get on about your business with no extra effort at all. On days when this syndrome is operative, traffic lights change to green as you approach; subway trains appear as if by magic just as you reach the platform; people smile at you for no reason at all; that waitress who always serves up some smart remark with your tuna sandwich tells you to have a nice day; casting directors love you; producers adore you; and directors can't wait to hire you. The trick is, you have really created these energies yourself—within yourself. Others are merely responding. What we must try for, it seems to me, is to make this not an occasional occurrence, but the normal, everyday way of life. Impossible? Not at all.

Its opposite, by the way, just so you get an idea by contrast, is described by Teillard de Chardin in *The Phenomenon of Man*. He tells us that whenever a species on the evolutionary scale develops a shell, it is bound for extinction. In other words, close in and die. Open up and live.

Now, how does this relate to the actor and the audition? It is my belief that the actor, when functioning at his most creative level, is an open channel through which feelings, energies and ideas pour out to be shared with people in an audience. These people then respond to these free-flowing energies themselves by opening up, if only just a little. They feel things more strongly than they usually feel them. How many times have you heard someone describe their feelings at a very moving play or film by saying things like: "I forgot I was in a theatre". Or, "It seemed as if I was only there a couple of minutes, but it was two hours." Better yet, listen to children's descriptions after a theatrical experience. Most children are freer than adults of defense mechanisms, and when they are transported by a theatrical event it's as if their freedom knows no bounds. They actually live in the whale's belly with Geppetto; they actually fly with Peter Pan. They really do believe in fairies. In other words, they are more open, more alive.

Now, what does this make the actor—the really clear, open vital functioning actor? He becomes an ideal, someone we strive to emulate. But more than that, he is a forerunner on the evolutionary scale of the highest reaches of expression and self that man is trying to make. Not a bad way to make a living and not a bad way to spend one's life. This then, in my opinion, is one of the prime causes of anyone's desire to throw themselves at the mercy of this crazy business we call acting—and to go through that trial by fire known as the audition.

Now, in order to act and to achieve any of the above one must, of necessity, have a part to act. This being the case, I now address myself for the rest of this epic to one very basic problem: How does an actor get a job?

"*Don't repeat don't . . . think you can go on stage and give 50% or 75% or 90% of your best. If you can't give it all, don't give at all. Because somehow that halfway effort will come back to haunt you.*"

Casting

One way to get cast is to be a friend of the producer or director or both. This can work in many ways, some good and some not so. There are directors who like to hire friends. Having familiar faces on the set or in the theatre gives them a certain feeling of security. But by the same token there are others who don't. Closeness is threatening to their security, or they feel ill at ease telling a friend what to do.

It is nice to have friends who can give you work. But in the interest of friendship as well as work, find out, in front, how your friends feel about working with friends.

Another way to be cast is, of course, to be seen. A lot of my casting is done from watching performances on T.V., in the movies, or on the stage. For those starting out, this last is the most reachable way to showcase their talents; mostly because the low cost of stage productions allows for the use of less experienced people, and the high cost of films and big stage productions just doesn't.

If you've taken the plunge and gone to New York to work as an actor or actress, the question is how to be seen. I suggest you consult the trade papers: *Variety, Backstage* and *Show Business.* They often carry casting notices and production listings. Also, listen to your fellow actors. They love to talk about readings they've been on, readings they are going to, and parts they are "up for". This is as good a way as any of finding out where things are happening.

One hint of caution: Be sure the play or film you go out on is one in which you really want to be seen. Sometimes, in a desperate attempt to be seen an actor will take part in a show or movie which calls for certain unorthodox public behavior. Without making any moral judgements (since I consider myself eminently unqualified to do so) I only caution you to be sure you want to be seen doing what some scripts or outlines call on you to do. Some actors have found out, much to their horror, that they have lost good parts in big films because when things were not so good, they accepted parts which, to say the least, did not show them off to best advantage. As a maxim I might say, the quick buck porno you do today could cost you that career later on.

Also in New York, if you belong to Actors Equity and want to be seen, look into the Equity Library Theatre. It is a first-rate showcase.

In Los Angeles there is less legit theatre activity than in New York, but all that is changing. There are more and more places for an actor to be seen. The restriction on smaller showcase theatres has been eased by Actors Equity, so there is now more volume, more product. And, there is getting to be an audience which regularly attends the theatre. Proof of this is that Gordon Davidson, Artistic Director of the Mark Taper Forum, has achieved what I once thought was impossible in Los Angeles...flourishing year-round professional theatre which is 70% subscribed each and every season.

One other word here about your work in one of these theatres in New York, Los Angeles, Pismo Beach or wherever you are appearing. If you are cast in a play, really do your job, and do it 100%. This may sound simple, but how many actors have you seen treat non-Broadway productions with a certain amount of disdain, as if they were doing the theatre a favor by just being there? How often have you seen them "dog" a performance because the house was small, because they have a hangover, because they "just don't feel it tonight". How stupid! You never...repeat never know the repercussions of a performance, or who is in the audience, or what casting position someone in the audience might be in six months from now or a year or two. You never know. One sloppy performance seen by a 19-year-old stage manager might come back to him three years later when he has become an assistant director, and when that actor's name is mentioned for a part, a simple raised eyebrow could cost that actor the part. Don't, repeat don't, once more don't think you can go on stage and give 50% or 75% or 90% of your best. If you can't give it all, don't give at all. Because somehow that halfway effort will come back to haunt you.

Another way to get cast is through the auspices of an agent. (If you already have one, skip this section and go on to the next)

The agent, in return for 10% of an actor's salary, theoretically at least, digs up information about who is casting what, where, and when. He sets up auditions and interviews for his clients. He advises producers and directors on casting...and serves generally as the business eyes and ears of the actor.

As there are all kinds of people, so there are all kinds of agents. They range from gentlemen and ladies who have a sense of taste, decency, and genuine care and concern for their clients down to quick-buck operators who could care less.

One word about agents: Too often an actor will get an agent, then sit back and wait for the phone to ring off the hook, and wonder why it doesn't. Here's why: You cannot expect an agent, or anyone else for that matter, to do the work for you. It is up to you to be informed about what's happening, to call your agent with information and ideas. Sometimes, if he has a creative sense, he might resent your "trying to do his job". If so, and if you respect him, allow him that reality, and just pursue those things you know he doesn't have the time or the inclination to cover for you. But otherwise, you must map out your own steps, then consult with your agent about them. If you want to pursue workshop productions, or showcase productions, your agent, since he will get nothing out of it, will probably be less than enthusiastic and energetic in this area, so it is up to you to create this activity for yourself. Don't expect your agent to be as interested in your career as you are, because he has a number of careers to concern himself with, including his own. (Though I must say one time I saw an agent, in New York, Susan Smith by name, become just as excited as her client, when she finally landed that client a really good part. It was a treat for me to see an agent who really cared). Anyhow...what I'm saying is, even though you have a representative, as with all things, what happens to you is determined in the long run by no one but you.

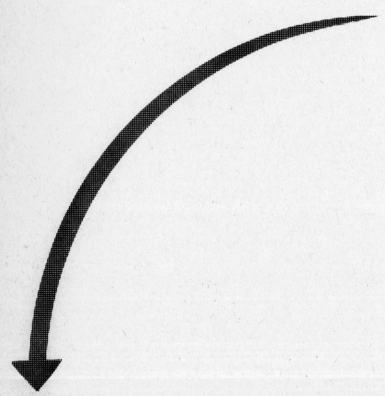

"*Those of us in casting often resent being told how great someone is, especially by that someone. Show us you are great and we love it. Tell us, and we have to wonder how great you really are.*"

Pictures & Resumes

There are two items actors must have when going on interviews and auditions—pictures and resumes.. . . . .

PICTURES

All actors need photographs. If you're a star you need them for publicity, for promotion, and for the delicatessen owner so you get a cut-rate on the salami for the party to which you will invite the producer who might give you your next job so you can remain a star.

If you're not a star, you need pictures to give to agents and casting people to remind them of who you are so they will cast you in bigger and better parts so you will become a star so you can give your picture to the delicatessen owner so you can get a cut-rate on the salami, etc., etc.

What should these pictures look like? Very simple—you! You as you are right now. How often I have interviewed ladies in their mid-forties—very attractive ladies I might add, who then proceed to hand me a picture of a 25-year-old ingenue which they claim is a picture of themselves. Maybe, but themselves 15 or 20 years ago is no help to me now.

The primary purpose of photographs is as a reminder to the casting director or director or producer. After he has seen 40 or 50 or 200 people for a specific part, he often needs to be reminded of who each actor was. For this reason, your pictures must, repeat must, look as you look today—right now.

13

If you grow a moustache, get new pictures with the moustache. If you had long hair in your old pictures and you have it all chopped off, get new pictures with short hair. If you are 20, look 20 in your picture. And if you are 55 look 55. What you are selling and what we need to know and be reminded of is you...not what you would like to be, not what you want others to see you as...but you.

The standard size for theatrical photographs is 8" x 10" and I recommend it be the size for you. I've received 12" x 15" and 18" x 24" pictures, obviously very expensively printed and mounted, but the truth is, the damn things don't fit in any files, so they hang around on the top of file cabinets, or at the bottom of a stack of photos, or leaning against a wall somewhere until finally one of us gets tired of dealing with them and throws them out. The same is true of undersized photos. They usually get lost in a pile of bigger pictures. So, save you and us a lot of hassle and get 8" by 10's".

I suggest also that your pictures be black and white. For one thing the cost of duplicating color is almost prohibitively expensive if you are going to have enough pictures—and I'll deal with what is enough in a moment. Also, I can't think of a time when I've been more disposed to call in an actor or gotten a clearer recall of an actor because I had a color picture in front of me instead of a black and white. That's not to say things won't change, and fantastically inexpensive color pictures will not be available, because I'm sure they will, but at least at this writing color is unnecessary, and if the cost limits the number of prints you have made, it becomes a liability.

The pose? That's a very individual thing, impossible really to generalize on here...but I do suggest you have at least one full-head close-up. Not cropped so we see only your face, but the whole head so we can see your hair and how it frames your face. You might want an even wider angle if you have some special features to display, but for the most part your face and head are what will remind us most of you.

The prints can be either glossy finish or matte finish. I prefer the matte finish, but that's merely a personal preference and since newspapers use glossies, if you want pictures for publicity as well as for getting work, get glossies. Or get some of each. One thing, I suggest you have your name printed on at least some of your pictures, or stamp it or write it on the back yourself. Too often I'll find a picture, the resume somehow is lost, and I have no idea whose interesting face I'm looking at. Don't let this happen. Identify yourself on each and every picture.

Who should take your pictures? I can only say, exercise caution in making your choice. In the first place, find someone whose work you really like. Check with other actors. Look at their pictures and see if they are not only clear and sharp and interesting, but more important do they really look like the actor they represent. Have they captured a kind of essence of that personality? When you find a photographer, then you must thoroughly investigate his prices. Not just the price of the sitting, which can range anywhere from 0 to $500.00; but also the cost of prints; who controls and has possession of the negatives, etc., etc., etc. Don't be shy. Ask questions. Evaluate. Comparison shop. Then make a choice depending on all the data you have accumulated. The point is, you can be careful about the cost of your pictures, but also you must be sure the ones you get will be the best, truest representation of you.

One personal note. As an amateur photographer I've come across a curious phenomenon. If someone really wants their picture taken, it is usually easy to get a good picture of them. Somehow, that flattering angle presents itself, that genuine smile is right there when needed, or that pensive deep look appears just as a small but artistic cloud in the background. But, if someone really does not want their picture taken (even though they might say they want it), it is almost impossible to get a decent shot of them. Something happens which prevents that terrific picture every time. So, be sure when you go for pictures, you've prepared yourself thoroughly...not only your hair and your clothes should be in order, but also your mind and your feelings.

How many pictures do you need? Simple. Figure out how many you think you need, and then get a lot more. You can never have too many. And since the cost finally breaks down into a few cents per photo, don't take a chance on not being remembered for a T.V. series or a part in a film or play. A few cents could help you net thousands. It's worth the gamble. Also, take a photo and resume with you on every, repeat every interview. Even if you are coming back to a production office for the third or fourth time, have the picture and resume with you. Usually, your pictures are filed away as part of a specific project, or maybe as part of one specific day's casting. If you come for a call back, or for a different role, or for a role in another segment or play or whatever, don't rely on us to have your photo and resume at our fingertips. We get thousands. So, always be armed with another one. There may well come a time in your career when you will no longer need one...some stars or well-known character people have achieved that kind of status. You will know instinctively when that day is at hand, but till then, bring pictures. It's important to us and our job, and important to you and yours.

A few don'ts regarding your photographs. Don't use:

a) An instamatic snapshot of yourself taken last summer at Jones Beach and blown up to a grainy and sandy 8" x 10".

b) A picture of yourself taken when you were a glamorous 25 years old, if you now happen to be a glamorous 45 years old.

c) A picture of yourself clean shaven, if you now sport a beard or moustache or both; or a picture of yourself with long hair if you now have short.

d) A production shot of yourself as one of the admirals in a little theatre production of MY SISTER EILEEN. We want to see you as you are now. Not you as a character, and not you posed with others.

e) A picture of yourself with chest bared, a cigarette dangling from your lips, dirt and grime strategically caked on your face, and an automatic rifle gripped in your hands if you happen to be by nature shy, retiring and given to deep sensitive thoughts.

As with everything, there is, I suppose, an exception to the above, and that is what we call a composite—a page with a number of pictures of you in varying attitudes, varying costumes, engaged in varying tasks.

These do serve actors for T.V. commercial interviews and for print work—i.e. stills for advertisements. I must say composites are of no real value to me, and to most of us in theatrical work because they show so many different "yous", I don't know which one is the real one. However, as I say, for commercial purposes, where your face might appear on the screen for a few seconds, they can help a casting director see the possibility of you stretching to fit a certain role.

But, for your basic theatrical photographs, I can't urge you strongly enough to take a look at yourself—look in the mirror and honestly describe what you see. Also look at your attitudes, feelings, the limits you have placed on yourself, your goals and where you think you are in relation to them. Do this, and then have some pictures taken. The photos which will best sell you will emerge. Then if a photographer wants to fake some poses to "make you look good", you can tell him what you think makes you look better—you!

RESUMES

A resume is a history of your life in art. It reduces hundreds of hours of work, sweat, blood, tears, joys and sorrows to a few mimeographed words on a piece of paper.

Resumes serve two basic functions:
1) When you are not present, they tell a producer, director, or casting director about your experience. One actor I cast in a leading role in the following way: I'd seen him audition twice. I liked what I saw, but I wasn't 100% committed. I was glancing at his resume one day and saw that he had worked with a director I admired. I called that director, he did a rave on this actor. That convinced me. The actor got the job. So, a resume can serve as a reference. It can also acquaint us with the kind of experience you've had, i.e. if you've done Shakespeare-in-the-Park and we're casting a classic, we might be more inclined towards you than if you'd done mostly dinner theatres. On the other hand if your training is almost all classical and we are casting a T.V.

situation comedy, we might have some concern about you and your ability to scale down your performance to T.V. size. So, your experience on your resume serves essentially as a guide to us as to what you've done and in what direction your career has headed to date.

2) When you come in for an interview or audition your resume serves as a kind of instant aid to communication. When I am interviewing an actor, I try so hard to find different ways of saying, "What have you done?", but it always comes out sounding like that even if the words are altered. The resume, however, can be a kind of springboard to further discussion. Maybe you have worked some place I have worked, or maybe with someone I know. Maybe you have studied with a teacher I admire. At least it helps to make a conversation seem as if we were starting more in the middle of a relationship than at the very beginning and this can make it much easier for both of us.

What to put into a resume and what to leave out:

First of all a resume should have your name, address, and a phone number where you can be reached. The name alone is not enough, because sometimes, if we need to quickly audition ten actors for a part, we grab ten pictures. If we have trouble finding a phone number of one of the ten, we might just drop his picture in favor of one which has a phone number on it. I'm not saying this happens often, but it happens.

The number can be your home phone. But if you don't want that given out, I'd recommend an answering service number or an agent's number if you have one, because sometimes people with more than business on their mind will use that phone number.

After that, the resume should contain nothing more or less than a brief outline of what you've done, where you've done it, and if appropriate— who you've done it with.

We'll see some examples of resumes—good and bad—in a moment, but first some words about resumes and truth.

A basic rule: Tell the truth on your resume (and elsewhere, too, if you ask me)...Here's why:

a) It feels better. Go on an interview and hand over a resume with some lies on it, and I guarantee a part of you will not be able to be in a full, open, present-time condition on that interview because you will be spending some of that time trying to figure out what to say or do if you are asked about that lie you put on your resume. One actor I interviewed who had some obvious inaccuracies on his resume, later told someone he resented the fact that I asked so many questions, and said he felt as if he was getting the third degree rather than being interviewed as an actor. Well, I will bet he felt that way before he came in to see me because of the lies he felt defensive about on the resume. Let's just look at the situation: He comes to be interviewed by me—at his own request. In order to impress me so I will hire him he hands me a document which contains a number of lies about himself. When I ask him questions about the document, really just in the process of trying to learn about him, he says he feels as if he is getting the third degree. That young man has a problem.

b) You can be caught—and sometimes in the most unusual ways. For example, I was casting for a season of summer stock. In response to a blurb in *Variety*, actors sent me pictures and resumes by the hundreds. I happened to be using my brother's New York apartment as an office. One day, for lack of anything else to do, he was helping me sort out pictures. He happened to come across one on which the actor stated he had played Brick in CAT ON A HOT TIN ROOF at the Hartford Stage Company. As it happens, my brother was one of the founders and for many years the lighting designer for the Hartford Stage Company. He had never heard of this young man, and was none too happy about the fact that someone whose work he didn't know was passing himself off as having worked at this theatre, as the theatre's reputation often relates directly to the actors who have worked there. He called the actor (who at least had the sense to put his phone number on the resume), asked him about his credits, and when the actor repeated his fictitious Hartford credit my brother told him point blank he was lying. The actor stammered, stuttered, even blushed over the phone, if that's possible, finally admitted his error, and apologized profusely. I suspect, or rather I hope he will not make the same mistake again.

    c) Tell the truth because sometimes casting people want new, unusual faces, so in these circumstances an overcrowded resume can be a handicap.

    d) Tell the truth because the purpose of the resume is to present as true a portrait of you as you can. If your resume looks to you as if you don't have enough experience, go out and get more experience.

Let me suggest that whatever you've done don't make an over-long resume. It can often have a reverse effect. Take this one for example:

ROBERT FOSTER

ADDRESS: 3786 Amalfi Drive

HEIGHT: 6'1"
WEIGHT: 180 lbs.
HAIR: Brown
EYES: Brown

TELEPHONE: (516) 483-8215

Educational Background: B.F.A. Degree Central City College

Special Studies: U.S. School of Performing Arts

Skills:Acting-Fred Conway. Ballet-Lisa Thomas. Dialects-Dennis Barner. Fencing-Henry Reilly. Mime-Rita Rogers, Bob Fielder. Theatre Dance-Jack Bright. Voice-Joan Von Stahl.

Instruments: Flute, Guitar, Harmonica

TRAGEDY

Diomedes	ANTONY AND CLEOPATRA	Shakespeare Festival Traverse City, Michigan.
Spurio	REVENGER'S TRAGEDY	Shakespeare Festival Traverse City, Michigan.

Duke of Venice	OTHELLO	Shakespeare Festival Dundee, Ill.
Montono	OTHELLO	Shakespeare Festival Dundee, Ill.
Iago	OTHELLO	Central City University
Henry VI	HENRY VI	Central City University
Horatio	HAMLET	San Marino Valley College

DRAMA

Uve Sievers	THE PHYSICISTS	Eagle Rock Theatre
First Patrician	CALIGULA	Eagle Rock Theatre
Jamie Tyrone	LONG DAY'S JOURNEY INTO NIGHT	Glendale Theatre
Cardinal Richelieu	THE DEVILS	Glendale Theatre
Bontemps	THE DEVILS	Glendale Theatre

COMEDY

Puck	MIDSUMMER NIGHT'S DREAM	Central City College
Lysander	MIDSUMMER NIGHT'S DREAM	Central City College
Newsman	LAST TO GO	Central City College
Solinus, Duke of Ephesus	COMEDY OF ERRORS	Shakespeare Festival Dundee, Illinois
Balthazar	COMEDY OF ERRORS	Shakespeare Festival Dundee, Illinois
Assistant to Pinch	COMEDY OF ERRORS	Shakespeare Festival Dundee, Illinois
Second Huntsman	TAMING OF THE SHREW	Shakespeare Festival Dundee, Illinois
Nathanial	TAMING OF THE SHREW	Shakespeare Festival Dundee, Illinois
Theseus	MIDSUMMER NIGHT'S DREAM	Glendale Theatre
Father Jack	JACK OR THE SUBMISSION	Glendale Theatre
Wyatt Earp	THE GREAT AMERICAN DESERT	Glendale Theatre
David Williams	WHO WAS THAT LADY I SAW YOU WITH	Oxnard Civic Theatre

Bo Decker	BUS STOP	Valley College
Lomov	THE MARRIAGE PROPOSAL	Salinas College
Matt Dillon	GO WEST YOUNG FAN	Salinas College

CHILDREN'S THEATRE

George, the Fisherman	THE BELL	Glendale Theatre
Palace Guard	PANG	Glendale Theatre
Dragon	PANG	Glendale Theatre
Bo-Bo Badura	ALI BABA AND THE MAGIC CAVE	Glendale Theatre
Prince Simone	THE UGLY DUCKLING	Valley College

MIME

Mephistopheles	FAUST	Monarch Mime
Huntsman	SWAN LAKE	Canadian Ballet Company
Duke	SWAN LAKE	Canadian Ballet Company
Notary	THE BARBER OF SEVILLE	Oregon Company Tour

Now, about this resume. The first part seems to be fine. Name clear, address and phone number right there. Educational background and skills also listed. But then we get into the actual credits and what do we have? A long, long list of college and community theatre credits, divided up into Tragedy, Drama, Comedy, and Children's Theatre. I get the feeling from this resume that this actor wants us to think he has much more experience than he actually has. It's as if he wants to make up in volume what he lacks in depth. I wonder, for instance, did he play Puck and Lysander in two separate productions of MIDSUMMER NIGHT'S DREAM? Also did he play Montono and Iago in OTHELLO? And so on...without questioning his veracity I wonder perhaps could we be dealing here with scene work he has done in class rather than full parts in full productions. It would seem so. One other thing, the sheer length of the resume makes me suspect a lack of real experience...that perhaps like the Player Queen he doth protest too much. I somehow get a feeling, without really knowing this individual, that perhaps he doesn't feel his experience is extensive enough.

As a matter of fact, though I don't want you to take this next bit of information literally and start throwing away your resumes, an agent once pointed out to me that the more "successful" (and we'll use that much abused word to mean here "active in your profession") you become, the less you need to put on your resume—because you have become more known, and so you assume others know you. Most of you are probably not at this point, as there are very few super-stars these days, but this is applicable when one reaches the third stage of an actor's six stages of life. The full six are as follows—A casting director is speaking:

1) Who the hell is Harry Kellerman?
2) Let's give Harry Kellerman a try.
3) We've got to have Harry Kellerman.
4) Get me a Harry Kellerman type.
5) Whatever happened to Harry Kellerman?
6) Who the hell is Harry Kellerman?

Let's look at a few examples of resumes. We've already seen one that is too long, and obviously contains only amateur credits. Here's one which seems to be inappropriate on any number of counts:

Hello:

My name is George Karp. I am an Actor, Singer, Dancer, Writer, Composer, Instrumentalist, Impressionist, Comedian, and a great entertainer. I would like to take this opportunity to tell you about my resume, and my ability to fulfill major starring roles.

I am 23 years old and from the very beginning of my career, I have been recognized as someone who will someday be a great star.

In 1971, Bobby Green of the U.S.O. saw the spark in me and compared me to a young Paul McCartney. Immediately after this I toured Europe with a U.S.O. Show called "Billy Jo and Me"—a vocal duo. I remember Billy Jo's words when he first saw me perform: "I don't know what the men will think of you, but the nurses will love you." As it turned out everyone loved me.

After that I began to write a new vital music, at least 60 songs which are all extremely fresh and exciting.

Later, I appeared in a musical revue at the Burbank Chamber of Commerce. I was highlighted in this revue, appearing in over half the revues, and spotlighted in several solos—more than any other cast member—including two which were the highpoint and finale of the show.

I placed second in the vocal division of the County Battle of the Singers. At this concert, before a packed audience, I received great cheers and signed autographs backstage.

I next toured the United States with "Smash", a recording group. Although I was not singing on these tours, I was shining perhaps even brighter than anyone else.

I was politely mobbed for an hour after each show by crowds of young teenage girls who asked for my autograph and took pictures of me. The girls were wonderful, we all enjoyed each other and everyone had a great time.

I began my solo career and was enthusiastically received at talent nights in San Francisco night spots.

I study ballet and modern jazz dancing from some of the top professionals in Los Angeles.

Since 1972 I have joined the ABC Agency and have been concentrating upon the total development of my talents: acting, singing, dancing, performing on musical instruments, composing, writing, comedy, and impressions (Teddy Kennedy, John Wayne, and Elvis Presley). I can pick up any impression quickly—almost instantly.

I have composed two lengthy vocal works. Each calls upon my ability to sing, act, dance, and carry the shows alone. People to whom I have shown them have expressed great awe and said that my performances were truly magical.

For one thing the resume is written out. The best resumes are designed so that a quick look will give us an impression of a performer's background and experience. The reason for this is that we in casting usually have stacks of pictures and resumes on our desks. If we are rushed, as we so often are, we want to be able to glance at a picture and resume, then put them in either the call or don't call pile. If the resume is not quickly legible, we often don't have the time to glean all the pearls from it.

For another, this particular resume has, in addition to the facts, a great deal of self-adulation. Such phrases as "...will someday be a great star.", "...60 songs...all extremely fresh and exciting.", "highpoint of the show..." etc. Things such as "I received great cheers and signed autographs backstage" are important perhaps to the young man in question for his memories, but they have no value at all for a casting director. On the contrary, it has the opposite of the intended effect. Those of us in casting often resent being told how great someone is, especially by that someone. Show us you are great and we love it. Tell us, and we have to wonder how great you really are.

The next one, I'd say, is a good example of a beginner's resume.

Mary Chambers

Age: 20   Actress, dancer, singer
Height: 5'2"   Message phone: 876-2100
Hair: Ash blonde
Eyes: Blue-grey

STAGE
Plays for Living—Don Porter, Director (Currently)

Hollywood Center Theatre/ The L.A. Youth Theatre

Los Angeles Drama Festivals

Fairfax High School

West Hollywood Auditorium

The Troupers—at Camp Pendleton and Service Bases

THE FANTASTICKS. . . . . Luisa
YOU'RE A GOOD MAN, CHARLIE BROWN. . . . . Patty
RUMPLESTILTSKIN. . . . . Princess Pettle
WHO THE HELL IS LYNN PERRY? . . . . Dancer
THE STAR SPANGLED GIRL . . . . Sophie
TARTUFFE. . . . . Marianne
MACBETH. . . . . Gentlewoman
CYRANO DE BERGERAC. . . . . .Sister Marthe
BYE, BYE BIRDIE . . . . .Kim
THE WIZARD OF OZ . . . . Dancer
PIRATES OF PENZANCE . . . . Chorus

FILMS AND TELEVISION

Student films for Art Center College
Let's Talk to Teens—KCET Educational T.V. Program

TRAINING

University of Judaism—with Benjamin Zemach
Los Angeles City College
Fairfax High School—with Marilyn Moody
L.A. Youth Theatre—with Gerald Gordon

AWARDS AND HONORS

First place at the 49th annual UCLA Shakespeare Festival—1969

Member of the National Thespian Society

Notice the biggest credit is first. Incidentally, I'd recommend that always. Don't arbitrarily use a chronological system, or a geographical one or whatever...use the biggest guns first, because, sometimes we only glance at resumes, and since we usually start reading from the top—let us see that first. Her credit also includes the name of a known actor which gives an added stamp of professionalism to the "look" of her career. (This is not always necessary or even desirable but where credits are slim it can help). There aren't a lot of credits here, but she has placed them in a very readable, orderly fashion and has spaced them on the page so they assume the look of a beginning-professional's resume.

What follows are two resumes of working actors. Both are in their mid-20's, both are pros. Their resumes reflect this. Note how easy each is to read—how easily one can look to a specific area (such as T.V., film, stage). Union affiliations are clearly indicated (AEA—Actors Equity Association, SAG—Screen Actors Guild, AFTRA—American Federation of Television and Radio Artists). Names and phone numbers are clearly printed. Presenting, two good resumes:

ROBERT DALE

AEA—SAG—AFTRA

PHONE: 340-0186 Height: 6'
SERVICE: 876-0400 Weight: 155
Hair: Black
Eyes: Brown

THEATRE: Broadway—FIDDLER ON THE ROOF-u/s Perchik

Off Broadway— THE BASIC TRAINING OF PAVLO HUMMEL- u/s Pavlo
MIDDLE OF THE NIGHT—Jack
BIG CHARLOTTE—Cafe La Mama
LOVING RELATIONS— Extension Theatre
POSTMORTUM—Assembly Theatre

MOVIES: *The Hot Rock*—Peter Yates
         The Hospital—Arthur Hiller
         The Gang That Couldn't Shoot Straight—James Goldstone
         John and Mary—Peter Yates

TELEVISION: *The Guiding Light*
           Love Is A Many Spléndored Thing
           The Secret Storm

STOCK: OF MICE AND MEN—George
       CAMELOT—Mordred
       WEST SIDE STORY—Bernardo
       WAITING FOR GODOT—Lucky
       AS YOU LIKE IT—Touchstone
       GLASS MENAGERIE—Jim

TRAINING: Acting—Uta Hagen, Stella Adler, Warren Robertson
          Musical Comedy—David Craig
          Dance—Jazz: Luigi, Matt Mattox
              Ballet: Aifredo Corvino
              Modern: Anna Sokolow
              Mime: Juki Arkin
          Speech: Alice Hermes

ABILITIES: Dialects—French, German, English, Cockney, Italian, Spanish, New York, Southern

           Sing, dance. sports, and 1st Trombone in High School Band

HARRIET GREEN

AEA—SAG—AFTRA—AGVA

Contact: APA—Bruce Savan
120 W. 57th
LT1-8860
APA—Hal Gefsky
273-0744

BROADWAY
PLAY IT AGAIN, SAM
(with Woody Allen)

Barbara
Dream Sharon

OFF BROADWAY
THE BALLAD OF JOHNNY POT

Desiree

PRE—BROADWAY
ON A CLEAR DAY
(with Van Johnson)

Flora

STOCK
GOODBYE AGAIN
(with Barry Nelson)

Julie

STAR—SPANGLED GIRL

Sophie

OKLAHOMA!
(with John Raitt)

Ado Annie

SWEET CHARITY
(with Gretchen Wyler)

Rosie

REVUE
DAVID MERRICK IS ALIVE & WELL

Playboy Club, N.Y.C.

WORKSHOP
KING LEAR
(Actors Studio)

Regan

TELEVISION
Kraft Music Hall, Merv Griffin, Tonight Show, M.A.S.H., David Frost Revue

FILM
Going Home (with Robert Mitchum)
Made For Each Other (Renee Taylor)

COMMERCIALS
List upon request

One final note: Be sure to staple, or somehow firmly attach that picture to that resume because we handle so many that if it's paper-clipped on, the clip will undoubtedly get lost and we'll be stuck with a face we like and no phone number, or a list of credits we like and no way of seeing who they belong to. Believe me, it's very disconcerting to come across a picture of a beautiful girl, turn over her resume and see that her claim to fame is the title role in a revival of THE HAIRY APE.

To sum up: A resume is a way of communicating, so make it clear, concise, truthful, interesting...and make it reflect you and your experience. Now let's move on to the basic procedures by which actors get jobs—The Interview and the Audition.

HOW TO GET AN INTERVIEW

HOW TO MAKE AN INTERVIEW WORK FOR YOU

A COMMERCIAL INTERVIEW

A THEATRICAL INTERVIEW

A NEW T.V. SERIES INTERVIEW

A T.V. SERIES OR SOAP ALREADY ON THE AIR

A MOVIE INTERVIEW

A GENERAL INTERVIEW

DOS AND DON'TS FOR INTERVIEWS

The Interview

How To Get An Interview

There are obvious ways such as asking your agent, if you have one, to make an appointment with a particular director or producer for a particular part. But if you are in the position of doing it yourself, there are three ways: writing, phoning, and "making the rounds".

Writing: When contacting a casting office by mail for an interview, always include a picture and resume. To repeat from Chapter 3, be sure the picture looks like you, and the resume is a reasonable facsimile of your work. Write asking for an appointment or for information regarding casting policies. You may or may not receive an answer. If you don't, a phone call is in order and that we'll deal with in a moment.

Be sure your letter is neat. Typing is preferable (though not obligatory). But a sloppy letter indicates a sloppy sender, and that does not interest us.

Be sure your letter states clearly what it is you want to find out. For instance: Are there open interviews and auditions, if so when and how does one apply? If not how does one get an appointment?

If you have something in common, a mutual friend or whatever, mention that in your letter. It could make the difference between a response or none. If you feel negative at all about being put in the position of having to ask for an interview, and you let that spill over on the page, you might as well save the postage, because our first reaction, mine and those I have checked with, is to throw those kinds of letters in the trash because we sense that the sender carries trouble with him. I've received a few letters which state or imply that we don't really care about real talent, or we're concerned with making money and not with people, or we're so exclusive we don't let real actors through our doors. And when I get such a letter, it quickly finds its way to the nearest trash can. Give me good vibes, and I'll give the same to you.

Making rounds: You can "drop in" to the Mark Taper Forum casting office (while I'm there, at any rate) occasionally. Also showcase theatres and little theatres in Los Angeles will often be receptive to an actor coming around to see what's happening, but for the most part "rounds" are not made in Los Angeles.

In New York, rounds are the actor's therapy...his way of feeling he is doing something to further his career. There are different kinds of rounds, and for the most part there is usually nothing to prevent you from dropping in and leaving your picture and resume with a reception-ist, but it will probably not get much further than that. Rounds are not really very valuable for film work in New York, except possibly for the smaller, independent producers since so much of this work is done through agents. The same is true of T.V. work, though there are some independent producers who might welcome a brief visit from you.

Legit rounds and commercial rounds are something else. A "drop in" is not out of line, unless you are specifically discouraged from doing so. When you do make legit rounds, here are a few tips:
a) Be sure your attitude is up and positive. Maybe I can describe what I mean by a negative version. A friend of mine, writer Jerry Devine, was once a kid actor in New York. His mother would send him out on rounds regularly. But since he was scared, no, terrified of going into those producers' offices, he would go up to the door, take a deep breath, open the door, poke his head in, wave at whoever was in the of-fice and say, "Hi! Jerry Devine. Nothin' today, huh?" and close the door again before they could answer. How many of you do your own version of that same thing today in one way or another?

b) Always leave your picture and resume. They are your calling card, your reminder to those people who might be casting.

c) Arm yourself with knowledge as to what the producing office does and what they might be doing in the future. Don't just blunder into a summer stock office wanting to find out if they are casting any Broadway shows.

d) Be aware of their problems. If they are busy, bow out graciously. If they will chat for a moment, do that. But be aware of them and their needs and chances are they will be aware of yours.

Making commercial rounds can be done in New York by stopping in to see commercial producers. They are scattered about the city in of—fices—some huge, some miniscule. Also, commercial casting is handled through commercial agents who free-lance talent to commercial producers. They have files with thousands of pictures categorized as to type. When they get a call from a commercial producer, they go through these pictures trying to fill the need as best they can. Since they do have so many pictures to go through, you will increase your odds with these people by not only sending pictures regularly but also by dropping in on your rounds "just to see what's going on". Again, don't overstay your welcome, but there's nothing wrong with making your presence known on a regular basis.

A last word about rounds. Don't go out because you feel you should. Don't go out if you are feeling bitter, angry, hurt, resentful, mean, ugly, or vicious. (If you are feeling any of those things, I suggest you find out why, any way you can, and then fix whatever it is that causes those feelings). Go out when you are feeling up, positive, joyous, eager and friendly. Those vibes will be transmitted, even if you just poke your head in an office door for a moment. Keep this up and maybe not the first time, or even the second or third, but somewhere along the line you will start a flow of positive vibes which will bring a flow back in your direction. Pollyanna talk? Practice it for a while and see the results. After all, as the man in the joke says, "It couldn't hoit".

The Phone Call: Some people have terrible trouble using a phone to call a casting office. They see the secretary on the other end of the line as a giant guard dog ready to bite off some vital parts if they say the wrong thing. And they fear the rejection of a harsh tone or a phone hung up in their ear.

I can only tell you, on the other end of the line is a person. A person who has his or her own fears and joys, angers and sorrows. Whatever that person says or does is not going to make or break your life. That person is probably not really concerned with you and how you feel, so that any fantasies you have about ruining your career and thus your life by saying the wrong thing, are just that—fantasies. Treat them as a human being and get on with the business at hand. Because that's what this casting thing is—a business, and though it deals basically with people, it is really a very impersonal business. I suggest you treat it as such. Don't think people in a casting office have strong feelings about you one way or another. To them you are another face, voice or body which they will use if it is to their advantage, and not use if it is not—and that is all. Think about that. It may sound cold, but, as a matter of fact, I'd say it is a good thing. It takes that giant personal pressure off the actor, and merely asks that he be himself—his best, most positive self—when he presents himself in person or by phone. Here are a few suggestions to use when phoning for an interview or for casting information:

1) See above regarding your attitude.
2) Don't take it personally if we can't talk to you. We might be very busy. Try again later. If we ask you not to call any more, take a look at your own approach before you condemn us altogether. Could it have been better? If not, fine. Then call the next on your list. If it could be improved, however, figure out how before you call the next place. Ask yourself: a) Were you free and open with whoever you talked to? b) Were you able to listen as well as to talk? c) Were you, in your own way, treating this business as a business, calmly, coolly and maybe with a dash of humor? d) Did you get to the point of your call, deal with that, and get off? If you were not doing the above, practice doing those things on the next call. It may not improve all at once, but if on the next call you take just one step in the right direction—just one step—that is a victory. Then use that as a technique for another similar victory on your next call—and so on. Before you know it, you'll be one terrific caller.
3) Have as much knowledge about what the office is doing as you possibly can. Don't call a network casting office and ask what commercials they are casting. Don't call a commercial production company and ask what dramatic shows they are doing. Find out from trade papers, friends, people on the unemployment line, or wherever, as much as you can, then call. If you want information, simply call and ask for

it. If you are reasonable in your request, you will probably get that information. For example: to call a casting office and to inquire if they have open auditions, and if not how does one best get an audition, is a perfectly sensible thing to do and you will usually get a sensible answer.

4) It will sometimes help (and I don't necessarily recommend this, but only throw it out as a suggestion) to use the name of someone—but only if it is legit. Someone who told you to call, someone who has worked there, someone you and the casting director know in common. As the fat man said after hors d'oeuvre, a little entre doesn't hurt. (Sorry).

5) When you call, be precise as to what you want to know, ask it, and get off. Don't waste the office time or your own.

To sum up: When phoning, be yourself as fully and freely as you can, know what you want, try to get it, then get off.

How To Make An Interview Work For You

First of all, let's define "interview".

Basically it is a chance for casting directors, agents, producers or directors, to get acquainted with actors. That's all. Usually jobs per se are not given out on the basis of an interview. Now it is possible that an interview can lead to a reading or a screen test, but the interview itself is only one preliminary step along the way—the "get acquainted" step. It is important to keep this in mind because too often actors will have very strong feelings about interviews. Negative feelings such as: "I'm talented, and I've proven it, so why should I have to sit here and sell myself to this son-of-a-bitch." Or: "This casting director asks the dumbest questions. I'm smarter than he is, so how come he's in a position 'over' me." Or: "I'm so inexperienced and tongue-tied I know he'll think I'm nothing, and tell me so and humiliate me so much I'll die ." Or: "I've been on so many interviews, if something good doesn't come of this one I'm going to quit the business or kill myself— whichever seems easiest."

Actors carry these and many other similar thoughts and feelings into interviews. No wonder they feel uptight. But think about it. You go on interviews because you seek employment. We see you because we need to cast shows. In order for both these objectives to be met we must first get acquainted. Ipso facto, the interview. That is all there is to it.

First of all, I suggest you think of every interview as being of equal value. This simply means you do the same preparation for a workshop interview that you would do for one at Universal Studios. Why? Because casting people talk a lot, and if this one interview goes well, the man you've talked to might just tell someone else about you. And so your name crops up here and there and before you know it you have a call for another interview. Another reason to prepare for all interviews is that today's little theatre director can be tomorrow's Orson Welles. Another is that you feel 100% better on the interview knowing you have done all you can to make it go well. If you've sloughed it off, that will show somehow in your interview. It may be a subtle thing, but it will show.

How to prepare:
1) I suggest some physical warm-ups before you go out on any interview. Many of you will call this ridiculous, but let me just point out that fifteen or twenty minutes exercising to get the blood flowing, and the mind more alert, the muscles loosened and the body toned, can be invaluable in giving you that extra "up" feeling which might make a difference between your getting the job and not getting it. Let me put it this way: Try it. If it helps you get the job it was certainly worth it, if not you're still a winner because you feel better the rest of the day. Also, do vocal warm-ups. That voice is one of your primary tools, and it should not only be free, it should be toned and ready to obey your commands. Just as a singer can't make beautiful sounds without warming up his vocal instrument, so an actor can't present himself at his best unless what he has to display—his body, voice and presence are tuned up, warmed up, and ready to play.
2) Put yourself in a proper frame of mind. There are any number of ways to do this, and if you reflect on it you will probably know the ones which work best for you. A few I've picked up along the way are as follows: If you find yourself panicking before you go on an interview, ask yourself what is the worst thing that can happen, and write down whatever comes to you, as crazy as what comes to you might seem to be. For example; you might think: "I'm afraid." What's the worst thing that can happen? "The casting director will think I'm worthless." Then what's the worst thing that can happen? "He'll yell at me and tell me to get out and humiliate me." Then what's the worst

thing that can happen? "I'll feel small and insignificant and worthless ." Then what's the worst thing that can happen? "I'll crawl into a hole somewhere and die". Then what's the worst thing that can happen? That's it.

After you've written these phrases down, read them over a few times, giving them all the reality you can, and chances are the emotional weight they carry will begin to diminish, and with it some of the fears about the interview.

Another way to put yourself in a proper frame of mind is to put this interview in its true perspective. It is a job opportunity, not a matter of life and death. Somewhere near where that interview is being held there is probably a hospital. And in that hospital at that very moment there is probably a new life appearing on the scene. Also, there is probably an old life passing on to wherever it is going. These things are important. So is your interview, of course, but how important compared to the others? Try to find a proper perspective.

Try these hints, or find your own, or use ones you already have, but whatever you do, get yourself into a frame of mind where you can show yourself off to best advantage.

One more thing you can do to prepare for that interview is to arm yourself with as much information as to what the interview is about as you possibly can. Since each kind of interview (film, T.V., stage, commercial) differs in what we can learn about it and the way we can learn it, I'll take a little time here to deal with each one separately.

Information for a Commercial Interview:

Find out what the product is. If your agent doesn't know, call the production office before you go on the interview and ask the secretary.

Find out what kind of commercial it will be—film? Tape? Live?

If possible, find out what kind of commercial artistically it will be. Comic? And if so, fully scripted? If not, do they expect the actors to improvise some of the material. Straight? There are different types of straight commercials. There is the spokesman, where a product is displayed and, in effect, sold by a spokesman or spokeswoman. Also, there are the straight situations, such as two ladies meeting over a clothes line, remarking on how sad it is that their neighbor's wash isn't as bright as theirs because she doesn't use Bold or Cheer or whatever-the-hell soap happens to be for sale that day.

On Camera Extra? In which case, you will probably be herded into a room with a number of other actors, then selected according to height, weight, and general appearance. However, if you really want that job, I'd say you prepare for the extra interview just as much as you prepare for that starring role. Somehow those vibes you bring into a room do carry to the one making the selection.

On Camera Part? This can be anything from a silent close-up to a spot where you do nothing but talk for one minute. It can be very reward-ing if you get a commercial which appears nationally over an extended period of time.

Voice Over? Voice overs are just what the name implies, a voice which is heard on T.V. as a picture of a product or event is being shown. It can be as short as one sentence, or as long as the longest commercial. Voice overs are not easy to get, because there are a few men and wo-men in New York and California who specialize in this kind of work and do it brilliantly. But if one does get a start, voice overs can be very lucrative. Casting for voice over: When new voices are desired this is often done by voice tapes. Sometimes, at an interview, a commercial agent will make a short voice tape. But if you really want to get voice over work, you should have a number of professional tapes made. To do this, select five or six different short passages to read—magazine ad copy is a good source for material. Make each one different in mood, style, content, etc. They needn't be longer than 30 seconds each. Re-hearse them well. Then go to a commercial recording studio and rent facilities for half an hour and make an audition tape. When you are satisfied you have your best work on tape, then get too many copies of the tape made so you don't risk losing a job because you don't have a tape to spare. This sounds expensive, and can be, but it is the best way to go about preparing for voice over interviews. Then armed with your tapes, go to agents' offices and commercial producers' offices and leave a tape as a sample of your work just the same as you leave a pic-ture and resume. I know all this is time consuming and, as I said, money consuming, but if you really want to work in this field, and are willing to take the time and make the sacrifices it takes to get established, the rewards can be fantastic.

Information For A Theatrical Interview

Is it for a specific play? If so, which one. Is it published? If so, get a copy and read it...not just once...but enough times so you are familiar with the whole play and not just the part you will be interviewed for. If the play is not published, call the office and without being too much of a bother try to see if you can get a copy of the play to read. If not, see if you can come in early and look at it in the office. If not, find out from the secretary or receptionist what kind of part it is so you have a clue as to how to dress, and what frame of reference you can bring to the interview. Incidentally, in terms of dress, I'd suggest you think of dressing appropriately for the part...which means dressing as you would dress for that part. Not as the character might dress, but as you would dress in that role. There are all kinds of variations on this suggestion... because I've seen terrific Shakespearian interviews given in blue jeans and tattered tee shirts, and terrible ones given by actors who dressed just right, so take the above as a suggestion rather than a rule. Another suggestion or variation on the above would be to think of that character when selecting what you are going to wear and with that in mind, choose what makes you feel most comfortable and most like you.

Also, find out as much as you can about the producer or director who will be interviewing you. What are some of the things they have produced or directed? Maybe you saw one of them, or appeared in a production of one. See if there is a connection. It could make conversation easier.

Information For A New T.V. Series Interview

Same as above regarding plays. If there is a script available, see if your agent can get it for you. If not, (either because he can't or because you have no agent), try to get it yourself, or set it up so you can look at it before the interview. If not, get as much information as possible about the part you're up for from the secretary. If you can't, go knowing you've at least done all you can to get information, which is a kind of comfort in itself.

Information For A T.V.Series or Soap Already On The Air

See as many episodes of the T.V. series or soap opera as you can before you go in. Ask your friends to tell you about episodes you haven't seen. Know the type of show it is—situation comedy, drama, whatever; who some of the production people are; etc., etc. There is nothing worse for me when interviewing an actor, than when he says something like, "Well, I don't really know what you do here, but my agent thought we should get together." My reaction is: "If you don't know what I do, why are you here?" Or, "I'd really like to work here. By the way, what kind of shows do you do?" My reaction is, "Find out. Then see if you do want to work here." On the opposite side of the pole, if you are being interviewed for something on a series you really like, don't hesitate to mention that. Don't be afraid to tell anyone you like their work. We all love to hear it. If someone puts you down for being enthusiastic, that's his problem. Not that you gush and swoon and fall down on the floor about it, but if there is something you like, mention it. It's much better than talking about things you don't like. There is something very unpleasant to me about an actor whose dialogue consists mostly of put downs of the work he has done or is doing and put downs of those he has done it with. I get the feeling that if I should hire him, he'd go around later telling everyone the same things about me.

Information For A Movie Interview

You probably won't have a chance to see a script in advance before an interview for a film, but again, if you can't get a script, ask a secretary if you can come in early and look one over. She might say no, and if so, so be it, but if not, go in early and see what it is you might be there for. Also, films are often based on material from other sources, especially books and plays. So if this is the case, scramble around and find a copy of whatever it is the movie is based on, and read it, get to know it. If there's no time try to find someone who has read it to give you a run-down on what it is about, what style it's done in, who the characters are, where and when it is set, etc., etc. If all else fails and there is no way to get information, again a call as follows to your (hopefully) friendly secretary: "Hi, I'm due for an interview for *THE CREEPING CRUD STRIKES BACK* on Tuesday at 2:00 and I wanted to find out what I can about the part. What age range and what type is she?" And, "How should I dress?"

If the secretary knows and is not overloaded with work, chances are she'll give you the answers you need. Often, for major film casting, your agent will give you these answers. If he doesn't volunteer the information, ask him. If he can't or won't get it, get it yourself, and think about getting another agent.

One problem I'll mention here—a problem common to all beginning film actors. Every time you go on a film interview it seems the question comes up: "Do you have any film on you?" If the answer is yes, fine. But most neophytes are faced with an insoluble dilemma: You have to have film on you to get a job, and you have to get a job to get film on you. Catch 22 all over again. How to solve it? I don't have a pat answer, but I do have one suggestion. If you don't have film on you, don't feel as though that's a crime, or some horrible deficiency. It is not. Sometimes it can even be an asset since we casting people do love to discover fresh faces...no matter what age they may be. So, don't lie and say you do have film when you don't because you might get caught in which case you could lose a chance at a job. Face it, everyone who has ever been on film, star or extra, has had to have that first frame of film shot on them at some time. So you are in the same position they were once in. Nothing more, nothing less, and certainly nothing to be ashamed of.

Information For A General Interview

Some organizations set aside time for their casting people to meet actors with no specific goal in mind, just on a kind of get acquainted basis. I'd suggest when you are getting ready to go out on one of these you do just as much information gathering as if you were up for the lead in a specific film. For instance, if it's a theatre, is there a repertory company or is each show cast separately. Are there other activities beside their regular season...labs, experimental work, play readings, etc. If it's for a T.V. company, what shows do they have on the air, and what shows coming up. (The trade papers will give you some answers to both of these questions). If it's a film company, the same questions would apply. In other words, even if you are going in there on a most preliminary basis, it would behoove you to know as much about the company you are dealing with as possible. For one thing, it helps you to keep a conversation alive, and also it makes whomever you are talking to aware of the fact that you are actively interested. That is very, very important.

So you go on your interview. What actually happens there can not be written down and preserved on paper, because ideally it is not programmed. It is a living, breathing, changing exchange between people which will take on a life of its own depending on the freedom, at easeness, and joy of one or both the participants. Now you can't do anything about the state of mind of the man across the desk, but you can do a lot about your own. I suggest you do all you can. As an aid, here are a few do's and don'ts:

1. Do present you...you in the most positive "up" way you know how. Without faking, or pretending, show the best you at this moment in time. One way to do this is, if you feel "scared," "nervous", "inhibited", or any of those other feelings we've all felt before interviews, is to follow the suggestion on page 38 where you trace what is the worst thing that can happen to its ultimate, writing it down as you do. Then look back over your answers, reading them over enough times so that some of the emotion connected with them and the threatening interview situation fades.

2. When being interviewed, be open enough to gauge the mood and frame of mind of the one who is interviewing you, and then see if you can put your own one step above. This is not a one-upsmanship tactic. It is an attempt by you to bring the tone or "vibes" of the conversation up to a more constructive, positive level. It also can be an attempt by you to help those of us who are doing the interviewing. We might seem sometimes like impenetrable father figures with the power to hire or not—which translated by the subconscious means to allow to live or not—which, of course, is totally invalid to the present situation. But we who are doing the interviewing have the same fears and uncertainties as you. Fears for our jobs, uncertainties about who we are— our masculinity or femininity, our mortality. So without gushing about it, an attitude of being helpful is a good one to bring in with you. You may never display it—and it probably is usually better left as an attitude rather than an action. But it is a good attitude to have toward casting directors and, come to think of it, toward everyone else. Anyhow, if you go into an office and the man is on the phone and ignoring you, or grouchy, or insensitive, or even rude, I don't advocate a huge cheery, "Good morning". For one thing, if he is that bear-like, he might grab you by the seat of the pants and throw you bodily out of the office. No, just gauge his feelings and his state and then place your-

self one positive notch above his, and then see if you can ease him up to your level. It's worth a try, and is certainly better, I'd say, than cowering in the corner, or matching his hostilities with yours. Be more aware of the person who is interviewing you, and less aware of yourself.

3. This may be part of 2 but I'll list it separately, as it has its own value. Listen. Look. See. I've seen actors do a "sincere" number in my office. I've then passed them on the street an hour or so later, started to nod "hello" and realized they didn't even know I was the one they were talking to. I have to conclude they didn't really see me... only what I could do for them. Better you see and hear, and get outside yourself a little.

4. Be prompt. If you have to wait, and you probably will, wait—that is if you want the job.

5. Dress appropriately. This is easy to say but impossible to generalize. I'd say wear what makes you feel best—what makes you feel attractive; what makes you feel free; what helps you to move easily. For David Merrick at Sardi's you might dress differently than for Ellen Stewart at Cafe La Mama...and maybe you wouldn't. I must leave this up to you. But use your sense of yourself to help you determine what to wear. Be open, and the right answer as to what that is will present itself.

Just remember, the outside is often a reflection of what is going on inside. After all, you choose your clothes. Look at them now. Are they dirty or clean? Sloppy or neat? Colorful or drab? Think about it. I've found for me, the clothes I wear...all the outer things of me, reflect me.

6. Bring a picture and resume even if it isn't requested. It's much better to have it and not need it than to need it and not have it. If it isn't asked for, then offer it. All we can do is say no, and we will probably take it gladly. Also remember, it can serve as an ice-breaker— a kick off point for a conversation when we first meet.

7. Have your credits arranged in your head in order of importance so when asked the proverbial "What have you done?" you have an answer. I don't mean learn and deliver by rote a set speech about your credits.

That can sound guarded, and the opposite of spontaneous. Just know the order of things as you would like them to be presented and freely present them that way if asked.

8. Treat secretaries and receptionists as human beings. They are, you know. Besides, though they can't hire or fire you, if you give them a bad time, it's easy for them to leave your name off a call back list, or forget to call you, or lose your picture and resume. But treat them well, and often they will do the same for you. If they don't respond appropriately, let that be their problem.

9. Do your best at every single interview, because you never know when or how the results of that interview will come back to you. If you are called for an interview, and you just barely manage to amble down there, go in, show them as little of yourself as possible and amble out again, you probably won't get the job. If you do happen to be what they need, O.K., but that attitude will back up on you sooner or later and that career will come to a screeching halt and you'll be wondering why. However, if you prepare for each interview as if it was the most important one you've had—and I don't mean get all fearful, I mean take the steps mentioned earlier having to do with preparation—you will reap some results. They may be for this job, maybe not; maybe for a future job; or maybe the results will come from you having set a pattern for yourself which you will be using when that really big job presents itself. There are a number of people I've interviewed who had obviously prepared and were ready and up for the occasion, but who just weren't right for a particular role. But I have since been able to find other parts for them, or refer them to other people I know who are casting. So if you treat every interview as an important one, you'll never know when the results will come in, but they will come in. If you don't, you'll never have the opportunity to find out. Here are a couple of don'ts:

1. Don't go on any interview with a chip on your shoulder, saying "Who does that guy behind that desk think he is, making me wait, making me nervous, making me ill-at-ease, making me talk about myself?" Better you try to like him rather than hate him. If the one you encounter is gruff, unthinking, and seems to want to humiliate actors, he's the one who really needs help, so give it to him, maybe by just a friendly hello, or maybe just by being open and free. Somehow,

somewhere in that closed-off, angry mind, he might get the message: he might even recognize that there is more to life than getting his job done. Maybe not now, maybe not till ten years from now, but it can and does happen. I've encountered a number of people who have had this effect on me...years later.

2. Don't just walk into someone's office even if the door is open if you can see they are busy talking on the phone, talking to someone else, or in the middle of some paper work...wait for them to see you. If they don't, a polite knock is in order.

3. When a secretary shows you in, a handshake, a hello—a decent greeting is in order. If you don't get the desired response, don't then turn the meeting into a "Why don't you treat me right?" session. Just go on about your business.

4. Don't mumble, hide your mouth behind your hand, or speak so softly we can't hear you. If you find yourself doing this, it means that for some reason you don't really want to be heard. It may be because deep down you feel you have nothing to say, or because you are afraid of what you might say. Whatever the reason, if you are doing this, find out why and fix it.

5. Don't be so self-concerned that you get in your own way. So often actors go into interview situations feeling, "Will he like me?" "Will I make a good impression?" "Will I be what he is looking for?" "What if he doesn't like me?" "What if he laughs at me?" "What if he tells me I'm boring and dull and throws me bodily out of the office?"

You see what's happening? It's total concern with "I" and "me" and nothing else. The truth is we casting people, at least most of us, don't really care about the "you" I just described. That is a self-oriented, self-centered "you" which when carried to any extreme at all becomes very destructive. We are rather concerned with the outgoing you, the alive and vital you, the you who sees and hears others, who is interested and attuned to life outside his own shell. Show us that "you" and let the chips fall where they may. If you persist they will sooner or later fall in your direction.

HOW TO AUDITION

WHAT IS AN AUDITION?

CATTLE CALLS

COLD READINGS

PREPARED AUDITIONS

PREPARING THE PREPARED AUDITION

JUST BEFORE THE AUDITION

FINAL PREPARATION

DURING THE AUDITION

AFTER THE AUDITION

The Audition

First of all, let me say that the audition process—that moment when the performer must stand up alone (the key word here), and deliver whatever he has to deliver in order to be hired to act—this process is one every, repeat every performer has had to go through at one time or another. Ask the biggest star. They all had to start somewhere. And chances are they went through the same number of "no's", the same "don't call us, we'll call you", the same indignities which you have suffered.

And it's not just an American phenomenon. I travelled halfway around the world to Australia to direct a musical...staggered off a plane after 26 hours flying time. Jet lag had thrown me into some weird time pattern where I dozed off at noon and woke up ready to go at midnight. My first day there, I was taken to a theatre for auditions. I sat down in "the stalls". There was a bare bulb work light, a stage manager with a script, and a pianist. The stage manager hollered, "Next". A performer came on, blinked in the light and sang his song. We said, "Thank you", and I suddenly realized this was the identical process we have at home, even down to the very same words exchanged. It's true, of course, in England and as far as I know in theatres in most western countries. At some time or other an actor must audition.

How To Get An Audition

The same thoughts on the previous pages regarding how to get an interview, i.e. writing, phoning, and using the auspices of an agent—apply.

One other thought. Consult your unions. Actors Equity on both coasts has audition notices posted on bulletin boards.

Also, check the trade papers.

One tip. Be persistent. Not to the point of obnoxiousness, but to keep up a steady stream of communication with those people who might be holding auditions. Let us know you are out there—not hungry and desperate—just ready and eager to go to work. This applies to each and every one of you. From time to time prominent film actors have called me and said words to the effect that, "Listen, if there's anything there you think I might be right for, please let me know. I want to do a play". So remember, whether star or beginner, wanting to work is no crime.

What Is An Auditon?

Webster defines audition as: "A trial performance to appraise an entertainer's merits". Look at those words: "trial", "appraise". No wonder you get terrified. So much for Webster. What about you? The one onstage in the dark, dusty theatre. A voice says, "O.K. Let's go, please". You fumble, open your script. At your side a short, fat little man with thick glasses also has a script. You realize this is the stage manager—the one you'll be reading with, and he is to play your lover, the man you can't wait to have carry you off and do all kinds of horrible, wonderful things to you.

You get yourself set to read, and suddenly realize you can't see the page because the only light in the place is shining directly in your eyes. You blink, you squint and finally somehow a few words drift into focus. You hear a voice: "All right, baby. That's the way you want it, that's the way I'll give it to you..." Your lover not only speaks in a halting monotone, his esses are startlingly sibilant. But you go on. You begin to gain a little confidence. You remember someone told you once it was important to relate to the other actor during an audition. You look at your lover. His face is buried in the script. The monotone and the esses drone on. But you're making it...not only that you're beginning to feel better about what you're doing...good actually ...as a matter of fact, that last line was terrific...and that little reaction afterwards...why, hell! This is a cinch. Not it's just a matter of... "Thank you". What was that? "Thank you, very much ." A voice from out in the black there somewhere. Saying thank you. But you're not through. You're just getting to the good part. The part where you can really let go. You want to stay now. To finish. But you find yourself, moving off, through the back door and out onto the street—and it's all over. You take a deep breath. You've survived.

But is that all an audition is? A test of your survival? For some it is. But if that's the case with you, I'd say the quality of your audition must suffer accordingly.

Find hope in one thing...the process is the same for everyone. No matter where you go, there is for the actor one moment when he must stand up alone in front of someone else and demonstrate his ability. This is an audition.

In our country, an audition is a procedure whereby two or more people come together to attempt to achieve mutual goals. Nothing more or less. For the producer and director, the audition is a way of getting the right actor for the part. As a director I'd say 80% of my work is done if the audition process is successful—that is if I get that actor who is just right for that role.

For the actor, the audition is the means by which he displays his wares, shows what he can do in relation to a specific role, or series of roles (as in a repertory company).

So basically, devoid of all the emotional factors, the producer wants something—the right actor for the role. The actor wants something— an opportunity to play a role. If these two wants come together and satisfy one another, fine. If not, each has spent some time and then goes on to look elsewhere to satisfy his wants. This is what an audition is—this and nothing more.

But is has become something more to a lot of people. Most producers, directors and casting people treat the audition as the businesslike activity it is...for better or for worse. But a few use it as a tool for acting out their own problems. A few play lord and master. A few laugh at others. A few will be downright brutal.

Still others will make the audition a cold, impersonal and consequently hostile experience because they are "too busy" to waste time with the simple amenities. One actor I know prepared two weeks for a Broadway musical audition, flew from California to New York, found himself on a huge stage singing his song, fluffed a lyric halfway through, and heard that loud voice from the dark yell, "Thank you". He started to explain about the lyric fluff, and again the voice: "Yes, yes. Thank you very much'" And that was that. A minute of someone's time might not only have made that actor feel a lot better, it might have showed that very busy man certain facets of a talented performer who soon after played the lead in a long-running Broadway show.

Still others look at actors as mere cogs in a machine—not human beings at all. And they treat them in the same cold, demanding way they deal with the engine of their Mercedes.

Now...you can be victimized by any of the above, or anyone else for that matter—if you so choose. But there is a big difference between being victimized and allowing someone their reality, and at the same time maintaining your own. When I was studying with director Milton Katselas, he repeated a maxim he had once heard. He said it took him about two years of ruminating for him to finally figure out what it meant to him. It took me about the same time. So, if you have a couple of years to spare, here it is: "You can never be the cause of anything you're not willing to be the effect of". As an example of what this meant, Milton described the days when he was a "gofer" for producer Kermit Bloomgarden in New York. Mr. Bloomgarden would send Milton out for cigars or coffee, errands which Milton greatly resented. He expressed his resentment by taking just as long as he could to carry out a particular order. As a consequence, Milton never progressed beyond the status of gofer as long as he was employed by Mr. B. Cut to a few years later. Milton has changed...grown, and he no longer has the same resentments. As a matter of fact he feels if asked to run down and get cigars he could do so, not only that but do so willingly. That is, he would be willing to be the effect of Mr. Bloomgarden. Not that he would give up his individuality. On the contrary it would be strengthened by the fact that carrying out a simple task would no longer threaten him to the point where he must resent it. So what happens when Milton realizes he has reached this stage? The phone rings. It is Kermit Bloomgarden calling to ask Milton to come over and discuss directing a new play. Milton maintains, and I agree, that that call would never come until Milton's attitude toward Bloomgarden had changed. This same syndrome has proven true in my life time and again. Check yours and see if it applies. Ask yourself if you resent the casting director, director, or producer who wants you to audition for them. If so, ask yourself what might happen if you didn't. No matter how difficult they are to deal with if, instead of getting uptight and defensive, you just said to yourself, "That's their problem", and continued on about the business of auditioning, how successful might you be? Isn't it worth a try?

Which leads us to the area of actors' feelings regarding auditions. And they are many and deep. Here are a few obvious ones we can label:

a) Hostility: Many, correction, most actors have some hostility toward the audition system—and its personification, the person they are auditioning for. Examples are legion, but here are a few. An actor I know who was studying singing, gave one of his first singing auditions for me. In the middle of his song he fumbled a little, then turned to the accompanist and said, in a nasty tone, "No, that's not it. Can't you follow the beat?" Another time, I asked an actor to improvise a little, just anything that came to mind. He looked at me. Suddenly, hatred poured out of him along with such words as, "Look at you sitting there. Who the hell do you think you are judging me? Who gives you the right?" I started to smile. "Look at you," he went on, "that stupid grin on your face. What's so funny? You think it's easy to get up here and do this, you try it sometime instead of sitting there with that self-satisfied look on your face..." And so on. He finished, and acted as if—no, really believed—he was only doing a simple improvisation. What he was really doing was telling me what he thought of me in no uncertain terms. Have you ever felt like that before, during or after an audition? Hmmm?

b) Resentment: This is a slow burning version of the above. It may be the result of many rejections, it may just be an overall feeling the actor, knowingly or unknowingly, carries around all the time. It can take many forms—holding back and not giving your all; sarcastic jibes in the guise of humor; an overall negative or non-enthusiastic attitude. In what ways do you express resentment? Hmmm?

c) Bluff: The "I'll show them a thing or two" approach. This is usually evidenced by a forced heartiness, a "pushed" reading or audition, a facade of stardom or "great actor" which doesn't let us in to see the human being underneath. Have you ever bluffed? Hmmm?

d) But basically, the predominant, or most prevalent negative feeling an actor has during an audition is fear, for it is the real cause of the feelings listed above. I'd say it's time we took a look at this fear. Webster defines fear as: "An unpleasant often strong emotion caused by anticipation or awareness of danger". I have come to know fear as a physical, mental and emotional jolt which serves as a radar-like warning system when we feel our lives are threatened. Since this need is less evident in our day-to-day lives today than it was in the jungle from whence we sprang (though one wonders when one walks down 8th Avenue at night if we have left the jungle, or just recreated it somewhere else), it is worth questioning why this system operates just as strongly as if our lives were being threatened in situations which, if viewed objectively, didn't really threaten our lives at all. O.K. Let's untangle that last sentence. You go into an audition with fear filling your whole being, your nerves strung taut. These are not the normal feelings which accompany a job-seeking situation. These are more appropriate to a life-or-death situation...a real blood-and-guts, live-or-die jungle battle. But it happens in an audition. Why? Because when we do audition—we often feel we are actually laying ourselves open, naked, alone and defenseless to some kind of horrible fate. The feeling of fear is, in my opinion, not a figment of the imagination, but a fear based on reality—a restimulation of past events. Some might call this racial or genetic memory, others would be more specific and say these events actually occurred back in time. However you look at it, this fear which overwhelms the actor is, if traced to its most basic element as I have done many times with students, a very real fear for survival, pure and simple. When placed in that solo spot, alone, we often become literally afraid for our lives on a purely emotional level. Sure, we know intellectually this audition will soon be over, we'll walk out on the street and resume our lives again. But somehow having to prove ourselves, having to do something for someone else with nothing more supporting us than our own talent, voice, body and presence, is often equated with some terrifying lethal result.

Here are a few examples of needless, yet painful audition fears we've all had in one form or another:

1) I am afraid they will say I'm not good enough, and by rejecting me they will reinforce my pattern of failure.

2) I'm afraid of not reinforcing my pattern of failure by being accepted. Take a look at this one. It does become comfortable for us sometimes to have a pattern of failure which we can blame our sorry state on. If we are accepted we can then no longer retreat to this safe place of failure, but must begin to take a step toward self-reliance. This can be frightening enough to make us adopt a crippling fear which can limit and often ruin an audition.

3) I'm afraid of getting the job because I know I'm worthless, and if I get the job, everyone else will know it too.

4) I'm afraid of getting the job because if I do it means I'll have to become an adult, and I'm not ready for that.

5) I'm afraid if I give my all at this audition, I'll uncover feelings of great joy, and if I do that I'll be so disappointed when they go away I could die. (Did you hear that last phrase? If someone feels that way at an audition, no wonder it becomes a life or death situation.)

6) Or, if I give my all at this audition I'm afraid of uncovering great feelings of sorrow because I could start crying and never stop.

7) If I give my all at an auditon, I'm afraid of uncovering great hostilities. I mean I'd probably kill those bastards out there who are putting me on the spot. (Look at the logic here. We blame—to the point of murder—those people who are auditioning us for our predicament, whereas the truth is we put ourselves there. No Nazi guard has stuck a bayonet in our back and said: "You vill audition, und you vill like it". We've volunteered, so we can blame no one for our being in this position but ourselves.)

8) I'm afraid "Daddy" out there with the pad and pencil won't like me. How often do you think of that auditioner as a father figure, judging you, praising or damning you? Loving you, or not loving you.

No wonder you get frightened. Because at the infantile level, the parents' approval means survival. If daddy and mommy like me they feed me and take care of me and I live. If they don't they have the power to not feed me or care for me, and I die. This is a genuine fear to a child. How many of us continue to feel this way to one degree or another when we are called upon to please someone—as in an audition.

Now I have a startling announcement to make. Are you ready? O.K. Here it is: I don't think you need any kind of fear at an audition.

Some nervousness maybe is natural, but the fear that cripples you, that takes you out of present time, that prevents you from really opening up and doing your best work, is what we want to get rid of...and not just for your benefit, but for the benefit of all of us in the theatre because (fanfare please, this is the big number): the less fear, the better the audition; the better the audition, the easier it is to cast; the easier casting becomes, the better the quality of the performance because there are less compromises; the better the quality of the performance, the better the show; and the better the quality of the show, the better it is for the theatre or TV or movies in general; and the better the TV show, movie or play, the more people will want to see more of the same; and the more people want to see more of the same, the more jobs will be available; which means more auditions, which means, better quality, etc., etc.

So, with this glorious goal in mind, let's investigate how to eliminate, (not minimize because that would be settling for something less than the best), unnecessary fears from the audition situation.

1) As we discussed earlier with the interview, one way to take the sting out of this situation is, when you are at home getting ready for an audition and you begin to feel anxious or afraid, ask yourself what is the worst thing that can happen to you.

If you really allow free rein, chances are your fear will be traced somehow to some form of dying since that seems to be our ultimate fear. Now I know this can seem preposterous, and you say to yourself sure I'm nervous as hell but I know I'm not going to die, even though it might feel like it. O.K., but if it feels like it, that means there is something lurking down there in the subconscious which links the audition experience with possible death, which makes it seem that you are literally putting your life on the line. So, as a way of at least temporarily short-circuiting this fear so the audition becomes not a trial at which your life is at stake, but an experience where you can be free and creative and show the very best you have to offer, I'd suggest the method just described above. Write it out, look at it till the immediate emotional impact is gone, then go on about your business. (If it persists, I'd recommend you look into it further in whatever way seems appropriate to you, since in my reality this fear is an unnatural and unnecessary thing and should be gotten rid of permanently.)

Another suggestion: if you have felt these nerves, these damaging fears and concerns during an audition, go home and write down what it was you felt.

Now, I don't want every aspiring actor to go into a deep death-like dive into his psyche and grapple with those fears that pull at us all. What I do want is for actors to see those fears for what they are—unnecessary burdens which hinder true, free-flowing creativity. Of course, there can be that edge of excitement before you go on, those little jolts of extra energy and drive which move you onto the stage with a certain vitality and out-goingness. That you want. What I'm talking about dealing with are those fears which take you out of present time and prevent you from doing your very best.

2)   Another way of easing fear is to get yourself out of the way. By that I mean, get rid of all that concern for self, for me, for I. When we are putting ourselves on the line we sometimes feel as if we can only deal with ourselves and nothing else. We get frightened or overly concerned and close in like a snail retreating into its shell. But, of course, that's the opposite of healthy, especially to an actor whose whole raison d'etre is open and free communication. When you feel that overwhelming self-concern, I suggest you do whatever works best for you. One way I've found is to put myself into the world around me. Here's what I mean. You are going to an audition. You're scared to death. It seems as if your life depends on it. But think about it. All you are going to do is read or test for a part. In the meantime, at that moment a couple on a beach somewhere are making love, someone is having dinner in Sydney while he looks at the harbor. In Hong Kong, an old man is struggling with a rickshaw. In Delhi kids fight for scraps

of food. All this and much more is going on at that moment when all
you can think about is your audition. But project your mind a bit out
into the world where life is happening, where death is happening, and
the event which is crowding you and making you so terribly fearful,
might assume its proper place, its appropriate perspective in the scheme
of things.

An exercise I've given my class is a very basic one, but it can tend to
awaken the senses and thus take one out of oneself. It's really very
simple. While waiting to audition (or for that matter to do any other
activity which causes you great, self-concerned anxieties), listen. Just
listen. You'd be amazed at how little of that you really do. Listen to
whatever there is to hear. Pick out each sound, separate it from other
sounds. For example, you're waiting backstage to audition. Listen.
Suddenly you hear the cars outside, and one which insistently beeps his
horn. You hear the chair of the person next to you creak whenever he
moves. Also his shoes scuffling on the floor. On stage you hear someone else reading, their voice rising and falling in pitch. Behind you,
through a wall somewhere comes the sound of a faucet dripping. A
page turns near you. Someone clears their throat. A deep sigh from
someone else. A door opens, someone comes in. You hear each step,
then their whispers to the stage manager, then their steps, and a chair
being moved, then creaking as they sit down. Sounds like these and
more are going on around us all the time, but we are usually so self-
absorbed, so tied up in our own limited world with our own limited
concerns that we rarely take the time or trouble to go beyond that.
But as a sensory exercise while going to, or while waiting for an audition, simple listening can be invaluable. It not only takes you outside
of yourself and your own small concerns, it also heightens your sensory awareness—and just simply gives you something to do to take your
mind off yourself.

Also, look. Make a conscious effort to see things you haven't seen before. You are waiting in an outer office before going into an inner office to read. It is a fifth call back. You've been in this same office, under these same circumstances four times before, but I'll bet if you
really look, there will be any number of new things to see, or old things
you just didn't see before. A flower on the receptionist's desk, the
look on her face, the color of the sweater of the girl next to you who is
also waiting to read; the thin spot where the carpet near the door has

worn down. The details on the abstract painting on the wall. The way the magazines are scattered on the table. You name it, it'll be different than it was the last time you were here. See. Be aware of what new things there are to see, and what things look like. You'll be easing your audition fears in two ways, heightening your sensory awareness, and just getting outside yourself.

Feel. Feel the temperature of the room. The coolness of the wood of the chair arm. The feel of the clothes you are wearing and how that feeling changes as you shift your body. The texture of the paper of the script you have in your hand. Be aware of how things feel.

Taste. If your mouth is dry, be aware of how that tastes or if you've just had water, taste the dampness. If you've just eaten a breath sweetener, taste the lingering sugary mint flavor which remains.

Smell. Is that a heady perfume that girl next to you is wearing? Smell that smell of hot dogs which just wafted in, or of cleaning solution from work the janitor has done the night before.

What I'm trying to say with all of this is instead of limiting yourself to you, and reducing the world to your size—open up and expand yourself to the size of the world. At the same time you'll be opening yourself up, making yourself more receptive, and more aware, and also helping to loosen those muscles which tense up when we have an over abundance of self concern, and prevent us from doing our freest most creative work.

3) Exercise. This is something I feel is a must before every audition. Why? Because if you do this, you are getting your blood flowing, your body moving, and generally toning yourself up, as opposed to just slopping through, or allowing yourself to go in a less than optimum condition. Also, by exercising you are doing something positive toward getting that job, and just carrying with you the feeling that you've done all you can, is a way of bringing a more positive, up feeling to the audition.

What kind of exercises? Physical warm ups. If you have a regular program, good. If not, I'd suggest at least some sit-ups, leg-ups, knee bends, toe raises, and a little jogging. The purpose of the above is to wake you up, get you in control of your body instead of the other way round, and get the blood pumping through the appropriate channels. Your brain will work better if it has a fresh pumping-through of blood, than if it has the same old toxins sloshing their way through there. I don't recommend, unless you're really into that kind of thing, a lot of pumping up of tired muscles with weights. If you are into it, and it's what gets you going, fine, but if not, those exercises which serve to stimulate you, and those which tend to relax cramped and tightened muscles are the best.

Vocal warm ups are another necessity before an audition...before an interview as well. If you can, go to a reputable voice teacher and pay to learn a set of vocal warm ups. If you can't, here are a few you can use:

Practice simple deep breathing and be aware of the breath. Inhale 5 counts, hold 10 counts, exhale 10 counts. Be conscious of the air going in, what it does when it's in there, and of it going out.

After a few deep breaths exhale, and as you do, allow sound to be added to the breath, so it becomes like a long sigh. After a few sighs, make this exhaling sound into the different vowel sounds , one at a time, exaggerating what the face does to make the "Ah", "Ee", "I", "Oo" sounds.

Then run through the consonants, being aware of what the teeth, tongue, lips, mouth and vocal chords do to make consonant sounds. As Joe Chaikin showed us in a workshop at the Mark Taper Forum, these consonants are nothing more than breath interrupted—interrupted by lips, tongue, teeth or any combination thereof. Sometimes the consonants are silent, as in the "sh" in "shame". Sometimes sound is added to the same formation of the mouth, lips and tongue so that "sh" with sound become "ge" as in gara"ge". Experiment with vowels and with consonants. Be aware of what the breath, voice, mouth, tongue, teeth, etc. are doing as you produce words. Go over these sounds.before you audition or interview.

Vocal awareness is a way or warming up the voice, warming up those muscles we use to form words so that forming words becomes that much easier. Sure, you can go off to an interview or audition without doing exercises, but maybe by doing them you will have just a little more control, a little more vocal power, a little more clarity in your speech...maybe just enough more of any of the above to get you the job. One other benefit: it will contribute to your sense of having done all you can to prepare for the audition, and if you carry in with you the feeling that you have done all you can to prepare, you have just a little more confidence than the guy who just shleps in and gives whatever is there at the moment. So, exercise your body and your voice before each and every audition. They are your most tangible assets. Believe me, there is nothing better for an auditioner after seeing actor after actor drag himself on stage and slog through an audition, than to see one come on filled with energy, power, and a sense of himself—with vitality and even a sense of joy. How much of the above did you bring to your last audition?

4) Find a way to make the day joyous. Sound like a lot of Pollyanna hogwash? Maybe. But maybe not. Here are a few suggestions as to how to do this:

a. Plan a fun evening after the audition so there is something for you to look forward to.

b. Make up with your boy friend.

c. Make up with your girl friend.

d. On the way to, or while waiting for the audition, look around you and see something funny. It is there, even on the worst days in the worst places. A couple of words someone says. A bit of graffiti on a wall. A practical joke some kid is playing on another. Look around. There is always something funny going on.

e. Help someone before you go on the audition. Make it a point to help someone. The help can be something as simple as a smile to a lonely man or woman—the newspaper man on the corner maybe. Call a friend who's in trouble "just to see how they are getting along". Help an old lady across a street...help a young lady across a street. I don't know. Who and how you help will be up to you. But, this must be genuine—not a gesture just to appease the "Great Audition God", but a real reaching outside yourself, however small or large the gesture may be. It will serve two functions: 1. It will help to get you outside yourself and eliminate a lot of this self-concern. 2. It will make you feel better, give you a lift and help you to be a positive participant in life— a giver rather than a taker.

f. Make up your own ideas on how to make the day joyous. But I think it should include some conscious action on your part, not just mental reflection.

5) Have something to go to, something creative to do after the audition. By that I mean a definite activity so that the audition is not the end of your day. For example, if you attend an acting class, set up a rehearsal of your next class scene for some time after the audition. Or maybe you can go to your dance class or singing lesson. If you don't have something set up, create something for yourself to do that day after the audition. Work on a dress, write a poem or short story: build a boat, paint the apartment—whatever it is, as long as it involves you in some creative, as opposed to destructive activity. The purpose is to give your mind something to dwell on other than yourself and the audition, to take that be-all, end-all feeling off the audition. So, when the audition is over you can put it behind you and leave knowing you've done all you can, at least for the time being, and go off in some positive direction. Otherwise you might, while waiting for the audition, subconsciously or consciously despair that you have nothing to do afterward, and this can drag down your audition performance.

6) Stay off drugs and booze and other substances which alter the consciousness. I can't tell you the negative vibes that fill a room when someone comes in in an altered state. I was casting a show in New York, and we thought of a well-known young character actor for the lead. We met him at 11:30 in the morning in a darkened theatre. He was half loaded. He talked haltingly trying not to slur words, he kept his hand in front of his mouth so we supposedly could not smell his breath, and what he said was terribly funny—but only to him. It was an ugly morning, ugly all the more because to this day, when that actor's name is mentioned to me, the first thing that comes to mind is not the brilliance of his work at other times, but his condition that morning.

Another time, a man came in to interview for a part. He was just right. He read brilliantly. We thought we'd found a new star. But as soon as the reading was done, he began to talk, at first about the script and the character, then about life. And the more he talked the more agitated he became, and the more hostile. He'd laugh at things that weren't funny, spend minutes on some bit of trivia which seemed to his altered mind to be very deep. In all, this pitiful, drug-induced soliloquy went on for for twenty minutes. I was recently asked my opinion of this actor by someone who was casting a show. I had to say that he was a marvelous actor, but the last time I saw him, he was a mess.

Then there are those who take just a few drags on a joint so they'll be "relaxed and casual" at the audition. The problem is that they are so relaxed and casual that time passes them by, and the essence of the audition process which is free-flowing communication and "getting to know you" process, is lost in lengthy pauses, and unconnected thoughts and sentences.

The point is this: Your best work is as a clear channel—able to receive, absorb, and then return all creative energies, thoughts, feelings and ideas which might come your way. While mind altering substances will sometimes bring a temporary clarification, they also bring an alteration in the time flow. Also, when the drug wears off the after effect is an abnormal constriction or dilation of the blood vessels (depending on what you took) resulting in a slow down of functions, some pain, a feeling of malaise, etc. In other words, a hangover. When you start fooling with mind altering materials, that is the natural outcome. You cannot perform to your fullest potential in that condition, and if you go to an audition with the idea either in the front or the back of your mind that you can get away with doing only 50%—or even 90%, forget it. That attitude will catch up with you sooner or later and deal you a crippling blow. If, as we said earlier, you, the actor, are a forerunner of a new evolutionary step where free-flowing energies lead to greater expansion and awareness, and you have the audacity to think you can fake your way into that select group, look at that, or get someone to help you look at that; and when you have decided to join the profession 100%, then come back and try again; but not until then unless you want terrible sadness and pain because that will be the result.

7)   Another way to eliminate fear is to get all the information it is possible to get.

If at all possible, know the script—play, movie, whatever it might be, and not just your part or your scenes. Know the whole thing. Its style, its period, what it is saying. How it is saying it, ie. tragically, comically, satirically, whatever. Go over it enough times so that the people in it are familiar, so that if asked, you can discuss not only your character, but the piece as a whole. You may never have the chance to, but just to know that you are ready will give you that much more confidence, and I'd be willing to bet it would help your reading as well. This does not mean you sit down with the material and try, try, try to get all the meanings and shadings crammed into your head as if you were studying to pass the bar. No. But it does mean reading the material over and over, and keeping yourself open as you do, so you can judge how it affects you and/or relates to you.

Find out all you can about the writer. If you are auditioning for a revival of THE HASTY HEART to be done at the Little Theatre of Eagle Rock, the author, John Patrick, will probably not be there. But even so it will help your audition to know what you can about Mr. Patrick's other plays, his style of writing, what kind of characters he creates, how he creates them, and so on. If you are auditioning for a new play, the same kind of research is invaluable. What other pieces has the playwright written? Is his milieu Greenwich Village or West Elbow, Texas. What does he say in his plays? Strange as it may seem, most playwrights actually do say something when they write. Neil Simon, whom most of us look at as the master of the one-line joke, and the slight, beautifully manufactured comedy, has for all these years, been saying something that is very basic, and very important to most of us as we struggle through a world of upheavals. He says, to me anyway, find that balance, that place that takes the best of two extremes, and makes your life and your place there. In COME BLOW YOUR HORN he finds the balance between the swinging bachelor life, and the stuffy dry, older married state. In BAREFOOT IN THE PARK, Corie's mother tells her in a beautifully simple speech, to live with love somewhere between her own wild impulsiveness, and Paul's conservatism. In STAR SPANGLED GIRL, Sophie finds a balance for herself. So, of course, do Oscar and Felix, the parents in the last act of PLAZA SUITE, and the couple in THE PRISONER OF SECOND AVENUE. The point being most writers write from their own experience. No one expects you to read the collected works of some author before you go to audition for his play, but I'd say the more familiar you can be with him, the better. For movies, the writer is often a part of the producing package these days, often producing or directing himself. But even if he isn't directly involved, a quick trip to the library or a few phone calls to friends who might know about him and what he's written, and what he writes about, could give you just that much of an edge when you audition. For T.V. it's harder because the writer is often long gone on other assignments by the time casting is under way, but here again, maybe you know someone who's done one of his scripts, or maybe you've seen one or two of his shows on other series. If so, try to put together what you can to make you familiar with this writer and his work. This brings to mind one thought. You people who act or want to act in T.V. and films, when looking at those screen credits, don't just look at the cast list. Who directed? Who wrote? Who produced? What does the show you just saw tell you about those people, and the kind of work they do? Maybe it would even help to keep a log of some kind so when you do have an interview or reading or test, you can look to see if the name of the writer or director you are auditioning for is there. If so, check whatever notes you took about the show they did. You might never use this log, but then again, if it helps you get just one good part, it's worth it.

Know your director. Know what he has done in the past that you might have seen. Finding out about the director is a conscious effort on your part to reach out and communicate, not just be a pawn shoved this way and that. You may never use the information you have, but just think how much more at ease you will feel having it there in your hip pocket if you need it or want it. Suppose he asks you a question or two about the play. If it can be done appropriately, without forcing, your answer might contain something which relates somehow to another play the director has done. As I say, this should not be forced, should not be done as a "clever" way to ingratiate yourself with that director, but if it can be done for real, in a way which is meaningful to you and the director, it certainly is a way of communicating. If you know someone who has worked with him before, ask about his way with people. Is he positive or negative? Easy to talk to or remote? Angry or friendly? What kind of work does he hope for from an actor—startling theatrics, or simple, personal work? Are his auditions brusque and businesslike, or are they work sessions where he takes time with the actors to develop things? Learn all this and more, bearing in mind that you will only be getting opinions from others about this man, opinions colored by their own experiences and prejudices; so you should not take their views as gospel, merely as possible modes of behavior you might expect. At the same time, you must be open enough to accept completely different behavior than that described if it should manifest itself. What I mean is, glean all the information you can about the director, then tuck it away for use only if necessary. If you've heard he is brusque and sharp with actors, and he is then brusque with you, rather than being unprepared and feeling you've done something terrible to warrant this behavior, you can feel, "Ah , yes. There he is being brusque", and still go on about your business. At the same time I must caution you against going in with such a preconception that it hampers your own evaluation. You can only really use your own intuition when meeting a director, but learning about him, without letting it prejudice you in advance, is a valuable tool to carry with out.

Know your producer. Know his past work. Know his temperament and personality. Here's why it can be helpful. A close friend of mine went to audition to replace the leading character in a hit Broadway musical. Sitting in the darkened theatre hearing him sing were the producer and director. He finished his song. The director asked him to look over a scene and come back in a few minutes to read. The actor shaded his eyes, tried to peer out to the dark theatre and make a little contact. "Is there anything you'd like to tell me before I read?" he called out. "Yea", boomed the producer's voice impatiently. "Be brilliant." My friend felt like someone let all the air out of him. He had sung well, tried to make contact, and been rudely "put in his place". If he'd taken the time to ask around, he might have learned that this is the way this producer behaves at auditions. No talk, no nothing. Just show me what you've got, and get off. If he'd had this information my friend might have felt, "Ah, ha, that's what I've heard about this guy. Well, I'll give him the best damn reading he's ever heard". Instead, he felt maybe he'd done something to offend the producer, and as a result gave a poor reading. The point is, take the time to find out about the producer if you can. His track record. The kind of show he does. How he behaves at auditions, etc., etc. Anything you can. Maybe you know someone who has auditioned for him before. If so, call them up and ask about their experiences, keeping in mind that it is only their opinion you are getting. If they should say he is fierce, and he does indeed turn out to be fierce, you'll be ready for it. Then just be the most positive "you" you can be. Not grovelling, just you there doing your job the best you know how. If he is still fierce, then that is his problem, but chances are those positive vibes of yours will communicate to him somehow.

If possible, know the place where you will audition before you actually audition there. Make a special trip if you have to. Ask a secretary as a favor to let you look in the office for a minute. Ask a stage door guard. However you do it, try to familiarize yourself with that space ahead of time. Here's why. Auditions can be held anywhere...anywhere from the stage of the Winter Garden Theatre to a small rehearsal hall across the street from the Music Center in Los Angeles; from a dingy back room in a small showcase theatre on Santa Monica Boulevard to the high-ceilinged stage of the Public Theatre on Astor Place in Greenwich Village. It may be in a huge auditorium in Richmond, or a little theatre in Traverse City, Michigan. Whatever it is, try to see it first—see and feel the environment. Check the acoustics, the sight lines, the rake of the stage if there is any. That way, when you come in to audition, any time spent adjusting to the new sights, smells and feels of this place (even subconscious time you are not aware of) can be dispensed with because you've already done it. The reasons should be obvious; the best way to get rid of fears is to turn the unknown into the known. Knowing the place where you will present yourself is one way to do this.

Finally, to help you get rid of those fears, know what's expected of you at the audition and prepare accordingly. Do as much as you can to prevent being caught off guard. Know if it's a musical or a straight play. Know if it's a pilot T.V. show or a one-shot. Know if the movie is a comedy or a drama. If it's a musical audition, have more than one type of song fully rehearsed and ready to go. If you think they will ask you to read cold, practice cold readings with a friend. If you've heard they ask for improvisations, get a couple of people together and go through some improvs. The point being, and with this I'll stop dealing with fears and their remedies, use your good sense, your abilities, and your efforts to know all you can about any audition and the people involved. Use that knowledge to help you prepare for each and every audition you go on. Sometime it will pay off. "But it takes so long", you say. "There's so much to do. How can I do all that?" In response to that, I can only answer your question with a question: "Whoever said being an actor was easy?" Do your preparation. Do it fully. It'll make being an actor, if not easy, at least much easier.

All right, now that your fears are, if not eliminated, at least eased somewhat, let's look at the different kinds of auditions and what one might expect to find at each:

CATTLE CALLS

You hear about an audition from a friend, or read about it in the trade papers. Or maybe you see a breakdown on the board at Actors Equity. Let's take a look at a typical breakdown for a revival of, say, THE GLASS MENAGERIE.

THE GLASS MENAGERIE
by Tennessee Williams

Roles

Amanda Wingfield—Mid 50's. A faded Southern beauty who lives in a world of graciousness and wealth—a world long gone. She is hard on her family, but soft when remembering days of her own youth and beauty.

Tom Wingfield—Mid 20's. Restless, anxious young man, stuck in a drab job, but determined to get out of it.

Laura Wingfield—Mid 20's. One leg crippled. Painfully shy, fearful and withdrawn.

Gentleman Caller—Mid 20's. A doer. A young man on the go. Nice looking, sure of himself.

You check over the list. What's right for you? Tom, obviously. You get dressed the way Tom might dress. You comb your hair the way Tom might comb his and off you go to the appointed place at the appointed time. You have studied a few of his monologues and you are ready. You arrive. Lo and behold there are 75 guys there already—75 guys your same age, same general type. A flustered man with glasses, pencil and clipboard takes your name and puts it at the end of a long list. According to your time of arrival, someone finally calls you inside—along with 15 or 20 others. They line you up across the stage. A man's voice calls from the darkened theatre, "Number 2 from the right step forward, number 8, you too. The rest of you—thank you". Incidentally, those last two words don't mean thank you at all. Well, they do mean thank you a little, I guess, but they also mean goodbye. It doesn't mean you lost the part necessarily when someone says "thank you", but it does mean go away—in the most polite way, of course. I remember the first day I auditioned actors in a Broadway theatre, one came on, gave a beautiful reading. I said, "Thank you, now if you could turn to the scene on page..." But by that time he was halfway out the stage door. He'd heard thank you, and started to go. The playwright explained to me that if I didn't want to lose a lot of actors I might be interested in, I'd better save the thank you for the end of the audition.

So you leave the stage and go on to your next audition—unless you happen to be number 2 or number 8. Let's say you are number 2. If so, the voice out there might ask you your name, and perhaps even the proverbial, "What have you done?" You then stumble out a few words, blushing and stammering all the while. If the voice out there thinks your voice sounds anything at all like Tom's he might ask you to read a few lines which, incidentally, brings us to our next category— cold readings. But first, a few dos and don'ts about cattle calls:

1. Do go with an "up" feeling. How do you know? You might meet a new sweetheart, get married and live happily ever after. Or, you might get the part and become a star. Or both. Anything can happen. Don't be disappointed if it doesn't happen, but don't be surprised if it does.

2. Do know you can't really do much about the choices made under cattle call conditions. You can prepare for an open call, and I suggest you prepare for it as you would for any audition by the methods spelled out in other parts of this book, because you never know when that kind of preparation might pay off. Other than that, all you can do is display you as best you can. The rest is out of your hands. Know that, and set your attitude accordingly.

3. Do expect to be part of a mob scene. Sure you are an artist and entitled to more personal consideration, but know you won't get that on a cattle call, and if you want to go on the call, expect to be part of a large group. That way you won't be disappointed or resentful

when the impersonal selection process is done.

4. Do be on time, even though chances are you will have to wait.

5. Do dress appropriately. If there are no guidelines, dress as much "you" as you can.

6. Do find some way to make the whole experience pleasurable for yourself. Maybe there's a book you've been dying to read and haven't had the time. Take the book with you. You'll probably have time to do some reading while you wait. Or maybe you knit, or sketch. Whatever you do that's portable, take it with you, so the time spent waiting at a cattle call can be filled if you indeed want it to be.

Now some don'ts:

1. Don't go if you resent the fact that you are on a cattle call. If you can't find a way to make it a positive experience, don't bother going. It will show, and you will waste your time and the time of those auditioning you.

2. Don't resent the fact they treat you as a group and not as an individual. I'm not, by the way, saying you should not protest rudeness or thoughtlessness by a stage manager or assistant, or a director or anyone else. Because you are on a group call it does not mean you have to be insulted. The best method for protesting is through your union, or by a letter to the producer (if he isn't the one being rude). You'd be amazed at the efficacy of such action. Not always, but often, a producer will be frightened of his image and his standing with the union, and act on such information. Make sure you don't use this method to take out some basic hostility of your own, but if you feel a real injustice has been done, you can be heard.

3. Don't cut up and make a lot of noise just to call attention to yourself, because that is almost always the wrong kind of attention. Not that you need be sober and serious. Just relax—be you at your best. If a quip comes and it seems appropriate, terrific. Don't force.

4. Don't call out over the footlights to the casting director or director or whoever is sitting out there, that some mutual friend says to say

hello. This is true of any audition, not just the cattle call. I've seen casting directors react to a feeble attempt by some actors to ingratiate themselves with a frosty, curt businesslike reply that would chill a sunburned Tahitian. I feel that the purpose of an audition is business— to cast a play. If an actor is right for a part, I will want him with everything I have, and if he is not he could be my long lost father (or mother) from Poland and we might sing and dance and have a joyful reunion, but he wouldn't get the part. If you have a little extra clout through a mutual friend and you have a chance to talk to those who are auditioning you, you can probably find a way to release that information. Also, if you follow up this audition with a thank you note, you could mention your mutual friend then. The point is, don't put your attention on ingratiating yourself, put it on doing the job.

A pause for a word about thank you notes. I think a thank you note is a terrific idea as a follow-up to any interview, meeting or audition. First of all it is a nice thing to do. Also, it continues the line of communication begun at the audition. Also, it serves as a reminder to the person you met with. I recommend these notes wholeheartedly. I'd suggest, unless you have a good reason to do them otherwise, they be informal and simply express your thoughts and feelings the way you normally express them.

Here is an example of a note I've received:

Mr. Gordon Hunt
c/o Mark Taper Forum Casting Office
135 North Grand Avenue
Los Angeles, Ca. 90012

Dear Mr. Hunt,

I just wanted to thank you for the audition last Tuesday. I enjoyed it. I hope you did, too.

Sincerely,

Write your own note...but write one. It can't hurt, and who knows? It might help.

COLD READINGS

Let's say you survive the cattle call, not only survive but—wonder of wonders—they thrust a script into your hands and ask you to read here and now. This is what is known as a cold reading.

I am opposed to cold readings in principle, because I think they put the actor at an unfair disadvantage, asking him to "wing" something he is totally unfamiliar with. However, I must confess, on a few occasions when I've really been pressed either for time or for an immediate result, to having actors read short scenes, if not cold, at least luke warm with just a few minutes to look over the material. Sometimes this is just to see if they can read a line, also to see how they handle a pressure situation.

A word to actors. If you are asked to read something cold, ask for a few minutes to look it over. If the reply is that it must be done now, so be it. But at least try for the time so you can know what the scene is about and get some attack on it.

If at any time you are offered the option of reading cold or taking a few minutes to look at the material, for God's sake take the few minutes. Other directors may feel differently, but for me, if an actor is given the option, and elects to read cold, I turn off at once. Either he doesn't know how to prepare, or he's afraid to prepare, or he wants to look super-capable, but whatever the reason, the actor who elects to read cold over preparing his work is, in my eye, the lesser actor. He only shows me he can read cold, not that he can act. What an actor does with material after he has looked it over—his attack, his point of view, his ability to personalize, at least a hint of his emotional range—these are the things I want to know. Cold readings don't help me know them.

Now, if someone insists you read cold, or with a very short preparation, here are a few suggestions:

1. Figure out the relationship between your character and the one the scene is played with and use it. For instance, you're asked to read cold this excerpt from PYGMALION.

PYGMALION

HIGGINS
(In despairing wrath outside)
What the devil have I done with my slippers?
(He appears at the door)

LIZA
(Snatching up the slippers and hurling them at him one
after the other with all her force)
There are your slippers. And there. Take all your slippers; and may
you never have a day's luck with them!

HIGGINS
(Astounded)
What on earth—!
(He comes to her)
Whats the matter? Get up.
(He pulls her up)
Anything wrong?

LIZA
(Breathless)
Nothing wrong—with you. I've won your bet for you, havnt I? Thats
enough for you. I dont matter, I suppose.

HIGGINS
You won my bet! You! Presumptuous insect! I won it! What did you
throw those slippers at me for?

LIZA
Because I wanted to smash your face. I'd like to kill you, you selfish
brute. Why didnt you leave me where you picked me out of—in the
gutter? You thank God it's all over and that now you can throw me
back again there, do you?
(She crisps her fingers frantically)

HIGGINS
(Looking at her in cool wonder)
The creature is nervous after all.

LIZA
>(Gives a suffocated scream of fury, and instinctively darts
>her nails at his face)

HIGGINS
>(Catching her wrists)

Ah! Would you? Claws in, you cat. How dare you show your temper
to me? Sit down and be quiet.
>(He throws her roughly into the easy chair)

LIZA
>(Crushed by superior strength and weight)

Whats to become of me? Whats to become of me?

HIGGINS

How the devil do I know whats to become of you? What does it
matter what becomes of you?

LIZA

You dont care. I know you dont care. You wouldnt care if I was
dead. I'm nothing to you—not so much as them slippers.

HIGGINS
>(Thundering)

Those slippers.

LIZA
>(With bitter submission)

Those slippers. I didnt think it made any difference now.

So , you are asked to read Liza cold. What do you do? Ask yourself
what is her relationship to Higgins at this point. Obviously one of sub-
servience, though she is fighting against it. Obviously one of caring or
she wouldn't be so angry and upset. Obviously one of wanting something from him—if only a drop of human kindness.

If you are asked to read Higgins, ask yourself the same questions about
him, then use the answers when reading the scene.

In other words, when given little or no time to prepare a reading, take

those things that seem obvious to you about a relationship and go with
it. Play it fully—as you might play that relationship with someone you
know. Make your choice, take the chance, and play it. It's much more
interesting than something safe, something played at 50% because
you're not sure of the relationship.

2. If it's a monologue or a scene, find out the emotional state of the
character. Is he or she sad? Frightened? Angry? Amorous? Then
express that emotion the way you express it. I mean, if the scene
calls for the character to be sad, and when you are sad your throat
constricts and you attempt to smile, then express the sadness that
way—your way. Try to open yourself and free yourself to the point
where that emotion will freely come through you. It may come from
the way the material makes you feel. Or you may use a sense memory,
or some other device to help you conjure up that feeling in yourself.

Say you're handed this monologue from Inge's A LOSS OF ROSES:

LILA

I remember my first day at school. Mother took me by the hand and I
carried a bouquet of roses, too. Mama had let me pick the loveliest
roses I could find in the garden, and the teacher thanked me for them.
Then Mama left me and I felt kinda scared, cause I'd never been any
place before without her; but she told me Teacher would be Mama
to me at school and would treat me as nice as she did. So I took my
seat with all the other kids, their faces so strange and new to me. And
I started talking with a little boy across the aisle. I didn't know it was
against the rules. But Teacher came back and slapped me, so hard that
I cried, and I ran to the door 'cause I wanted to run home to Mama
quick as I could. But Teacher grabbed me by the hand and pulled me
back to my seat. She said I was too big a girl to be running home to
Mama and I had to learn to take my punishment when I broke the
rules. But I still cried. I told Teacher I wanted back my roses. But
she wouldn't give them to me. She shook her finger and said, when I
gave away lovely presents, I couldn't expect to get them back...I guess
I never learned that lesson very well. There's so many things I still
want back.

Obviously there's a lot of pain and sadness there. If you dredge up a
similiar instance—and chances are as a child something like this happen-

ed to you at one time or another—be specific with it. See your schoolroom and teacher—really see them. Are there others in the room? Is the sky outside clear or cloudy? Smell the smells—the lunch boxes, the teacher's perfume; and hear the sounds—the teacher's voice, the kids yelling at their recess games outside. Open up all those senses, it will make it easier for the feelings to come in and be real for you.

3. Find out what the character wants in a particular scene, and make whatever that character is after of vital importance. Otherwise, the character is only half interested, the actor is only half interested and we in the audience begin to doze off. I don't mean, of course, that you play a "Pass the Rinso" scene as if it was LONG DAY'S JOURNEY INTO NIGHT, but if the scene is about someone who is rushing to get the wash done and who needs the Rinso now, you could create a situation in your head where if she doesn't get the wash done her husband won't have any clean shirts, and if he has no clean shirts, how can he do his best at that big meeting where the boss will either give him a raise or fire him? In other words, develop your own logic for the particular scene, and in the context of that logic, play the hell out of it. Make it (almost always) a matter of life and death.

Say you are cold reading Corie in this scene from BAREFOOT IN THE PARK. How vital is all of the following to you?

BAREFOOT IN THE PARK

PAUL
What crisis? We're just yelling a little.

CORIE
You don't consider this a crisis? Our whole marriage hangs in the balance.

PAUL
     (Sits on steps)
It does? When did that happen?

CORIE
Just now. It's suddenly very clear that you and I have absolutely nothing in common.

PAUL

Why. Because I won't walk barefoot in the park in winter? You haven't got a case, Corie. Adultery, yes. Cold feet, no.

CORIE

(Seething)
Don't oversimplify this. I'm angry. Can't you see that?

PAUL

(Brings his hands to his eyes and peers at her through
imaginary binoculars. Then looks at his watch)
Corie, it's two-fifteen. If I can fall asleep in about half-an-hour, I can get about five hours' sleep. I'll call you from court tomorrow and we can fight over the phone.
(Gets up and moves to bedroom)

CORIE

You will not go to sleep. You will stay here and fight to save our marriage.

PAUL

(In doorway)
If our marriage hinges on breathing fish balls and poofla-poo pie, it's not worth saving...I am now going to crawl into our tiny, little, single bed. If you care to join me, we will be sleeping from left to right to-night.
(Into bedroom and slams door)

CORIE

You won't discuss it...You're afraid to discuss it...I married a coward...!
(Takes shoe from couch and throws it at bedroom door)

PAUL

(Opens door)
Corie, would you bring in a pail? The closet's dripping.

CORIE

Ohh, I hate you! I hate you! I really, really hate you!

PAUL
(Storms to head of stairs)
Corie, there is one thing I learned in court. Be careful when you're tired and angry. You might say something you will soon regret. I-am-now-tired-and-angry.

CORIE

And a coward.

PAUL
(Comes down stairs to her at R. of couch)
And I will now say something I will soon regret...Okay, Corie, maybe you're right. Maybe we have nothing in common. Maybe we rushed into this marriage a little too fast. Maybe Love isn't enough. Maybe two people should have to take more than a blood test. Maybe they should be checked for common sense, understanding and emotional maturity.

CORIE
(That hurt)
All right...Why don't you get it passed in the Supreme Court? Only those couples bearing a letter from their psychiatrists proving they're well adjusted will be permitted to be married.

PAUL

You're impossible.

CORIE

You're unbearable.

PAUL

You belong in a nursery school.

CORIE

It's a lot more fun than the Home for the Fuddy Duddies.

PAUL
(Reaches out his hand to her)
All right, Corie, let's not get—

CORIE

Don't you touch me...Don't you touch me...

>   (PAUL very deliberately reaches out and touches her.
>   CORIE screams hysterically and runs across the room away
>   from him. Hysterically)

I don't want you near me. Ever again.

PAUL

>   (Moves toward her)

Now wait a minute, Corie—

CORIE

>   (Turns away)

I can't look at you. I can't even be in the same room with you now.

You look at it, call it a marital squabble, and read it as such. O.K. But how much better it would sound, how much more urgent and exciting if Corie feels she is going to die—literally die if her marriage doesn't work out. The scene then becomes one of great intensity, where small issues are blown way out of proportion. Therein lies not only the energy of the scene, but also its humor. More of this in a minute. First let's look at another scene and see just how vital it is to you at this moment.

You're asked to cold read Edmund's following speech from LONG DAY'S JOURNEY INTO NIGHT:

EDMUND
(Then with alcoholic talkativeness)

You've just told me some high spots in your memories. Want to hear mine? They're all connected with the sea. Here's one. When I was on the Squarehead square rigger, bound for Buenos Aires. Full moon in the Trades. The old hooker driving fourteen knots. I lay on the bow-sprit, facing astern, with the water foaming into spume under me, the masts with every sail white in the moonlight, towering high above me. I became drunk with the beauty and singing rhythm of it, and for a moment I lost myself—actually lost my life. I was set free! I dissolved in the sea, became white sails and flying spray, became beauty and rhythm, became moonlight and the ship and the high dim-starred sky!

I belonged, without past or future, within peace and unity and a wild joy, within something greater than my own life, or the life of Man, to Life itself! To God, if you want to put it that way. Then another time, on the American Line, when I was lookout on the crow's nest in the dawn watch. A calm sea, that time. Only a lazy ground swell and a slow drowsy roll of the ship. The passengers asleep and none of the crew in sight. No sound of man. Black smoke pouring from the funnels behind and beneath me. Dreaming, not keeping lookout, feeling alone, and above, and apart, watching the dawn creep like a painted dream over the sky and sea which slept together. Then the moment of ecstatic freedom came. The peace, the end of the quest, the last harbor, the joy of belonging to a fulfillment beyond men's lousy, pitiful, greedy fears and hopes and dreams! And several other times in my life, when I was swimming far out, or lying alone on a beach, I have had the same experience. Became the sun, the hot sand, green seaweed anchored to a rock, swaying in the tide. Like a saint's vision of beatitude. Like the veil of things as they seem drawn back by an unseen hand. For a second you see—and seeing the secret, are the secret. For a second there is meaning! Then the hand lets the veil fall and you are alone, lost in the fog again, and you stumble on toward nowhere, for no good reason!

> (He grins wryly)

It was a great mistake, my being born a man, I would have been much more successful as a sea gull or a fish. As it is, I will always be a stranger who never feels at home, who does not really want and is not really wanted, who can never belong, who must always be a little in love with death!

Now obviously, this is a memory piece—a reflection of times past. So how vital is this to Edmund? There are a couple of possible choices. (I'm sure there are a lot more, but two occur to me): It was vital to him then, at those moments when he became one with nature—it was a live or die situation, and as such of total importance to him. Another approach is that in order to survive it is vital to him to tell this story, make sure the listener knows just how it was during those moments he describes. There are a number of choices one can make for any piece of cold reading material. Make your own. If one isn't readily apparent, create one. It will probably work for you, and the reading will then have a goal and a direction. That is vital (there's that word again) for a cold reading.

What I'm saying is, give a drive and a thrust to the scene. I don't mean be loud and bombastic, but I do mean give it the intensity and emotion which makes a reading come to life. To do this you must create your own reason for excitement and be very specific about the details you create to make that excitement.

4. This now leads us to another hint about cold readings, one which, though it might seem to, does not contradict the above. That is, don't go overboard. Find a direction and an emotion, and use them fully, but with your own taste and you own good sense as guides. Don't try to rant and rave us into submission. Rather, show us you and those feelings appropriate to the scene coming through you. Let us fill in the rest. For example, Jack in this scene from THE GREAT WHITE HOPE could pour it on at top volume, the anger inherent in it, hammered at us over and over:

THE GREAT WHITE HOPE

JACK
Move! You through widdit now—

ELLIE
(Kneeling, D.R. end of table)
Jack—

JACK
No mo lousy grub you gotta puke up, no more a ya lookin like a wash out rag here, wid you eye twitchin alla—

ELLIE
Don't—I don't care—

JACK
Juss MOVE—

ELLIE
(Rises)
I'll take better—

JACK

Hangin on me, dead weight—

ELLIE

No, not for you—

JACK

Start—

ELLIE

Jack, I'll find a job, please—

JACK

Ah toleya when mah momma die, Ah toleya leave me be a while, now—

ELLIE
(Goes to JACK)
Jack, I can't run any more, not by myself—

JACK

You got you people an you a —

ELLIE

No, listen—

JACK

You a young woman an you gonna—

ELLIE

Please, I'd never—

JACK

Gonna fine—

ELLIE

No one else, I'd—

JACK

Tough titty—

ELLIE

Just—

JACK

Move, or goddam you—

ELLIE

Why can't you wait at least! Wait till you've given me a chance to make
you happy—one chance, only one—I swear I've never had one—

JACK

Too big a order all aroun!

ELLIE

No, I won't go—

JACK

Wanna drag it out, huh—

ELLIE

I won't, I can't—

JACK

Den Ah goona wise you up good now, you gray bitch—
            (Leaps onto table, grabs towel and jumps to floor,whipping
               ELLIE with towel. Pushes her against table and steps back
               C)

ELLIE

You can't make me go, stop doing this—

JACK

Why you think Ah ain't put a han to ya for how long, why ya think it
turn me off juss lookin atya—

ELLIE

Stop it—

JACK

You stayin, stay fo it all—ya know why? Does ya, honeybunch? Cause evvy time you pushes dat pinch up face in fronna me, Ah sees where it done got me, dass whut Ah lookin at, the why, the wherefore an de Numbah One Who, right down de line, girl, an Ah mean YOU, an Ah doan wanna give you NOTHIN, unnerstan? Ah cut it off firss!

ELLIE

Oh, I despise you—

JACK

Right, like alla resta ya—
        (Moves U.L.)

ELLIE

Oh, I'd like to smash you—

JACK

        (Comes back)
Me an evvy udder dumb nigger who'd letya! Now go on home an hustle one up who doan know it yet, plenty for ya, score em up—watch out, brudders! Oughta hang a bell on so dey hear you comin.

ELLIE

You mean this?

JACK

Look in mah purple eyes.

ELLIE

You win, daddy.
        (Turns and goes off L. Pause)

It seems to me rather than blasting this through at full volume anger (as I've seen it done) you would be better off to let a sense of the different feelings in the scene come to you. Sure there's anger, but there's also sorrow, irony; even a little humor. And if you allow some of those feelings appropriate to the scene to come through you, it's better than trying to blast us into accepting you. By this I don't mean you mumble and fumble your way through a reading, waiting for the feelings to overtake you. Oh no. Make your choices and act them. But make them not necessarily the obvious "hit 'em on the head"

choice. Make them yours. How to do this? One way is to practice
at home. Look at a short scene or monologue—using a timer, allow
yourself, say, three minutes to look it over and make some choices.
When the timer goes off, plunge ahead with the reading based on the
choices you've made. At first it may seem you've only had time to
decide one thing—such as "she's angry". But I think if you practice this
a few times you can get in the habit of picking out other values...and
incorporating them into your reading.

5. This next is something I consider necessary to any audition, but I'll
state it here. Look for the humor in any scene or monologue. It will
be there. But this is a serious drama, you say. I can only tell you humor is a basic ingredient of life and of art and I have yet to hear of a
serious play that has lasted for any length of time that didn't have it—
by the car load. Here are a few examples:

This opening monologue from RICHARD III could be delivered with
the usual venom and evil:

RICHARD

Now is the winter of our discontent
Made glorious summer by this son of York;
And all the clouds that lowered upon our house
In the deep bosom of the ocean buried.
Now are our brows bound with victorious wreaths,
Our bruised arms hung up for monuments,
Our stern alarums changed to merry meetings,
Our dreadful marches to delightful measures
Grim-visaged war hath smoothed his wrinkled front,
And now instead of mounting barbed steeds
To fright the souls of fearful adversaries,
He capers nimbly in a lady's chamber
To the lascivious pleasing of a lute.
But I, that am not shaped for sportive tricks
Nor made to court an amorous looking glass;
I, that am rudely stamped, and want love's majesty
To strut before a wanton ambling nymph;
I that am curtailed of this fair proportion,
Cheated of feature by dissembling Nature,

Deformed, Unfinished, sent before my time
Into this breathing world, scarce half made up,
And that so lamely and unfashionable
That dogs bark at me as I halt by them—
Why, I, in this weak piping time of peace,
Have no delight to pass away the time,
Unless to see my shadow in the sun
And descant on mine own deformity.
And therefore, since I cannot prove a lover
To entertain these fair well-spoken days,
I am determined to prove a villain
And hate the idle pleasures of these days.
Plots have I laid, inductions dangerous,
By drunken prophecies, libels, and dreams,
To set my brother Clarence and the King
In deadly hate the one against the other;
And if King Edward be as true and just
As I am subtle, false and treacherous,
This day should Clarence closely be mewed up
About a prophecy which says that G
Of Edward's heirs the murderer shall be.
Dive thoughts, down to my soul: Here Clarence comes!

Take a look some time at Lord Olivier's film of this play. His Richard
is not some monster filled with hate, he is a vital alive man who enjoys
to the nth degree the intrigue and evil deeds he has done and is going
to do. He enjoys them to such an extent that we too get sucked into
the evil. We find ourselves almost rejoicing in what he does. We find it
all very hard to resist. And there is great humor in this contrast of
evil, and the thorough enjoyment of same. Only later do we realize
how far he is willing to go with his murdering (the two princes may be
your cut-off point), and thus show us how far we are willing to go
along with him. This then shows us the deadly serious point Olivier
is making. But his approach is filled with humor, and this allows us to
relax, to express ourselves through participation (ie. laughter) and thus
to lower our guard and join the actor in what he is about. This you can
do, too, if you look for the humor in the scene you are going to read
cold.

Another example is this scene from THE WOMEN:

THE WOMEN

OLGA

Funny, isn't she?

MARY

She's a darling.

OLGA
(Filing MARY's nails)

She's a writer? How do those writers think up those plots? I guess the plot part's not so hard to think up as the end. I guess anybody's life'd make an interesting plot if it had an interesting end—Mrs. Fowler sent you in?
(MARY, absorbed in her book, nods)

She's sent me three clients this week. Know Mrs. Herbert Parrish that was Mrs. Malcolm Leeds? Well, Mrs. Parrish was telling me herself about her divorce. Seems Mr. Parrish came home one night with lipstick on his undershirt. Said he always explained everything before. But that was something he just wasn't going to try to explain. Knows Mrs. Potter? She's awful pregnant—

MARY
(Wants to read)

I know.

OGLA

Soak it, please.
(Puts MARY's hand in water. Begins on other hand)

Know Mrs. Stephen Haines?

MARY

What? Why, yes, I—

OLGA

I guess Mrs. Fowler's told you about that! Mrs. Fowler feels awfully sorry for her.

MARY
(Laughing)

Oh, she does! Well, I don't. I—

OLGA

You would if you knew this girl.

MARY

What girl?

OLGA

This Crystal Allen.

MARY

Crystal Allen?

OLGA

Yes, you know. The girl who's living with Mr. Haines.
          (MARY starts violently)
Don't you like the file? Mrs. Potter says it sets her unborn child's teeth
on edge.

MARY

          (Indignant)
Whoever told you such a thing?

OLGA

Oh, I thought you knew. Didn't Mrs. Fowler—?

MARY

No—

OLGA

Then you will be interested. You see, Crystal Allen is a friend of mine.
She's really a terrible man-trap. Soak it, please.
          (MARY, dazed, puts her hand in the dish)
She's behind the perfume counter at Saks'. So was I before I got fi—
left. That's how she met him.

MARY

Stephen Haines?

OLGA

Yeah. It was a couple of months ago. Us girls wasn't busy. It was an awful rainy day, I remember. So this gentleman walks up to the counter. He was the serious type, nice-looking, but kind of thin on top. Well, Crystal nabs him. "I want some perfume", he says. "May I awsk what type of woman for?" Crystal says, very Ritzy. That didn't mean a thing. She was going to sell him Summer Rain, our feature anyway. "Is she young?" Crystal says. "No," he says, sort of embarrassed. "Is she the glamorous type?" Crystal says. "No, thank God", he says. "Thank God?" Crystal says and bats her eyes. She's got those eyes which run up and down a man like a searchlight. Well, she puts perfume on her palm and in the crook of her arm for him to smell. So he got to smelling around and I guess he liked it. Because we heard him tell her his name, which one of the girls recognized from Cholly Knickerbocker's column—Gee, you're nervous.—Well, it was after that I left. I wouldn't of thought no more about it. But a couple of weeks ago I stopped by where Crystal lives to say hello. And the landlady says she'd moved to the kind of house where she could entertain her gentleman friend. "What gentleman friend?" I says. "Why, that Mr. Haines that she's had up in her room all hours of the night," the landlady says. —Did I hurt?

      (MARY draws her hand away)

One coat, or two?

      (Picks up a red bottle)

MARY

None.

      (Rises and goes to the chair where she has left her purse)

OLGA

But I thought that's what you came for? All Mrs. Fowler's friends—

MARY

I think I've gotten what all Mrs. Fowler's friends came for.

      (Puts coin on the table)

OLGA

      (Picks up coin)

Oh, thanks.—Well, goodbye. I'll tell her you were in, Mrs.—?

MARY

Mrs. Stephen Haines.

OLGA

Mrs—? Oh, gee, gee! Gee, Mrs. Haines—I'm sorry! Oh, isn't there something I can do?

MARY

Stop telling that story!

OLGA

Oh, sure, sure, I will!

MARY

And please, don't tell anyone—
          (Her voice breaks)
—that you told it to me—

OLGA

Oh, I won't, gee, I promise! Gee, that would be kind of humiliating for you!
          (Defensively)
But in a way, Mrs. Haines, I'm kinda glad you know. Crystal is a terrible girl—I mean, she's terribly clever. And she's terribly pretty, Mrs. Haines—I mean, if I was you I wouldn't waste no time getting Mr. Haines away from her—
          (MARY turns abruptly away)
I mean, now you know, Mrs. Haines!
                    (OLGA eyes the coin in her hand distastefully, suddenly
                    puts it down on the table and exits. MARY, alone, stares
                    blankly in the mirror, then suddenly focusing on her image.
                    She leans forward, searching her face between her trembling
                    hands).

This could be a simple expository scene where Olga rattles on and Mary learns the terrible truth. However, if the actress thinks of Olga as someone who thinks of herself as a born storyteller—who embellishes everything with her own little touches, the scene can have two edges— one of awful reality as Mary finds out what's happening, and one of great humor as Olga busily does her nails and tells her story in all its colorful detail. Get a partner and experiment with this one. I think you'll see what I mean.

One final example. This opening monologue of John Adams from the musical 1776.

JOHN

I have come to the conclusion
that one worthless man is called
a disgrace—that two are called
a law firm—and that three or
more become a Congress. And
by God, I have had this Congress!
For ten years King George and
his Parliament have gulled,
cullied and diddled these Colonies
with their illegal taxes—Stamp
Acts, Townshend Acts, Sugar Acts,
Tea Acts,—and when we dared
stand up like men they stopped
our trade, seized our ships,
blockaded our ports, burned our
towns, and spilled our blood—
and still this Congress refuses to
grant any of my proposals on Independence,
even so much as the courtesy of
open debate! Good God, what in hell
are they waiting for?!

There is humor here. The reference to the law firm and Congress are obvious examples. The rest of the speech can be read like a speech— an oration, or it can be filled with the genuine outrage of a little bandy rooster who is sick and tired of the way things are going. It is this real, human attack which gives this the bite which makes it funny.

Now, as an exercise, you find the humor in this passage. Don't make it an intellectual exercise. Just fool around with the material and see what comes to you:

THE GLASS MENAGERIE

JIM
(Puts out cigarette. Abruptly)
Say! You know what I judge to be the trouble with you?
(Rises from day-bed and crosses right)
Inferiority complex! You know what that is? That's what they call it
when a fellow low-rates himself! Oh, I understand it because I had it,
too. Uh-huh! Only my case was not as aggravated as yours seems to
be. I had it until I took up public speaking and developed my voice,
and learned that I had an aptitude for science. Do you know that until
that time I never thought of myself as being outstanding in any way
whatsoever!

LAURA
Oh, my!

JIM
Now I've never made a regular study of it--
(Sits armchair right)
--mind you, but I have a friend who says I can analyze people better
than doctors that make a profession of it. I don't claim that's neces-
sarily true, but I can sure guess a person's psychology. Excuse me,
Laura.
(Takes out gum)
I always take it out when the flavor is gone. I'll just wrap it in a piece
of paper.
(Tears a piece of paper off the newspaper under candela-
brum, wraps gum in it, crosses to day-bed, looks to see if
LAURA is watching. She isn't. Crosses around to day-bed)
I know how it is when you get it stuck on a shoe.
(Throws gum under day-bed, crosses around left of day-
bed. Crosses right to LAURA)
Yep--that's what I judge to be your principal trouble. A lack of confidence in yourself as a person. Now I'm basing that fact on a number of
your remarks and on certain observations I've made. For instance, that
clumping you thought was so awful in high school. You say that you
dreaded to go upstairs? You see what you did? You dropped out of
school, you gave up an education all because of a little clump, which
as far as I can see is practically non-existent! Oh, a little physical

defect is all you have. It's hardly noticeable even! Magnified a thousand times by your imagination! You know what my strong advice to you is? You've got to think of yourself as superior in some way!

>   (Crosses left to small table right of day-bed. Sits. LAURA
>   sits in armchair)

LAURA

In what way would I think?

JIM

Why, man alive, Laura! Look around you a little and what do you see? A world full of common people! All of 'em born and all of 'em going to die! Now, which of them has one-tenth of your strong points! Or mine! Or anybody else's for that matter? You see, everybody excels in some one thing. Well—some in many! You take me, for instance. My interest happens to lie in electro-dynamics. I'm taking a course in radio engineering at night school, on top of a fairly responsible job at the warehouse. I'm taking that course and studying public speaking.

LAURA

Ohhhh. My!

JIM

Because I believe in the future of television! I want to be ready to go right up along with it.

>   (Rises, crosses right)

I'm planning to get in on the ground floor. Oh, I've already made the right connections. All that remains now is for the industry itself to get under way—full steam! You know, knowledge—ZSZZppp! Money—Zzzzzpp! POWER! Wham! That's the cycle democracy is built on!

So much for humor. Obviously I don't mean you try to be a Vegas comic with every cold reading you perform, but in almost any selection you are given to read or choose to read there is a vein, or a moment or at least one brief flash of humor. Look for it. It will be invaluable.

6. All right, you finish your cold reading. Then what? If you hear a

voice say "Thank you". Then go. It is best not to stand there and explain how you might have done it if you didn't have the flu. Or how you knew you didn't give your all, but after all this was only a cold reading, and besides, you know this character and could do it now with your eyes closed. If you do get a call back and it then seems appropriate you might say any or all of these things, but we out in the house have things to do, and it would help you—and our image of you—if you finish, say your words of farewell, and go. As Milton Katselas so often told his acting students don't "Q and A" it. That is, don't question and answer and stand there and play word games which are really designed to cover up nervousness, or to delay actually plunging in and acting, or to try and keep an audition situation alive or to accomplish any number of things an actor wants to accomplish—other than acting. Don't Q and A. Just do it, do it the best you can at that time... and get off. To sum up cold readings:

If you're asked to read cold, ask for a few minutes to look at the material. When you do read:

1) Set a relationship between your character and the one you read with.

2) Set the emotional state of the character and then let your version, your means of expressing that emotion carry you through.

3) Find out what is vital, really vital to the character in that scene, and play that as fully as you can. If there is nothing evident, create something so you have something definite to play.

4) Don't try to astound us with your force, power and range. Do the material simply, appropriately, fully. Let us fill in the rest.

5) Find the humor.

6) Do your cold reading as best you can, then get off.

One final hint about cold readings. One of the tricks is learning to read, and relate to another character at the same time. The simple problem of eyes on script, eyes up, eyes back to script again without losing your place is a technical trick you must learn. One exercise I'd suggest is to practice doing this at home with any kind of material—plays, newspapers, novels, the phone book—use different size books with different size type and practice reading, looking up from the page as often as you can, and then going back to your place without interrupting the flavor and sense of what you are saying. At first it may seem slow and difficult but keep trying. Practice makes this not necessarily perfect, but a lot easier for you.

So—don't treat your cold readings as the big trauma of all time. If you must do a cold reading, do it the best you can, then go your merry way knowing you've done that. If you get the job or a call back—so much the better. If not, go on to the next one.

Prepared Auditions

These can come about in a number of ways:

You've passed the aforementioned cattle call and cold reading tests, you are handed a script and asked to come back in a few days, or a few hours and read a scene.

Or, you've worked for the producer or director before. They send you a script, and ask you to come in and read at an agreed upon time.

Or, your agent arranges for you to audition for a particular part at a particular time.

Or, you prepare a scene or monologue for a general audition such as we have at the Mark Taper Forum. A general audition is not for a specific part, but is rather an opportunity for an actor to present himself and his talent, and for us casting people to see that actor, make notes on him and his presentation, and then have those notes on file so we can consult them when we are casting a specific play. At the Taper we have these auditions once a month. Appointments are made by phone or through interviews on the first Monday of every month. We then set aside a ten minute time span for each individual. We ask them to bring a picture and resume, and to prepare two monologues—one classic and one contemporary, two and a half minutes each. The reasons for the time limit are that we want to have time to see all those who want to audition; we also want to have time for at least a brief moment or two of talk so we can meet the actor, not just the character he plays. Also, and this some of you may find hard to believe, we can tell a lot in two and a half minutes. As a matter of fact we usually have most of the data we need after one minute. Sometimes we can be fooled, but usually two minutes is plenty of time to show us what we need to know. The fallacy that you need ten or fifteen minutes to show us all your facets and shadings is indeed a fallacy. If you've ever watched auditions—and I strongly recommend that you do every chance you get—you'll know what I mean. We can be startled in two and a half minutes. After that, if one is sitting through a day or two of auditions, anything else becomes a soporific. And though we try not to, we do come to resent those who deliberately ignore the rules. The vaudeville phrase "Always leave 'em wanting more", is also valid in auditions.

T.C.G., or Theatre Communications Group, headquartered in New York, carries on similar auditions on a broader scale. The purpose of T.C.G. is to service regional theatres throughout the country. One of its most important functions is as a casting consultant.

T.C.G. casting is done in two ways. One is by audition in New York at the T.C.G. office. Pictures and resumes are accepted. Appointments can be made. The usual two monologues are requested—one classic and one contemporary, no more than three minutes each. Notes on your audition are kept on file there. If you are a tall, striking looking 35-year-old lady with a decent credit or two and you give a whopping good audition and someone then calls in from, say, the Alley Theatre in Houston and needs a tall, striking looking 35-year-old leading lady, you will probably be recommended to them. Sometimes a regional theatre will get in a casting bind and call T.C.G. for emergency help. This happened once when I was visiting the office. Jon Jory, director of the Actors Theatre of Louisville, had to let an actress go after a few days rehearsal and needed a replacement flown down that evening. He spent a lot of money on long distance phone consultations with T.C.G. while they threw out ideas to him of people whose work they knew.

A thought intrudes here, so let me put it down. If you have done a general audition somewhere, and the person you have auditioned for leaves for one reason or another, do not assume their replacement will merely consult the old files. Get in there as quick as you can and audition for the new man or woman as if you've never auditioned before.   A live audition has value for us, someone else's notes on a piece of paper do not.

The other way T.C.G. casts is through annual student auditions. They are handled as follows: Representatives of T.C.G. hold preliminary auditions for people recommended by qualified schools throughout the country.   Then in the spring, there are finals in Chicago.   To these finals come the best talent the T.C.G. reps. have been able to uncover, and it is sometimes startlingly good.   Viewing the auditions are representatives—directors, producers, casting directors, etc.,—from most of the regional theaters.

The procedure is as follows.   Saturday morning at 9:00 a.m. the sleepy-eyed representatives of the theatres file into a rented auditorium. It is quiet, subdued.   Sitting together in the left hand corner near the stage are the first group of young auditioners.   After a word of welcome, the first actor climbs on the stage—cold-turkey—faces a darkened auditorium of people with pencils poised—and introduces himself and his selections.   Then, after a moment's preparation, is expected to astound us with his brilliance.   Easy?   Not at all.   He does the usual two monologues, says a subdued "Thank you", gets a "Thank you" back from casting director Michael Fender in the house, and goes off as the next actor comes on.

Why mention this here?   So you young actresses and actors will be aware of these auditions.   So you more experienced people will be aware of T.C.G. and what it does.   And also so you get a sense of the prepared audition—what it is, and what it is used for.

Preparing The Prepared Audition

Some of the suggestions for cold readings apply here, and perhaps bear repeating in the context of doing a prepared audition.   Also, some new ideas apply:

1. Get information.   Read the whole work—play, movie or whatever it is. Be familiar with all of it, not just the scene you will read. That scene will be affected by other events in the play. The director might ask you to read another scene just to see a different color. If so, and you are prepared, it might really surprise him. Also, he might want to ask you

some questions about the play or the part and you'll be in a fine mess if you can't answer them. One other reason it helps to be familiar with the whole play is that there is an added sense of confidence when you are fully prepared, much more so than if you go with an "I'll get by" attitude. Being better prepared just helps you to do better work. It's that simple.

2. Even though it is a reading, be familiar enough with the material so you are not dependent on the script. Memorize it if at all possible. Then hold the script anyhow, and refer to it if you need to. But with the words learned, you can give a much better sense of acting and re-acting than you can without.

3. Get help preparing your audition if you think it might be needed. With practice and experience you often can do the preparation yourself but don't be hesitant about getting help if you think it will be of value. The most professional performers will often seek help in preparing an audition. The prime example in recent Broadway history is that of Alexis Smith who auditioned for the role of Jessica in FOLLIES. She did not get the part the first time out so she went to the man most noted for preparing musical auditions for actors, the brilliant teacher David Craig. Once of New York, now in Hollywood, David is known throughout the business as the man who knows how to teach actors and singers to audition and to perform songs for musicals. Needless to say, Miss Smith, after working with Craig, went on to win the role, the Tony Award, and a whole new career. One note of caution: Beware of the kind of help you get. The most well-meaning friend might be a frustrated director who sees a chance to express all his creative drives through you—with little or no regard for what is appropriate to the audition. Use your own logic, your own good sense to guide you to the one who can help you prepare your audition. Remember, audition-ing is not a "do-it-yourself" contest. Get help if you need it.

4. Prepare an attack. Let's say you will be preparing this audition without help. I suggest you look over the scene a number of times, af-ter becoming familiar with the whole play, of course. Without pushing or forcing or trying to do anything or make anything happen, just read the scene, leaving yourself as empty as possible. You'll find the second, third or fourth time through an idea, perhaps just a flash of feeling for one passage, or even one line, will come to you. Let it. Then go back

and read the scene again. Now put down the material for a little while, and let ideas come to you. If you want, jot them down. If ideas don't come, do something else, some activity which involves you and doesn't allow you to think of the scene at all. Then go back to the material and without trying to get ideas or an approach, read it over again. Just read it. Sooner or later a thought or feeling will come to you...then another, and another. Not all these ideas will be useful, but as you go on, you'll select those which make sense to you and discard those which don't. Slowly, if you let it happen and don't force, a pattern or point of view or attack on the material will emerge.

You need this in an audition. It will give your work some interest. It will show us you can take a part and do something with it. It will give you assurance. And during the audition, rather than floundering from approach to approach, you will have an overall feeling or concept to serve as your guide.

Some of the best auditions I've seen have been given by people who work in —hold on—soap operas. I know we of the "theatah" often look on soaps as one of the lower forms on the evolutionary scale. But the soap opera does serve some functions and in some cases serves them very well. One of these is that it is a place where actors can learn and develop. One way they develop is by having to deliver a performance— a thought-out, logical, and hopefully moving performance—almost every day. They learn to look at a piece of material, make a choice, and go with it. No Q. and A-ing. Just find an attack and do it.

One word to my fellow directors and casting directors (You actors can listen too). Be sure the audition you're seeing is not the final performance. Be sure that the actor, after he gets the part, will take that initial approach and work it and mold it till it becomes more vital, more exciting, more him. But (and actors, we're back to you now) an attack, a specific attack is one of the requisites of a good audition.

As aids in developing this attack, let me repeat a few points, and maybe even add a couple of new ones:

Determine how the situation in a particular scene is truly vital to the character you're playing. Often it can be broken down into a life or death situation (see "cold readings" and the example of BAREFOOT

IN THE PARK). Then play the reality of that life or death situation fully.

Find the humor in any scene. (See "cold readings" and the example of RICHARD III.). There can be humor in just about any scene you play. Not necessarily Marx Brothers routines,sometimes it's just a warm smile of humanity, but it is there. Find it.

Make your attack on the scene as clear as possible, or conversely, don't play obscurities. Make a choice, a clear-cut choice and go with it. This opening scene from Pinter's OLD TIMES can serve as an example:

ACT ONE

A converted farmhouse.

A long window UP CENTRE. Bedroom door UP LEFT. Front door UP RIGHT.
Spare modern furniture. Two sofas. An armchair.

Autumn. Night.

Light dim. Three figures discerned.

DEELEY slumped in armchair, still. KATE curled on a sofa, still. ANNA standing at the window, looking out.

Silence.

Lights up on DEELEY and KATE, smoking cigarettes.

ANNA's figure remains still in dim light at the window.

KATE
(Reflectively)
Dark.
(Pause)

DEELEY
Fat or thin?

                          KATE

Fuller than me. I think.
          (Pause)

                          DEELEY

She was then?

                          KATE

I think so.

                          DEELEY

She may not be now.
          (Pause)
Was she your best friend?

                          KATE

Oh, what does that mean?

                          DEELEY

What?

                          KATE

The word friend...when you look back...all that time.

                          DEELEY

Can't you remember what you felt?
          (Pause)

                          KATE

It is a very long time.

                          DEELEY

But you remember her. She remembers you. Or why would she be
coming here tonight?

                          KATE

I suppose because she remembers me.
          (Pause)

DEELEY

Did you think of her as your best friend?

KATE

She was my only friend.

DEELEY

Your best and only.

KATE

My one and only.
          (Pause)
If you have only one of something you can't say it's the best of anything.

DEELEY

Because you have nothing to compare it with?

KATE

Mmnn.
          (Pause)

DEELEY

          (Smiling)
She was incomparable.

KATE

Oh, I'm sure she wasn't.
          (Pause)

DEELEY

I didn't know you had so few friends.

KATE

I had none. None at all. Except her.

DEELEY

Why her?

KATE

I don't know.
(Pause)
She was a thief. She used to steal things.

DEELEY

Who from?

KATE

Me.

DEELEY

What things?

KATE

Bits and pieces. Underwear.
(DEELEY chuckles)

DEELEY

Will you remind her?

KATE

Oh...I don't think so.
(Pause)

DEELEY

Is that what attracted you to her?

KATE

What?

DEELEY

The fact that she was a thief.

KATE

No.
(Pause)

DEELEY

Are you looking forward to seeing her?

KATE

No.

DEELEY

I am. I shall be very interested.

KATE

In what?

DEELEY

In you. I'll be watching you.

KATE

Me? Why?

DEELEY

To see if she's the same person.

KATE

You think you'll find that out through me?

DEELEY

Definitely.
　　　　(Pause)

In this scene, Pinter is telling us a great deal. One could choose any number of things to play if one were asked to audition for Deeley. That's the problem. It is not a clear-cut "I love you" or "I hate you" scene. But I think, in an audition it's important to make a choice, a simple choice. For instance, one could say Deeley is trying to make contact with his wife, or even stronger, Deeley feels he has to make contact with his wife. The scene then becomes something more than two people exchanging information. It also allows for colors, humor, intensity, etc. If you are asked to read for Kate, you could choose, for example, to deliberately withhold yourself as much as possible from your husband. This is an action—a negative one. But an action nonetheless. Or you could choose to infuriate him. There are many choices which you as actors can make with this scene. I'm just saying better to make clear one and go with it, than to flounder or to play some deep dark obscure meaning. We want to see what you will do with the material. And the clearer you make things for us, the easier it will be for us to see you.

Next, find ways to make the scene or monologue vital and alive. For example, many Chekhov plays begin with people seemingly bored to tears. They talk about how bored they are, and how boring life is, and how boring everything is. But hold on! These seemingly bored people often turn out to be real swingers underneath it all. I mean later we learn that they are drunkards, lechers, greedy landlords, ex-courtesans—in short real people with real problems. Boredom, if indeed it does exist for them, is merely a surface feeling. Other things are going on inside of them. In auditioning, it's good to be aware of these other things—the affair that is brewing; the self-disgust and hangover which are a result of last night's debauch; the real concern a mother has for her wastral son—whatever is going on at the same time they profess boredom. Be aware of these things. Use them, without, of course, clobbering us over the head with them, and your audition will take on a life and vitality far removed from the boredom the characters talk of.

Relate the material to you. Express the feelings of a particular scene as you would express them, not as you've seen others do it, or as you are "supposed" to do it. For example, I know one man who, whenever he gets angry, always smiles and spews out his anger through a kind of forced laugh. It's as if he gets very angry, but feels the need to shield it, or hide it somehow. How much more interesting for him to play an angry scene this way, than to do the conventional yelling and shouting. I underline "him" because that's his way—your might be very different. But it's important, I think, to know how you express fear, joy, sorrow, rage, lust. What is your unique way of reacting when dealing with or expressing these feelings. Be in touch with that and use it when you audition. You are much more interesting than your version of someone else, so show us you.

Create a place for yourself as called for in a particular scene. When reading for a scene you will probably be doing it on a bare stage, or on the set for some other play, or in an empty rehearsal hall or in someone's office. Wherever it may be, you can be sure (unless it is as a replacement for someone in a show already running) that you will be reading in some place different from the place where the play takes place.

But, the place where the play takes place will be a definite factor in the behavior of the character you are reading. It is up to you as an actor to give at least some thought to this, and while it may never come out in overt behavior (or it may) the sense of your physical surroundings is a factor you can't ignore if you want your audition to have all the color and vitality it must have.

Let's say you have been asked to read for the part of Private Collucci in Harry Brown's A SOUND OF HUNTING. The scene is the opening one:

ACT ONE

SCENE: The living-room of a war-ruined house on the outskirts of Cassino, Italy, in January, 1944. It is just after dawn. Light, gray and unhealthy, turning everything the cold color of an oyster, comes through a shellhole pounded in the side of the house facing the audience. The pile of rubble made by the shell has been formed into a rough seat by the hole. The roof of the house is shattered, and shelter-halves have been joined together to keep the rain out of the interior. There is a broken door to the left, and a small, shattered window flanks the shellhole. To the right is a fireplace, also shattered, but still in some sort of working order. On the ledge above the fireplace are canteen cups and other necessary articles, as well as a telephone connection—the soundpower. A jerrican, half full of water, sits in the fireplace. A rickety table, together with two chairs and a stool, stands in the middle of the room. Scattered about the floor are the bedrolls of eight men. Each bedroll marks the "home" of the man it belongs to. On a wire, strung near the shellhole, are several grenades. Near the door are boxes of ammunition, boxes of rations, and about twenty mortar shells. On the wall, right, is a pin-up picture, the only one in the room. There is also an ugly chromo of the Virgin, framed and hanging over the fireplace. On the wall under the window is the hastily scrawled word "Achtung". The Germans had been here before. This, then, is the present quarters of one squad of the 34th Division.

AT RISE OF CURTAIN: Only one member of the squad can be seen. PVT. DINO COLLUCCI is asleep at the right, under his pin-up picture. He is wrapped in a torn blanket. There is the sudden whine of a ricocheting bullet. Then, as though hurled from a catapult, PFC.CHARLES

COKE dives through the shellhole, picks himself up, takes a quick look behind him, and swears softly under his breath. He hangs two grenades on the wire, stands his tommy gun by the shellhole, and starts to remove some of his equipment, then walks over to COLLUCCI and prods him with his toe.

COKE

All right, all right. You're in the war.
>(COLLUCCI stirs and groans, but does not wake up.
>COKE scrapes his leg with his hand)

COKE

Rats! Look out for the rats!

COLLUCCI

Huh.
>(He sits upright very suddenly. Then he becomes relaxed
>and a little annoyed)
Goddamn it, Coke, cut that stuff out. I told you before.
>(He shakes his head, and wipes the back of his hand across
>his mouth)
You spoiled a beautiful romance. You know what I was dreaming?

COKE
>(Crossing to the shellhole and looking out, not turning
>as he speaks)
I always know what you're dreaming.

COLLUCCI

This one was different. Totally different. If the Army don't do nothing else it provides very interesting dreams. How long I been asleep?

COKE

I busted my watch.

COLLUCCI

Everything gets busted around here. Ah, I got a headache. I got a stomach-ache. I got a bad taste in my mouth. I can smell myself coming twenty feet away. Now I know how the dumb animals live.
>(He gets stiffly to his feet and stands there, rubbing his cheek

Geez, what a beard I got!

                              COKE

What a face you got!

                           COLLUCCI

Listen to Dream Boy.
                    (He stands with his hands on his hips)
A fashion plate. An awful fashion plate.

                              COKE

Okay, I'll bring you a mirror.

                           COLLUCCI

Never mind. Geez, it's cold in here.
                    (He walks to the table and sits down)
Well, what's for breakfast? Caviar? Too expensive. Lamb chops? I
ain't interested. Big, thick, juicy steaks? The hell with big, thick,
juicy steaks.

                            • COKE

How about a little of the K rations?

                           COLLUCCI

                    (Wearily)˙
Yeah, I'll have a little of the K rations. I got to have a little of the K
rations.
                    (He crosses to the box of K rations, takes one, and brings
                    it back to the table)
If the whole human body could stand as much as the human stomach,
we'd of been in Berlin a week ago Tuesday. At four o'clock.
                    (He gets up and goes to the fireplace, picks up his canteen
                    cup, and pours himself a drink from the jerrican)
Hey, Cokey, where the hell is everybody?

                              COKE

Ain't you got nothing to do but ask questions?

                           COLLUCCI

Keep your shirt on. All I wanted to know was where is everybody. I

miss my friends.
> (He returns to the table)

COKE

I don't know. Out somewheres is all I know.

COLLUCCI

Any trouble?

COKE

Naw, it's been quiet.

COLLUCCI

That's nice. This place is getting to be like a lousy country club. I should of brought a mashie.

COKE

Why don't you go back and get it?

COLLUCCI

The honest fact of the matter is, I ain't got a nickel for the subway. You wouldn't want me to walk the hell and gone down to Eighth Street, would you?

COKE

I sure as hell would.

COLLUCCI
> (Opening the K ration)

That's love for you. One of my own friends puts the zinger on me.
> (He shakes out the contents on the table)

Some day I am going to meet the guy who invented the K ration and we are going to have words. We don't see eye to eye on a lot of things.

Now, you've read the description of where Collucci is, and you've read over the scene a few times. How to incorporate this into your audition? Well, think about it. A bombed out house is no doubt going to be one very dusty place to be. The dust, permeating your mouth, making it always dry, caking in your eyes so maybe you have to rub them to get it out, that dust could be used as an aid in acting the scene. Since Collucci is asleep on the floor when the scene starts, his awakening must be more than just someone getting out of bed and getting up. He has spent the whole night huddled on a stone floor. That does things to the body—makes joints ache, makes muscles stiff. The reality of those feelings can heighten your audition, making it a moment of reality rather than just another reading. And what about the temperature of the room? Since one whole wall has a hole blasted through it, and since it is January, it must be very cold. Collucci even comments on it. The unthawing of fingers and toes, the rubbing of a face, pinching a nose to make sure it's still there—all can be part of your audition. Let me repeat, that you don't necessarily act all of these things out. Maybe a few, maybe one or two, maybe none. But be aware of them. Know they exist, and use them if it seems appropriate.

Another more commonplace example to illustrate this point might be the living room for Edward Albee's A DELICATE BALANCE. You will probably be reading as I said, on a bare stage. The chairs you have to work with may be wooden straight-backs, or folding metal chairs. But this living room has been lived in for a long time. The people in it sit in their favorite chairs or on their favorite sofa. They sink into the pillows a little. The lighting in the room, unlike the one worklight you may have to audition with, is probably a muted warm glow. These are things you can use in your audition. Just open up and be aware of them.

In other words, to ignore where a scene takes place, makes you just another actor reading a scene. To be aware of it and to use it, can give your reading the life and richness it needs to make it and you something special.

Create a time for yourself. There are two facets to this, one is the time in which the play takes place. Obviously one's behavior will be somewhat different in the time of, say, the court of King Henry IV as set down by Shakespeare, than it will in the men's room of today as set down by Le Roi Jones in THE TOILET. The other facet is the time of day. Again, one's behavior is different according to what time of day it is. An obvious example is the Tyrone family in LONG DAY'S JOUR-

NEY INTO NIGHT. In the first act, they all seem to be at least reasonably fresh and able to cope. But by the last act, it is late at night, they are all tired, nerves taut to the breaking point, eyes burning, mouths tasting bad, and heads aching. Not only the tensions and events, but the lateness of the hour has a decided effect on their behavior.

Here is an example of both in one: From Schulberg and Breit's THE DISENCHANTED, the first meeting of Manley and Jere:

JERE dances in Up Left, leaves her partner for another. Down left, runs to another center. They pick her up and carry her around the table.

JERE

I declare a holiday throughout the realm! Let the slaves drink wine!

HALLIDAY

    (Now reliving the past)
You are the most beautiful woman I have ever seen.

JERE

    (Crosses to HALLIDAY's right, with a bad French accent)
That is not important.

HALLIDAY

    (Down center)
Perhaps Mademoiselle will be good enough to say what is important?

JERE

Dancing. Pleasure. To be gay—these are the only truths.

HALLIDAY

But are you not too attractive to bother about definitions of truth?

JERE

Ho-hum.

HALLIDAY

I bore you?

JERE
(Crosses to below table, around and back to HALLIDAY)
Being told I'm beautiful? Why shouldn't it bore me? Generals and privates tell me. Even handsome captains. I have eyes. I can see that I am beautiful. I look into the glass after the bath and I say to myself, "how much more beautiful you are than those stupid pink nudes of Renoir".

HALLIDAY
Perhaps some day soon I shall be fortunate enough to be permitted to agree with you.

JERE
(Crosses to right of HALLIDAY)
Ish ka bibble.

HALLIDAY
Hah. So you've picked up some of our slang.

JERE
Yes, these slang is, how you say, very funee of uz—What you call bed-pillow French.

HALLIDAY
You're not French. Come clean now. Who are you? What do you do? Why aren't you in uniform?

JERE
I will tell you a secret but do not be frightened. I am a sorceress.

HALLIDAY
Apprentice or professional?

JERE
It's Armistice Night—let them court-martial me—If I have to face a firing squad I'll die as a woman—not as a corporal—

HALLIDAY
Rebellious and lovely corporal —I salute you! Don't leave me! Don't vanish.

(The music stops. She moves toward the door. He takes
her to table)

Sitten-sie! I have got to talk to you.
(Sits her right of table)

JERE

I like intense men. Who are you?

HALLIDAY
(Sits on front edge of table)
Some days I'm Christopher Wren building my own cathedral. Some
nights I'm Toulouse-Lautrec on the prowl with paints and brushes. I
might even try to be a writer.

JERE

That's it. You are a writer.

HALLIDAY

How do you know?

JERE

It's the one you find hardest to say.

HALLIDAY
(Rises, moves left, his back to JERE)
You won't believe this—one day I met a German soldier leaning against
a shattered tree, writing a sonnet and we talked about Schiller.

JERE

In the very eye of the holocaust two enemies meet and talk quietly together about Schiller. And your commander would have hated you
both.

HALLIDAY
(Sits left of table)
If I could be a novelist, that's what I'd write about.

JERE

"Friends and Foes" That's your novel!

HALLIDAY

"Friends and Foes" by Manley Halliday. I like it.

JERE

(Rises)

Then, Manley Halliday, write it! I'll make you write it. If you don't,
I'll haunt you.

(Crosses above table, around and front of table, weaving a
spell)

HALLIDAY

(Rises to her, dances with her to Down Center)

Who are you?

JERE

I am me and me is I—
Lawless, flawless, Lorelei—
If I should die before I try—
Will you put a penny on my eye?

HALLIDAY

You'll never die. You're my eternal jazz-baby Lorelei.

JERE

Oh, I love writers. I've loved hundreds of them.

(HALLIDAY retreats from her)

Such a grim look, m'sieur. You are not by any chance an agent of the
Surete?

(Retreats right)

HALLIDAY

(Moving to her)

Madam—I have been shadowing you for years. Your name is Hilda von
Fruhling-Spitzel Horsthausenschaft, Operator 32x!

JERE

Ach, Ausgefundet!

(Music, an old waltz, is played)

That's the last song, I have to leave you and say goodnight to everybody.

HALLIDAY

Don't be so gregarious.

JERE

It's my job. I'll tell you a secret—I love my job. I wish that wars would go on and on and on, only without any shooting, so that these patriotic orgies would go on and on too. It makes me feel so conscientiously promiscuous.

HALLIDAY

Just be promiscuous with me.

SOLDIER

(Left of them)

Come on, Jere, we're going on to the Ritz bar.

HALLIDAY

(Sits JERE at desk, right. Ushers CROWD out)

We'll catch up with you in an hour. Just tell them at the Ritz that the Armistice isn't official until General Pershing and Gracie Fields arrive.

(The CROWD goes off, leaving them alone. At door)

I never imagined that there were eyes like yours. Blind as turquoise and seeing as a cat.

(Kneels left of her)

Or as though your eyes were made to see something other than objects. You do see, don't you, Jere?...What do you see?

JERE

I see spinning. I see the world spinning. I see inside you spinning.

HALLIDAY

Shall I take you seriously?

JERE

Never completely—but always a little.

HALLIDAY

I'll always remember that.

JERE

O terrible frisson des amours novices sur le sol sanglant! Oh, the agony of new love on bleeding earth. Rimbaud and bright lights never seem right together. He wrote by the light of hell-fire!
(HALLIDAY turns out the overhead lamp)
One of these days I'm going to astonish the world with my translations. But when I try to put it into English it goes so dingy and—blah!

HALLIDAY

(Crosses back to her)
Then why try?

JERE

(Rises)
I love to dive deep. I need to climb high.

HALLIDAY

I never wanted anyone or anything so much.
(He embraces her)

JERE

It's three in the morning, my lipstick's all smeared, my hair's a mess, I feel older than Elsie Janis' mother—and you still want to seduce me?

HALLIDAY

(He kisses her)
Your mouth is my hunger. I can hear the wine singing, and you're the youngest old enough girl in the world. And I'm all the determined young men.

JERE

And I'm all the undetermined young women. That's dangerous.

HALLIDAY

(Kisses her)
Jere...Jere.

JERE

(Pulling away from him)
Mannie, I hate that feeling...fingers under my clothes.

HALLIDAY

Jere...please. Please.

JERE

When it happens we'll both know and we'll come to each other and our clothes will fall away.

HALLIDAY

Jere, you must. You must.

JERE

There isn't anything in this world that I must. Except die. And I'll never forgive God for that.

HALLIDAY

You'll never die. You're ageless and timeless. Promise me you'll look exactly as you do this moment a hundred years from now.

JERE
(Backing slowly off, down right)

Mannie, I promise...I promise.

The time is a big factor in this scene. Armistice Night, 1918. People finally feel free to laugh, to drink, to dance, to love. So the overall time is important and can be used. Now the specific time: 3:00 a.m., the cap on a night of fun and games. Champagne has flowed. Jere and Manley are young, healthy, attractive and lusty. At 3:00 a.m. there's probably a moon and stars outside. At 3:00 a.m. they are probably just drunk enough to be carefree and happy and without inhibitions. If you should ever be called upon to audition for the part of Jere, or for any other part in any play, film or T.V. show, the time of the play, and the time of day or night of the scene will affect your reading if you let it. Let it.

One final note on preparing an attack. Be aware that something has happened before any particular scene begins. Find out what that is, and bring it on with you. Some teachers call this "the event". What happens to characters before a scene has a decided effect on how people will behave in a scene. Here's an example from Neil Simon's COME BLOW YOUR HORN:

At rise: ALAN BAKER, in a short Italian suede ski jacket, is standing
in the doorway being his charming, persuasive best in attempting to
lure PEGGY EVANS, pulling her into his bachelor apartment. PEGGY
is in a ski outfit that fits her so snugly it leaves little room for skiing.
ALAN puts down his valise (L. in foyer), then slides PEGGY's over-
night bag out of her hand without her even noticing it and places it on
the floor. ALAN is very adept at this game. Being good-looking,
bright, thirty-three and single, against PEGGY's twenty-two years of
blissful ignorance and eagerness to please , it appears that ALAN has all
the marbles stacked on his side.

                              PEGGY
Alan, no!

                              ALAN
Come on, honey.

                              PEGGY
Alan, no.

                              ALAN
               (Taking off her ski jacket. Puts on luggage)
Just five more minutes. Come on.

                              PEGGY
Alan, no. Please.
               (He pulls her into the living room. He R. of her—D.C.)

                              ALAN
But you said you were cold.

                              PEGGY
I am.

                              ALAN
               (Embracing her)
I'll start a fire. I'll have your blood going up and down in no time.

                              PEGGY
Alan, I want to go upstairs and take a bath. I've got about an inch of the

New York Thruway on me.

ALAN

Honey, you can't go yet. We've got to have one last drink. To cap the perfect week-end.

PEGGY

It was four days.

ALAN

It's not polite to count—Don't you ever get tired of looking sensational?

PEGGY

Do you think I do?

ALAN

You just saw what happened at the ski jump. They were looking at you and jumping into the parking lot—Come here.
(He bites her on the neck)

PEGGY

(Giggles)
Why do you always do that?

ALAN

Do what?

PEGGY

Bite me on the neck.

ALAN

What's the matter? You don't think I'm a vampire, do you?

PEGGY

Gee, I never thought of that.

ALAN

If it'll make you feel safer, I'll chew on your ear lobe.
(He does)

PEGGY

    (Giggles)

Kiss me.

ALAN

I'm not through with the hors d'oeuvres yet.

    (Nibbles—then he kisses her)

PEGGY

    (Sighs and sits on sofa)

Now I feel warm again.

ALAN

Good.

PEGGY

Thank you for the week end, Alan. I had a wonderful time.

ALAN

Yeah, it was fun.

    (Crossing U.L. toward bar)

PEGGY

Even though he didn't show up.

ALAN

    (Stops and turns)

Who?

PEGGY

Your friend from M.G.M.

ALAN

    (Continuing to bar. Quickly)

Oh, Mr. Manheim. Yeah—Well, that's show biz.

PEGGY

Did it say when he expects to be in New York again?

ALAN

Did what?

(Picks up carton containing Scotch bottle)

PEGGY

The telegram. From Hollywood.

ALAN

(Crosses D.L. by window)
Oh! Didn't I tell you? Next week. Early part.

PEGGY

It's kind of funny now that you think of it, isn't it?

ALAN

What is?

PEGGY

Him wanting to meet me in a hotel.

ALAN

(Taking bottle out of carton)
It was a ski lodge.

PEGGY

Was it? Anyway, it was nice. I've never been to New Hampshire before.

ALAN

It was Vermont.
(Putting down carton on sideboard)

PEGGY

Oh, I'm terrible with names. I can't imagine why an important man like that wants to travel all the way up there just to meet me.

ALAN

(Puts bottle back on bar. Crossing above R. and to R. of sofa)
I explained all that. Since this picture he's planning is all about a winter carnival, he figured the best place to meet you would be against the natural setting of the picture. To see how you photograph against

the snow. That makes sense—
          (Not too sure)
Doesn't it?
          (Crosses R.)

PEGGY

Oh, sure.

ALAN

Sure.
        (Pulls PEGGY up from couch and embraces her)

PEGGY

We ought to go again sometime when it's not for business. Just for fun.

ALAN

That should be a week-end.

PEGGY

Maybe next time I could learn to ski.

ALAN

I wouldn't be surprised.

PEGGY

It's a shame we were cooped up in the room so long.

ALAN

Yes. Well, I explained, we had that bad break in the weather.

PEGGY

You mean all that snow.

ALAN

Exactly—But you make the cutest little Saint Bernard—
        (He is just about to kiss her when the buzzer rings)

This could be a simple seduction scene. But then consider the event.
Alan and Peggy have just driven hours on the thruway so they are tired.
That can be used. Also, they have spent four glorious, very sexy days

and nights holed up in a ski lodge. The after-glow of all of that sex, adds a dimension which seems to me necessary to the life and humor of the scene. Add to that the stiffness that the long drive (and the long weekend) has given to their muscles, the foggy, warmly hung-over feeling they both feel, and you have a scene which has some truth and interest to it.

Another less obvious example is this scene which opens Clifford Turknett's one-act play DADDY'S DUET:

THE SCENE: A waiting room of a hospital maternity ward. CHARLES enters from Delivery doors. After a moment NELSON enters the waiting room from hallway. He studies CHARLES. He takes a cigarette from his airline bag and lights it. This is merely a device to trigger a response from CHARLES. CHARLES does respond. He looks at NELSON, then the NO SMOKING sign, then back to NELSON. NELSON looks at the sign, then looks at CHARLES. And then:

NELSON

Smoking bother you?

CHARLES

No bother to me much. My wife smokes. But you know. The sign. They'll just make you put it out.

NELSON

As long as it doesn't bother you. Cold enough for you?

CHARLES

Certainly is.

NELSON

I'll say.

CHARLES

That wind.

NELSON

And so forth.
        (Pause)
Whew! Boy! Been here long?

CHARLES

Not long.

NELSON

Guess I'll have a good wait. Understand this kind of thing can go on forever.

CHARLES

Hhmmmmm, yeah. Depends on the mother, and any complications of course.

NELSON

Oh, right. Well, they're all different I guess. Do this often?

CHARLES

Excuse me?

NELSON

Do this often?

CHARLES

I'm sorry I don't unders—

NELSON

Have any other children?

CHARLES

OH! Yes, yes, a girl.

NELSON

I'm here to watch it.

CHARLES

What?

NELSON

The birth. I'm here to watch it.

CHARLES

Oh, well,...good for you.

NELSON

Watch your first one?

CHARLES

Uh...well...matter of fact...yes.

NELSON

What did it look like?

CHARLES

Well...it felt good.   Actually, it was a highly personal experience.   I'd rather not talk ab—

NELSON

Oh, sure, sure, right.   Not going to watch this one?

CHARLES

Not this one.   A complication involved.   A natural childbirth is preferred, but—

NELSON

Natural?   Ha!   I'll be damned.   Natural.   Ha!   I'll be damned.   Natural.
    (Silence)
What do you want?

CHARLES

What do you mean?

NELSON

A boy this time?

CHARLES

Oh, well, anything would suit us.   A boy would be nice though.

NELSON

Good...and so forth.
    (CHARLES tries very hard to concentrate on his work,
    avoiding NELSON, but NELSON studies him.   NELSON
    then extends his hand for a handshake)
My name is...for want of a better one...Nelson.

> (CHARLES shakes hands with NELSON. NELSON hangs onto CHARLES' hand longer than is necessary)

CHARLES

Charles. You can call me...Charles.

NELSON

> (NELSON now brings out a bottle of beer from the bag, opens it, and takes gulping swigs. This, too, is a device to gather a response from CHARLES. And CHARLES looks up)

Bother you?
> (Belching)

CHARLES

No. No bother. My wife drinks. Uh...could be this isn't really the place for it though.

NELSON

As long as it doesn't bother you.

CHARLES

Oh, no. No.

NELSON

You wouldn't want one?

CHARLES

No, no. Not at all.

NELSON

Cigarette?

CHARLES

No. No thank you.

NELSON

> (NELSON discards the cigarette. It's use is over)

Really clean liver, huh?

CHARLES

Oh, no, not that. Just...uh...don't care for stimulants. You know. Alcohol and tobacco, it's...it's bad for the system. You really going to drink that in here?

NELSON

I like you.

CHARLES

Who? Me?

NELSON

I like you. You're a very, very interesting man.

CHARLES

Oh, really? Well...In what way?

NELSON

O.K. Look, I'm an actor....right?

CHARLES

Actor.

NELSON

Right. Exactly. And I observe people. It's my business to observe people. That's how I perfect my craft, see, when I'm not on stage. I observe people, the way they behave, any oddities, and what not. Then later, in a part I'm working on or something, I'll think back on something I've seen, observed, and I'll use that to make myself more believeable. See? It's that extra something that makes me more believeable, more natural. And when I see that I jump on it...an actor has always got to be perfecting his craft, even when he's not on stage. Or he dries up. See? He dies. That's how it's done.

CHARLES

Oh? Well...that's very interesting.
                (Pause)
To be or not to be.

NELSON

What?

CHARLES

Something I remember from school. Shakespeare.

NELSON

Well now that's beautiful, it really is.

CHARLES

The whole world is an entire stage.

NELSON

What? Oh, yeah, right. You're getting it. So I observe people. Take mental notes. Store it all up. For future use.

CHARLES

That's really fascinating. That would really take some practice. But what is it about...me?

NELSON

Everything. The way you work over those papers. The way you comb your hair. Your clothes, your funny shoes, everything.

CHARLES

And what does that tell you?

NELSON

EVERYTHING!!

CHARLES

I see.

NELSON

Yeah. And so forth.
          (A beat)
Do you like what I'm wearing?

CHARLES

Well...yes...it's...okay.

NELSON

Just my everyday clothes.

Let's say you are reading for the part of Nelson. Here it's not nearly as clear cut as in the Neil Simon play. Turknett has given you clues, that's true...such as the fact that Nelson is an actor. Also, he appears to be waiting for the arrival of his new child. But, since the playwright is no more helpful than that, it's up to you and your imagination. Has he been at a bar drinking before coming to the waiting room? Has he just been out with the boys to celebrate the impending arrival? Is he a young husband who is out of work and fears the responsibility of fatherhood? Has he just committed a burglery to get money to pay the hospital? I don't know. Any of the above could be appropriate choices—and there are hundreds of others. He can have been anywhere, and done anything you choose. My only suggestion to you is that, out of your own background and experience, you settle on an event—something which happened to this man or something he made happen before the scene starts. Be specific with it and let whatever influence it might have on his behavior shine through during the scene. Without it you will be doing just another audition. With it, you will be creating a life on stage.

5. If at all possible, get familiar with the place where you will audition. I know I said this before, but let me add one trick used by a young actress, who gave a superb audition for me. She says she tries to pick an object—a chair is often best—and touch it for a moment, or move it slightly, or whatever. But consciously she makes that object familiar, treats it as a friend. Reassures it, and lets it reassure her. In other words, even though the time this takes may be only a few seconds, try to find one object in the environment and make friends with it. This then becomes your ally, and the environment consequently becomes less strange.

6. Choice of material. This concerns those general auditions where you are asked to select material. The first suggestion I have is if you are given specific guidelines such as a time limit and a certain type of material, work in response to those guidelines. They are there for a

reason. Also, a deliberate violation of rules often shows an actor's resentment or hostility, which is not the most desirable facet one would want to show. I'd say, choose that material which shows off *you* to best advantage. I emphasize "you" so hopefully it will be communicated that I mean you as you are. Not you as you wish to be, or you as you want others to see you, but you right here and now. This is often a most difficult concept to grasp; especially for beginners. The actor's art seems at first blush to be purely imitative. We see somebody do something, and then try to do it ourselves. And in our society, with T.V. and movies forever staring us in the face, our young actors (and too many of our older ones) more often than not will imitate not an action, but some other actor's imagination of an action. So we get a doubly filtered version of an event, when the event ideally would be something fresh, vital and new.

As an example, think of the number of death scenes you've seen on your T.V. this past week. What happens? Gunfire, someone falls and is instantly dead; or he manages to say a few very pertinent final words—exhales, and dies; or someone in a bed who is very sick stares weakly at the one she loves, closes her eyes, and fades off amidst many violins to a sleepy state which we assume is death. These are actors copying other actors' versions of that very real, very dramatic event; and consequently giving us a watered down version of that event. I mean, what really happens when someone gets shot? There is probably internal hemorrhaging. Perhaps a filling up of the lungs. A kicking, croaking, clawing feeling as the victim tries by any means at all to get just a bit of air into his lungs. Perhaps bleeding from the mouth. Now granted, directors have limitations. There are things which people don't want shown on T.V. O.K. But when you are auditioning (and now we are getting back to the concept of you being you) and you have to do a death scene, it might be worth investigating how you might react to a bullet wound, or a fatal illness or whatever...and bring us your version of that event. I've given you a negative example. Let me give you a positive one. In Zefferelli's film of *Romeo and Juliet* , when Mercutio—John McEnery—is stabbed by Romeo, everyone, including Mercutio, thinks it's only a scratch. The others laugh and carry on. Mercutio begins to feel weak. The others don't even notice. He discovers blood. This gives him pause. He puts his hand over the wound as if this might stop the flow. He gets weaker. The others are still oblivious. He tries to get up. Can't. He begins to realize it's serious. He tries to get the attention of the others. Can't. The others gather around and look down at him. Slowly, they begin to realize he is really hurt. He moves. He gets weaker and weaker, still only half-believing this is happening to him. The others now look down silently. Mercutio, now frightened, again tries to move. He is too weak. He kicks as if to prove he can still move. The kicks grow weaker and finally in a spasm of agony he goes under.

This is not your usual Robin Hood—eek!-I'm-stabbed-fall-down-and-die death. This is a man suffering the physical and mental agonies...the pain and the fears of facing that moment. It has truth.

Now I've used a most graphic example of you using you and your reactions. There are many others. It merely behooves you to look. How do you feel when you fall in love? How do you feel when you are so angry you could spit...or kill?

Well, all of this began with us talking about choosing material with which to audition. I'd say you should use as a guideline a role in which you might actually be cast. For instance, if you are 21, don't try to impress us with your great versatility and prowess by choosing to do a speech of King Lear's. We will not be able to see you at all, no matter how well you do it. Or, if you are a lady who is short and, let us say, somewhat stout, don't choose to audition as Helen of Troy.

Another suggestion. Stay away from dialects. I will except from this some regional suggestions of dialects—such as Blanche in A STREET-CAR NAMED DESIRE or Gittel in TWO FOR THE SEESAW. These we can deal with since they are just slight variations on the speech of most Americans. But anything more is a no no. Dialects tend to call our attention to the dialect and away from you. We either question the authenticity of a dialect if it's not too good, or wonder at it if it is good; but while we are doing one or the other, we do it at the expense of seeing you. It often seems to me that the actor using a dialect is hiding behind it. Come out and show us you.

Don't select material which calls for elaborate costuming, props, sound effects or music. For one thing, at most auditions time is at a premium, and the time it takes to set these things in motion does not sit well with auditioners, not because we begrudge you the time but because we are conscious of our obligation to you and to the 25 people waiting behind you. Also, (and if I'm beginning to sound like a broken record, good!) we want to see and hear you. Not the you under a costume. Not the you bolstered by background music. The actor's job is to act, pure and simple. The professional does that with as few trappings as possible. The amateur feels a need to tell his audience everything as if they might not understand. The professional leads them, giving them only that information which will catch their interest, grip their emotions, and make them feel they are watching a heightened moment.

Don't select material which needs an explanation. Maybe a short sentence or two if absolutely essential, but preferably nothing. If you find your monologue absolutely must be preceded with an explanation, throw it out and get another one. The less experienced actor, feeling that his audience won't "get" what he is trying to do, will often feel compelled to do a plot summary leading up to his monologue. (One actually took 3 or 4 minutes to tell me the plot of HAMLET leading up to "To Be Or Not To Be".) The work should stand on its own merits.

A thought. Do prepare each and every audition if you want the part. Unnecessary advice? I think not. I've seen it ignored many times. I know a marvelous young actor who had just finished doing a play for us at the Mark Taper Forum. He was on very good terms with the casting office and with the directors. Immediately after his play closed another part came up which he was right for. He expressed interest, we sent him a script, and he then came in to read. Everything was first names and smiles—jokes about the last show and so on. But when he began to read it was obvious he'd done little more than glance at the script beforehand. He was totally unprepared. You ask, since we had worked with him recently, why couldn't we judge from that? Well, every part is different. Every director is different—and different when he works on different material. (For example, just watch how the same director will function when he has a star in the company and when he doesn't). The point is, we need to see what the actor does with this part in this play. So don't...again don't take for granted that we know your work so you don't have to show us anything. If that was the case we'd offer you the part over the phone. But if we ask you to read, and you want the part, really prepare a terrific reading. Do your best...always.

Just Before The Audition:

Do your acting preparation during the time you are waiting off stage or in that outer office. Don't wait till your name is called to start getting in the mood. Some people use that time to gossip with the other actors who are waiting, but often that is merely the exchanging of pre-audition insecurites, and I'd suggest you avoid it. A pleasant "hello" and then back to your script, and the others will get the message. One exception (there are probably more) is the actor who needs to feed off others and is preparing to go on to do, let's say a comedy monologue. He might need that contact to get his juices flowing...but for the most part I'd suggest actors do their preparing before an audition, and their socializing after.

If, while waiting, fear begins to take you over there are a few ways to deal with it. Most have already been set down earlier in this chapter, but here are a couple of additional thoughts.

Don't be alarmed at simple nervous energy. This can be useful and give you the "charge" you need to spark what you do in the audition. What you want to get away from is that crippling, agonizing terror we have all faced at one time or another. As mentioned before, practice listening and seeing. Also think of those things going on in the world around you and put the audition in its proper perspective.

But most important, make the audition a joyous occasion for yourself. "That's easy for you to say," you say, but it can be done. Some people try to do it by hating "those bastards out there" and they anticipate great glee in "showing them what it's all about". Others imagine the auditioners sitting there in their underwear in an attempt to strip them of any dignity they might have. But I say rather than putting the auditioners down, you'd do much better to put yourself up. Find out how you can be joyous. Some do this by looking on the audition as an opportunity to do something they love—i.e. to perform. If you go out with this attitude you will probably get off to a good start. If so, let that feeling of joy which accompanies doing something well, generate more good work, thus more joy, etc., etc. This might sound impossible to some, but if you take it one step at a time it can be done. Maybe when you first walk out on the stage, you flash a brief trace of a grin (more than that if at all possible, but if not settle for a brief trace). It might not seem like you're doing very much at all, but if you manage a genuine grin, it's one step farther along than you were before. The next time you might manage a whole, sustained smile. And if you continue to try this—just one step at a time, don't push or force—you could get yourself to the point where you really enjoy an audition. It is possible.

The stage manager or his assistant will probably be the one to call you on stage. When they do, take a deep breath or two and let each breath help to generate a feeling of anticipation and eagerness to get on the stage, and then go. Once there the stage manager will probably introduce you. Often there will be lights shining in your eyes and you will have no idea if there are two or two hundred people in the house. I suggest you treat that group as one person until you find out differently. If the stage manager fails to introduce you, or if there is no stage manager, the best approach is a simple friendly, "Hello. My name is—." Then if you are reading a scene they have asked you to prepare, you are ready to go. If it's a general audition and you have chosen your own material, state the name of the play, the author, and if necessary the part you'll play. For example, "Hello, my name is— and I'm going to do one of Hotspur's speeches from Shakespeare's HENRY IV Part I" I'd suggest you not rehearse this introduction so it comes out as a prepared speech because then it will sound stilted and unnatural. Just simply give us the information so we can then adjust ourselves to the style and content of what we are about to see.

If you are reading with someone it will probably be a stage manager. This can be a problem because stage managers usually come in one of two shapes: a) The frustrated actor who uses auditions as a chance to emote. This kind will huff and puff and bellow his way through your audition secretly hoping it is his as well. b) The technician who hates being on stage and would much rather be back with his light board where he feels safe and secure. This one will bury his nose in the script and rarely speak above a whisper.

How to deal with them? I know only one way. Believe that the person opposite you is the world's greatest living actor, and play the scene as if he were just that. He is Olivier or Brando or Hepburn or Duse. Just choose your favorite and use your imagination to make him the greatest. Then, since you are playing with the greatest, let your talent rise to meet the challenge.

Final Preparation

You are on stage and you have introduced yourself. Now a final moment of preparation is in order. Some actors do this in just a couple of seconds. They pause, take a deep breath and then are off to the races. Others turn their back for a moment just to collect themselves before they begin. Still others feel they need a longer time.

One of the longest I've seen was a young lady who, as soon as she came into the audition room began to sniff. The sniffs soon turned to tears, the tears to sobs. Suddenly she screamed, "God damn it, this is humiliating. Why should I have to go through this? I've got talent. I've got talent, God damn it, and to have to come here and beg for a job..."

She looked at me, hate shining through the tears. "What do you know about how we feel? The humiliation. You just sit there. You don't know. You don't care" and so on for at least three minutes of complete hysterics.

However, at one point she looked at me through the tears and sobbed, "You know what I'm doing, don't you?"

I nodded. She was preparing. The only problem was that her preparatin, as out of control and destructive as it was, was more interesting than the audition which followed.

This, of course, was an extreme...and there have been others. One man, undoubtedly on drugs of some kind, before he began, stared for a full 120 seconds directly at the stage manager he was to read with. This was not just a stare. It was a vacant, wild, hostile look—chilling to see.

I've seen young girls reach in and yank off bras. Others take off shoes and socks and anything else which might get in the way. But all of this seems to me to be incidental to the job at hand.

As a rule of thumb I'd say the less time one takes for this final bit of preparation, the better. However, do not rush yourself. Take what you need, no more but no less. You will, of course, run into some auditioners who don't want to wait and who tell you to just get on with it. Then you must evaluate the situation and, if it seems appropriate, cut down that last minute preparation time to a minimum.

But all in all, even if it's only a deep breath, I'd say a moment of preparation just before you begin is a valuable thing.

During The Audition

It is, of course, impossible to tell you how to do the audition itself, as each audition situation is completely different from any other, but there are things you can do during the audition to make things easier for yourself and consequently for those auditioning you. Let's look at a few.

1. Be cooperative. Generally speaking an aura of cooperation will be contagious. If you have been trying it and it hasn't seemed to work, don't be discouraged. It is an attitude I would suggest for the rest of your career. Now you will run into people—people in a position to hire and fire such as producers and directors—who have adopted non-cooperation in its many forms as a life style. When coming up against this attitude we sometimes will automatically assume the same stance, if only subconsciously, in an attempt to achieve that same power for ourselves. It doesn't work that way. My advice? Let their problems be their problems, not yours. Don't assume their attitude if it is negative. Who knows, they might even learn a bit of cooperation from you.

Being cooperative does not mean you have to give up your identity. Quite the contrary. In my reality the person with the most positive identity is the one who can afford to be cooperative. He doesn't need to close up defensively and say, "Don't tell me what to do". That attitude carries with it the opposite of strength, because inherent in it is a fear that someone is going to try to take away something which makes you "you". If you have a sense of self...a real sense of self... you don't lose anything by cooperating with others. Actually you gain. If you don't have it, take whatever steps seem appropriate to get it. One way might be to plunge into activities which make you fearful and prove to yourself that you can survive them. Another is to seek help. Still another is to give up something you are dependent upon. It might be as simple as not having dessert because that means extra pounds. Or finally give up cigarettes as you've said you were going to do for the last five years because cigarettes represent that dependency which makes you feel less than capable. Whatever it is you feel dependent upon, try doing without it. If you persist your auditions will be a lot better—to say nothing of your life. .

One more word about your cooperative attitude. The editors of *Esquire* magazine a few years ago devoted an entire issue to sophistication—true sophistication as opposed to the phony, bored, cigarette-holder caricature we see so often—and they came up with the following, perhaps slightly paraphrased, definition: "The true sophisticate is one who can adapt himself to any environment or social situation without losing his identity." I'd say that's a good goal to shoot for at your next audition.

2. Be alert and alive. Sitting out in the darkened orchestra of the 46th Street Theatre afternoon after afternoon, I've seen auditioners, myself among them, sink farther down in their seats, the corners of their mouths turning down lower and lower as one after another, actors slump on stage, mumble their auditions, and slump off again.

But then something happens: someone strides out of the wings, a purpose in his walk, a smile on his face. When he talks his voice is loud and clear. When we talk, he listens. There is a bounce and vitality he brings on which is infectious. We sit up. We lean forward. We find our mouths have formed into a grin. Some life has come into the theatre.

Please note, this sense of alertness and vitality is not something to be faked. That's worse than not having it at all. But it is something you can develop...slowly, perhaps,...or not so slowly depending on who you are and what you are about. But if you are interested try first being aware of your own attitude. Is it down? Lacking vitality? If so, take just one aspect of your demeanor...say, for example, your walk, and infuse it with a little more drive than it had before. Or maybe your posture. If you find yourself slumped over like a scarecrow after the rain, be aware of this and straighten up.

In other words, take an aspect of you which seems to need revitalizing, and give it an injection of life. When that's done and feels comfortable, try it with another aspect, then another, and so on.

3. Be flexible and ready to change. Say you have prepared your audition the way you want to do it. Not as an imitation of what some other actor does on T.V. but you shining through those words on the paper.

Then, surprise? The director wants you to try a completely different approach. "Oh, my God," you say. Or, "I've done all this work presenting me and now he wants me to change," you say. Or, "How dare you," you say. Or, "I can't do it," you say.

But you can. If you want the job. Don't be angry or insulted. Just try it. What have you got to lose? Your identity? Your creativity? Horse feathers! Be flexible. Be adaptable. It's vital for your survival as a human being, why shouldn't it be vital for your survival as an actor?

Don't look on any legitimate suggestions or ideas as hostile. Rather, approach them as a challenge...one you can't wait to tackle. If you do, the audition can be fun rather than fearful, exciting rather than routine...a challenge rather than a mechanical procedure.

One hint. Even if we've loved your audition, sometimes we casting people will give you a different way to tackle a scene just to check out your adaptability, your willingness to dare something new, your range and/or your cooperative spirit.

To sum up. Be ready, willing and eager to try, to change, to re-think, to branch out. Instead of dreading the new or untried, welcome it.

4. Be happy. Even if you are auditioning for the darkest tragedy and and have fully prepared yourself, be aware of that joy which can come to you when you are doing well.

Let's put it this way: When you are auditioning, what is there to be unhappy about, unless you are not in present time?

"What do you mean," you say. "My knees are shaking, my heart is pounding, my throat is dry, and those guys out there hate me. Why shouldn't I be miserable?"

But take a look at this situation. You are displaying all those symptoms because you are afraid. Why are you afraid? (We've already dealt with fear, but a moment's recap as we talk about actually doing the audition might not hurt). Three possibilities occur:

a) This situation where you must prove yourself puts you in that familiar childlike position where you are helpless and alone and dependent on others for your care and feeding and for your very survival. If you do not please them, they could be angry, or oblivious and you could die.

b) If you don't get the job, your career will take yet another blow, your feelings of self-worth will drop yet another notch, and you will have to drop all those dreams of being an actor and begin a paper route.

c) You might end up getting the job...and this we've already explored.

If any of these three fears, (or any others, for that matter) rings a bell, then take a good hard look at them, for while they have the power to shake the strongest man or woman, they all carry one fallacy: THEY HAVE NOTHING WHATSOEVER TO DO WITH NOW.

What is actually happening now (in the audition) is that those producers and directors want very much to cast their show. The sooner it's cast, the sooner they can rehearse and open and make themselves rich and famous. So they would like nothing better than to have the next actor or actress—you, for instance—be just the one for them.

You, on the other hand, are there presumably because you want to be cast in a play or film or T.V. show.

Now, one of two things can happen as a result of your audition: Either your goals and the auditioners' goals will be achieved. Or they will not. That is all. Other outcomes such as feelings of rejection, deflated ego, etc., are not really a part of what is going on.

"Easy for you to say," you say. "You're sitting out there, while I'm up here baring my soul and my guts to the world, just asking someone to shoot me down."

But the truth is, an audition is best performed when you want a job, not when you need it. The having to have something, carried to the extreme some actors carry it to, is something which should be done away with. For the most part, I think "want" is healthy, "need" is un.

To summarize, during the audition: 1. Be cooperative. 2. Be alert and alive. 3. Be flexible and ready to change. 4. Display joy in your work.

After The Audition:

One important thing to remember is that the audition doesn't end when you finish reading. I have seen actors give marvelous readings, and then as they leave, I've heard a loud, "God Damn it!" from the wings. Whatever I thought about this actor's work can be affected seriously by an off-stage temperamental outburst.

I've also seen actors blame, if only slightly, stage managers or accompanists for some real or imagined error. I can't say I look on this with much favor either.

What I'm saying is, your audition is not over until you are out the door. Maintain that up attitude we've talked about past the audition, through the "thank yous" and the "goodbyes" and out into the street. For that matter what would it hurt to maintain it the rest of the day, or the week, or your life?

I now have some advice as to what to do after your audition—advice most actors will agree is very sound except when they try to practice it themselves. The advice is this: Once you've done your audition, forget it.

If you have mentally and physically prepared your psyche and your body; if you have gone into the audition, committed yourself fully and freely to it, and presented yourself in the most positive way you can... then you are a success. Later on, if you also get the job, that's gravy. But you have "made it" if you've done the audition as described above.

So, my advice is, when the audition is over, take a look at what you've done. If it could have been better, piece together why and how and work on those things before the next audition. If not, if you really did everything you could, forget about it, because the truth is, what happens after that is completely out of your hands.

Here are a couple of examples of what I mean:

I saw a young lady give a fabulous audition for the touring company of a hit Broadway musical. She sang with guts and passion. Musically she was superb. She had worked on her reading and it was full, rich, funny, sad and warm. In short, she did everything she could. But when she left the room, the producer and director arrived at the conclusion that she was too close in personality and power to another performer already cast in the show. They had to say no. What else might this girl have done? Nothing, because the factors which resulted in her not getting the part were factors over which she had no control. Was her audition a success? Many actors would say no. I say yes. A huge one. She did all she could. That to me is a success.

What about the job? She didn't get it, but she did demonstrate to a number of people not only her talent but her commitment. As a matter of fact I've called her in on a number of other jobs since then. I also have referred her to others, and this is another point to remember. We people in casting have big mouths, and when we find talent we like to let others know about it. So, do all you can at every audition, and if you don't get the particular job you are there for, you still win in ways you may not even know yet.

Even if you give a 100% perfect audition there are still so many factors beyond your control. As examples:

Your size. I saw a man 5'6" be brilliant, and still lose a part because his lady love in the play had already been cast, and she was 5'8". I've also seen men lose parts because they were too tall.

Sometimes directors want to balance a production racially. I've seen whites lose parts because blacks, chicanos or orientals were desired—and the other way around.

Sometimes, especially in casting a big production, our minds get fixed on one certain area of casting. For example, in doing a big Shakespearian play we might, on one particular day, be concentrating our attention on the low-lifes and overlook a good actor for a nobleman. We don't do this often, but we do it. This is another reason to forget the audition after it is over. There are just too many elements you can't control, including our all too human errors.

Sometimes actors get roles by default. By this I mean a director makes a list of, say, three choices for a particular role in order of preference and you, without knowing it, are number three. He offers the part to number one, but he's been offered a bigger part and more money by someone else and turns it down. The director tries number two. He has suddenly been signed to do the lead in a horror film shooting in the Philippines. So he turns to number three—you. What does this tell us? First of all, it's another example of the actor's inability to control factors other than his own preparation and audition. It also says something about how actors feel about other actors getting jobs, and I'd like to side track on that one for just a minute.

If you feel a jolt of envy, anger or bitterness when you hear of another actor getting a job, come to terms with that. That is, in my reality, a most destructive way of approaching your career. That bitterness, when broadcast out to the world, has a curious way of bending back and kicking you in the pants when you least expect it. Whereas if you can be glad, really glad when someone takes a step forward, it somehow makes your next step forward that much easier. I can't tell you specifically how that works, but I've seen enough examples of it (as in the case described above where you got the part because the other two actors got jobs) to state it as fact. Be happy for others' success, and before you know it, they'll be happy for yours.

Your audition is over. Before I deal with call backs, I'd like to, for the benefit of those who are skimming the pages, do a brief recap, on how to do your best audition:

1. Prepare The Audition.
    a) Know the scene and the whole script well.
    b) Learn what you can about the people you will audition for.
    c) Get help if you feel you need it.
    d) Work to do the audition fully and freely.
        a. Prepare an attack.
        b. Relate the work to you.
    e) If possible, know the place where you will audition.
    f) Prepare every audition as if it was the most important one. It is.
    g) If you must choose the material, choose something for which

you might be cast, and make it something you really like to do.

h) Find ways to make the audition a joyous occasion for yourself.

2. Doing The Audition.

a) Do your acting preparation before you go on.

b) Do the audition simply, without elaborate accoutrements.

c) If you get upset, angry, or overly frightened at an audition, find a way to deal with that right now. Chances are the audition is only the immediate cause, not the real cause of those feelings.

d) Be of help to those you are auditioning for.

e) Be alert and alive.

f) Be flexible and ready to change.

3. After The Audition.

a) Remember, you're not finished till you've left the theatre.

b) When you've done the very best you can, consider yourself a success because you are. The rest is out of your hands.

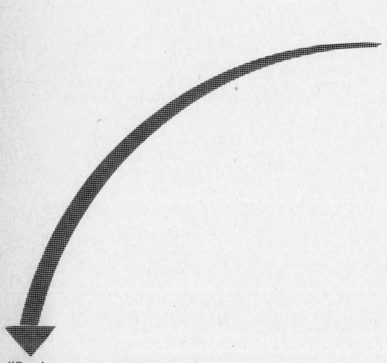

"Don't come in with that chip—on—the—shoulder 'Whatsa matter? You gotta drag me in here again? You couldn't make up your mind the first time?' attitude. If you feel we are 'dragging you in here,' don't come. If a call back seems to you (as it does to me) to be a legitimate part of the audition process, then come . . . and enjoy."

Call Backs

All right. You did the audition. They said, "Thank you," and you left. It's been three days. They've obviously chosen someone else. But what's this? The phone? For me? They want me for a call back?

The reactions to call backs vary from a feeling of victory and euphoria: "I've got the part! Now let's see. First I'm going to move to a bigger apartment. And I think I'll sell that V.W. and get a new Audi. Audi? Hell, why not a Mercedes?" to panic and despair: "Oh, God. A call back! What'll I do? It was all an accident at the first audition. They'll see right through me this time for sure. Oh, God. Why me?"

Now calm down. What is a call back after all? On its simplest level it is an attempt by the auditioners to see you and your work again so they can make a better judgement as to your suitability for a specific role. Nothing more.

Why should you, the actor, be put through all that again? There are a number of reasons for call backs. Here are a few:

1. As a reminder. We saw 75 people that day. You were one of them. We have written good comments next to your name but we need to be reminded just who you are. (Sorry to bruise your ego, but the truth is we don't always remember you.)

2. As a field narrower. We have to cast the part. We've seen 30 people. Sooner or later we have to make a choice, so we call back the 5 most likely candidates.

3. As a possible reserve candidate. Sometimes we are not sure if our first choice for a part will be available, so call backs sometimes give us back-up candidates.

4. As a dispute settler. The producer hates you and the director loves you. Each wants to prove the other wrong so, you are called back.

5. As a test. We know the call back situation can be a pressured one. But so is opening night. So is the out-of-town chaos when the show is being born. So is 6:55 p.m. on the set, when a film must be wrapped by 7:00 p.m. and the last shot is a 3 minute close up of your complete mental and physical disintegration. So we call you back to see how you handle a pressure situation.

6. As a check of other facets. We liked you, but we need to see more humor. Or more emotional release. Or more spontaneity. Or greater use of your body. Or how you improvise. Or a hundred other things we might have missed the first time around.

7. As a test of how you work. For example, we might want to see if given more time than you had before, you will do more work on the audition—dig deeper, add layers, find humor, find more of yourself in the part.

There are many more reasons, of course. If it's for a musical we might want to hear you sing a different kind of song. If it's a dance audition we might want to see which groups of people work best together.

The upshot is, the first audition is often just a preliminary step, hence the call back.

How do you prepare for a call back? Here are a number of do's and don'ts.

DO more work on the script. Really dig into it. Prepare as if it is for the greatest part of your career. Get help in preparing if you think you need it. Work on a dialect if that is called for. Open yourself emotionally if that's what you think is needed. Find the laughs, etc., etc.

DON'T assume that because you are called back you are almost cast so you don't need to knock yourself out preparing. I've seen too many actors lose jobs just because of that attitude. They sidle in for a call back, give just enough to let us know they're in the room, and sidle out again. Forget it. If you don't do more work, don't bother coming back.

DO attack the call back with the same or even more energy than you did the first audition.

DON'T, however, change the basic approach you had at the first audition—unless, of course, you are asked to. (There were obviously some good things there already or you wouldn't be called back). I've seen lovely little ingenues, on call backs for ingenue roles, come bombing into the room like incipient Raquel Welches. Wrong! You were close to the mark the first time or you wouldn't be called back.

DO wear the same thing you wore to the first audition, unless asked to dress differently. Remember, that overall impression including your clothes, was part of what made us want to see you again.

DON'T come in with that chip-on-the-shoulder "Whatsa matter? You gotta drag me in here again? You couldn't make up your mind the first time?" attitude. If you feel we are "dragging you in here," don't come. If a call back seems to you (as it does to me) to be a legitimate part of the audition process, then come...and enjoy.

At the actual call back, the same suggestions made in the "audition" chapter apply. Namely, plunge in, take a chance, show us you, find the humor and be flexible. And when you are through—go.

So you've done the call back. What's that? Phone for me? A second call back? Oh, my God!

Why would auditioners want another call back? For all the same reasons they wanted the first, only by now the field is even narrower.

And so it goes. Some people have been called back six, eight, ten times, and lost out. But let me remind you of what we said earlier. You are not auditioning just for that role. The people you audition for will no doubt be doing other things, so if your audition is wonderful, but for some reason they choose someone else, you can be sure that wonderful audition will bring its reward sometime in the future.

All right, you've heard enough from me. The next voices you hear will be those of professionals from theatre, films, television, educational theatre, and dance. You will also hear from some actors, and learn how they deal with auditions. These opinions, as you will see, vary considerably. Some agree with mine, many do not. I'm including as wide a variety of thoughts about the audition process as possible so that you can see the different kinds of people you will be auditioning for. Also, I hope these interviews will help to lift at least a bit of the cloak of mystery which seems to surround the audition process.

The following interviews have been edited to eliminate repetitious and irrelevant material, but the essence of what was said remains intact.

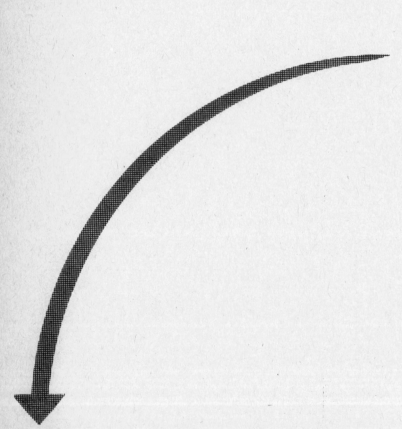

"... if I see an actor who is too rigid and I want him to bend a bit I'll take the part and bend it in another direction just to see if he can be loose — if he can loosen and change and take direction."

Gower Champion

**A DIRECTOR/CHOREOGRAPHER
TALKS ABOUT AUDITIONING**

GH: How about singing or musical auditions? I just wonder if there's anyone that really knocked you out.

CHAMPION: Well, I can tell you one about a star, Carol Channing. It has to do with her wanting the role of HELLO, DOLLY! and I'll tell you the story and you can use it or not, whatever it's worth. I had decided to do the show, David Merrick and I went to see her in THE MILLIONAIRESS which was playing in Long Island—and I felt that she was wrong for the part of HELLO, DOLLY! because she was still playing Lorelei Lee. And because I knew Carol from before I went to her hotel that night, back in town, and I said, "Look, Carol, I love you— so-and-so and so-and-so—but I don't think you are right for this particular thing." And she said, "I'll do anything. Let me work on the script. Let's work on it right now. Tell me what you want. I will do anything." And her husband, Charlie Loewe, went to my hotel to get a script and brought it back to their hotel and she and I worked—just going back and forth, and back and forth. She was trying to understand why I felt she wasn't right for the role. And we spent—Oh, we worked until about one or two o'clock in the morning and I began to get a glimmer of what this lady could be in that particular role. So then I said, "O.K. Let's sleep on it." I went back to my hotel and said, "I'll see you about 11 o'clock the next morning." Which I did. And she had been up all night, she had not been to bed—I found out later—because she wanted it. And she worked her ass off for it. And I came back to work some more—I had Lucia Victor come with me, to read with her. I began to see it was going to happen and I phoned Merrick, and I said, "David, maybe this is going to work. Set up a theatre for me and I'll come down with Carol and we'll read on stage so we can take a look at her." Which we did. We went down to the Imperial Theatre and Carol got on stage and was reading with Lucia and she was doing quite well and mid-way through the audition she stopped—having done a kind of Lorelei Lee-ism—and looked up and said, "Wait a minute! That's what you mean. That's what I'm not supposed to do. Isn't that right, Gower?" And I said, "Right" and she went ahead. Now, the only lesson to be gained from that was a total gut want and fight! She would have killed to do that part and she was right because she was marvelous in it—and the show was marvelous for her. Plus which, she listened to her director, took direction and understood what he meant in the terms of that particular role—and found it. And once she found it, when she fell out of it she, as an actress, was smart enough to know she had fallen out of it. That was the most exciting audition that I ever had in my life because—well, as I say, she would have killed for it.

GH: I think to me, that's the most important thing that an actor can do—is to have that kind of enthusiasm or drive or desire. I mean, more important than any technique.

CHAMPION: Right, right. You'll forget technique, you'll excuse bad technique—if they have the need, the desire and the gut thing.

GH: Do you use any technique yourself, as an auditioner?

CHAMPION: Yes. No specific—but if I see an actor who is too rigid and I want to bend him a bit I'll take the part and bend it in another direction just to see if he can be loose—if he can loosen and change and take direction.

GH: Do you have any pet hates about things people do in auditions?

CHAMPION: Lack of preparation is the main one. I would say 60% of the people here, in California, I'm talking about stage people, who are headed for New York, maybe, will be not as well-prepared as the New York people.

GH: So that tells you, in effect, that they are not interested—or as interested as you'd like them to be?

CHAMPION: Not interested and number two, not trained. They don't have the background. So many Hollywood stars who want to go into musical comedy will go out and play summer theatre—like Debbie Reynolds did, like Anna Maria Alberghetti did, like Carol Channing did. They go out and they want to get into theatre and they'll play St. Louis and Dallas and all those places and really work and sweat and find out what it is to play with an audience. Then you know they've got that experience. And there's only one way to do it, that is to get experience, to get it under their belts, and you know you have that experience to draw upon when they have got to get in front of an audience on stage. Like, Debbie is incredible because she knows how to play an audience because she's done it. You don't learn that in front of a camera, you just don't.

GH: One last one. Do you like auditions?

CHAMPION: No, I hate 'em.

GH: May I ask why?

CHAMPION: Well, I think they are demeaning basically. It is very tough on the performer. They have got to get up there under a bare work light and then sell themselves to the director or the choreographer in a way. It's always very tough...it's tough for them, mainly. Sometimes you get people, who are quite good, who are lousy auditioners. They just can't...they may have prepared, done all they can do, but they just tighten up or they get nervous or they need the comfort, the safety, the inclusion of a play in a dark theatre and an audience and so forth.

GH: Yes, yes. You empathize then with them—I mean, as a performer yourself...

CHAMPION: Yes, yes, and it's very tough to make a decision. Sometimes somebody will walk out on that stage and BAM! you know it right away. One of the worst auditions I ever had in my life was Pierre Olaf for CARNIVAL. Pierre had been in PLUME DE MA TANTE and Mike Stewart said, "You've got to remember that guy who hit the bells." "Yes, fine." So Pierre came in and walked onstage at the Imperial Theater and he had a script and he had these little glasses on.

And he tried to read with these glasses, and he dropped the script. Now, the script is all over the stage—spread around—and he eventually (I swear!) he got down on his hands and knees and was reading—this is the way he auditioned for me reading the page like that. Now, it happened that he was ZAP—he was so gorgeous and right on it that before he even read I said, "Oh, my God, he's it!" That's Jocko of CARNIVAL. So it worked—in contradiction to everything I've said. He just had the right quality and was that little nebbishy man, and French and all of it.

GH: Does it take you long to know, when somebody walks on, whether they are even in the running?

CHAMPION: Generally you know pretty quick. And you get vibes. You get vibes—and in a room like this if someone walks in and says, "Hi!"—there's something there. Then you may find they are not right but usually first impressions have a lot to do with it.

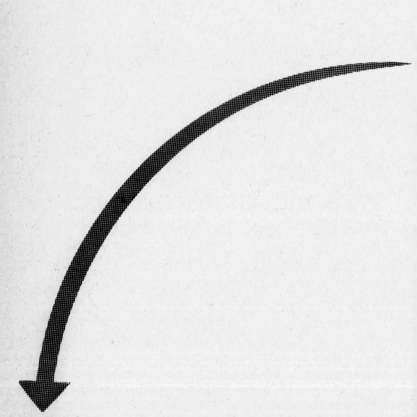

"*I do believe in one thing, very strongly, and that is that unless you are painting the blackest of villians—there has to be something, aside from the person's acting ability, something appealing, something magnetic...*"

Peter Hunt
A DIRECTOR TALKS ABOUT AUDITIONING

GH: What's the difference between auditioning for a play and auditioning for a film or television show?

HUNT: A stage audition, I think, is much more demanding on a person than just sitting across a desk in a very relaxed atmosphere reading a script. Also, actors tend really to underplay everything for film because that's really motion picture technique, anyway. To do nothing is usually very effective in a movie. You can't go wrong if you do nothing. But I like to know that there's that emotional reserve, there's that power, you know?

GH: Do you also look for a kind of sympatico in actors?

HUNT: I think it's important to me, personally, that I feel I can get along with a particular actor—but I think that's a bit of a handicap on my part. I think that I should be more daring—and be willing to go with somebody I don't really like but know is right for the part. You know? I do believe in one thing, very strongly, and that is that unless you are painting the blackest of villians—there has to be something, aside from the person's acting ability, something appealing, something magnetic in any part—even if it's a maid that comes on and says, "Dinner is ready." That's kind of a prerequisite with me for any part...and...I can only go on my own hunches, my own feelings about a person when they walk in a room. Or in the case of New York, when they come out on stage. My favorite audition of all time was Richard B. Schull who has, as you know, been in a lot of commercials. All he did was come out and somehow he exuded this aura of—"You can do anything you want with me. I'm just here and whatever." And you just smelled good things when he walked out from the wings. He wears like a suit and a funny bow tie and sneakers—and it gets to be bizarre, but it isn't bizarre—that's just it. And he always sings "Lost in the Stars" and he can't quite sing it and so you start laughing at him and you think it's a clown act and then about halfway through you realize it isn't. It's more like Walter Houston singing—and it grabs you and you get a lump in the throat and you realize this guy is really serious. But when he finishes the audition you know he's just kind of a nice guy. It's a wonderful audition. Best one I've ever seen. You have a feeling he wants the job but the audition isn't the first and last audition he's going to do. There's that marvelous balance between "I'd love to be in your play but this isn't the end of the world." So he puts you at ease. I think that's one of the hardest things—if the actor can put the director and the producer at ease, because they're just as nervous, they have a terrific chance of at least being heard, you know. There's such a difference between that and a girl who once came out and sang for fifteen minutes in a terrible voice and I finally had to cut the audition because—and I hardly ever do that—but she just wouldn't stop. Finally when I cut the audition, she reached under her skirt and pulled out a trumpet and started playing the trumpet—now it was very, very funny and had nothing to do with getting a part but I must say I laughed hysterically. See, that's the funny thing. We laughed about it because—we didn't feel comfortable because we felt there was a maniac up there on the stage.

GH: Are there other ways you find actors besides auditions?

HUNT: So often, in my case, I have seen a person's work before—in stock, regional theatre, Off-Broadway or another show on Broadway or in a movie. And I make a note of it—I keep a file of actors that interest me.

GH: Have you gone back to that over a period of time?

HUNT: You bet. I go back to it all the time. For some people— I guess the audition is the whole thing. For me, it's just kind of something that I use in conjunction with a lot of other things, like things that other people have said about an actor. I would say that Bill Daniels is a case in point in 1776. His audition did nothing for him, but there was a good smell about him, and the people around me, who knew much more than I did about his past performances, knew that he was absolutely right. And so the audition was only a part of the whole sum total of the casting.

GH: How about the 1776 auditions?

HUNT: We took more time on that than anything I've done since.

GH: Really.

HUNT: There's a chorus in it but the chorus people all have to know how to act...so, we had all the usual chorus auditions—singers on stage left and actors on stage right and all that sort of nonsense—and we got it down to about 30 people. We took them down to the lounge of the theatre and had a reading bee—and everybody kept switching parts and reading—back and forth it went on for about 5 hours—and we just did it by process of elimination. One person would just overpower the other person for the part and you see one person grow and another person stay at the same level—and that's really what I was looking at— to see if there was a sign of growth or intelligence, because then we could work together. And that's how we did that—and it worked. That was the one time Stuart Ostrow thought I was going crazy. It just seemed a little self-indulgent, I think. He was certainly a great help during the main auditions—because half the time I didn't know what I was doing. I was very nervous.

GH: Were you really?

HUNT: I was nervous because it was my first show.

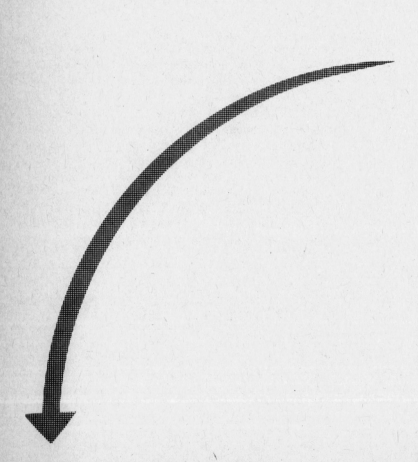

"Now for a newcomer, the best thing he can do is come out **and** give as much energy as he possibly can."

Stuart Ostrow
A PRODUCER TALKS ABOUT AUDITIONING

GH: Do you like to go to auditions?

OSTROW: Yes, because as you and I found out, it teaches you so much about your show. I think that's where the show really gets done—because it teaches you what works in dialogue and what works in song...based upon a variety of opportunities and options. For me, it's the golden moment in the show.

GH: Really?

OSTROW: Oh, yes. Auditions. A most important time. Not only to find people but, as I said before, to tell you what your show really is and what its weaknesses are—and strengths.

GH: What about cold readings?

OSTROW: It's the best of a worst lot—it's not entirely satisfying and it fools you a lot of times but—I think I have to answer: yes, it does help. What it does first and foremost is tell you about the intelligence quotient of the actor. And I would always opt for an intelligent actor, even though he may be wrong for the part. In the creation of a play, that cold reading leads to an understanding about the actor's capacity for imagination and creativity.

GH: What are your pet peeves about auditions?

OSTROW: The irresponsibility of the actor to research the play he is coming up for—the part he's coming up for. All that information is easily available—easily available—and they just do not prepare correctly. They don't call the producer's office, or call the casting director. It's usually the terrific, intelligent actors that find a way of dealing with this problem. That's my pet peeve—that people are lazy—actors are lazy.

GH: Any others?

OSTROW: No, it's a pretty brutal business, you know, it's the most uncivilized thing in the world to ask somebody to come out and stand there and say—sing for me, dance for me, make me laugh—it's terrifying.

GH: Do you feel empathy?

OSTROW: Yes, very much so. Well, we've been through it together. I try—notwithstanding my wisecracks, you know—I try to hear them out. Most of them are defeated before they begin.

GH: Why?

OSTROW: Because they haven't thought about what they are up for—so they are coming in on the Lana Turner principle: which is, they think, "Somebody's going to discover me and make me a star in Schwab's Drugstore, without me doing anything." I can smell those people and, unfortunately, it's the majority of people that audition.

GH: Really.

OSTROW: I think so. It's hard to get the good people to audition because that's a lot of work. Almost all of the people that we cast in PIPPIN were people that we had to drag in—John Rubinstein, Jill Clayburgh...They didn't want to come. They didn't think they were right for it.

GH: Did they all audition?

OSTROW: Eventually, yes.

GH: They had to come to that moment of truth.

OSTROW: Yes. Now for a newcomer, the best thing he can do is come out and give as much energy as he possibly can. That's very important for me—the ability to take stage and deliver energy—because theatre is energy—for me, theatre is energy. It is not closeups and not subtleties, it's energy, but I'm a musical producer as opposed to a drama producer.

GH: You're talking about "size" then?

OSTROW: Yes, that's what I mean by "taking stage"—exactly— and that comes from energy. I don't think it comes from anything else. Even with a song like "Momma Look Sharp" it takes an enormous amount of concentration and energy to make it work. It's the energy and the concentration that's apparent in an audition.

GH: Can you remember what the best audition you've ever seen was?

OSTROW: Irene Ryan gave a sensational audition. (For PIPPIN) She knew what the part was, she came in and she did a vaudeville turn—it just killed me.

GH: Her own material.

OSTROW: Her own material. She had material written for her—she did a sensational five minutes, from her nightclub act. She knew it was an old, vaudevillian lady. How she smelled that out from the script and without hearing the songs, I don't know, but she did. Maybe she got some help along the line but she made it her business to find out and she came in prepared. She was wonderful.

GH: Was there any question in your mind after that?

OSTROW: None whatsoever. We had gone, literally, through 600 old ladies. It was a terrible problem—that particular part. Because there is a song about "being over the hill and coming back again" and you can't get a lady who's fifty—and not over the hill.

GH: How often do you get sucked in by the song?

OSTROW: A lot.

GH: And clobbered by the reading?

OSTROW: Yes. A lot of people audition very well and then, as you say, when it comes to the new material, they die. Because the song is something they know—so you get, as you say, clobbered by it and then along comes the reading and they have to use their head and their talent and their intelligence—there's that word again. And, it's not there.

GH: How long do you think it takes you to tell whether they are possible or not?

OSTROW: For me it's very quick.

GH: Like, within the first minute?

OSTROW: The first minute—yes—I would say so. I'm fooled many times but not that many. Again, it's knowing what you hope for out of the part and, until somebody comes along and completely turns you around—by their talent, you stick to what your image of the part is and try to match it up on the stage.

GH: Can you tell of any instances of somebody that's taken your concept of the part...?

OSTROW: Sure, Paul Hecht—Dickinson, the original Dickinson (in 1776.) The concept of that part was always a kind of fop—elegant. That was the way Peter Stone wrote it—and Hecht came and and Hecht is a burly, almost lumberjack—and completely made it his own. And all of a sudden we found what was essential in 1776 which was a masculine, leading man playing the antagonist. As opposed to casting it the way we had written it, which was really kind of predictable. Paul gave the part dignity. There are many who still say that Dickinson was a much stronger character than Adams was. You know, you've directed it. And that problem sometimes comes into play.

GH: Oh, yes.

OSTROW: The problem in the theatre is that there are not enough talented actors. That's the central problem in the theatre. Everyone has a reason, I'll plump for this one: If there were more gifted, remarkable actors and singers there would be more people writing for them.

There'd be more people directing them, there would be more producers wanting to make money off them. But the craft has ebbed, I think, I really think that's the center of the theatre problem—that the younger people are going into television, movies—or—there's a lack of training, a lack of dedication, there's a lack of culture—an avoidance of those things. Don't you think that's a possible explanation for the kind of laconic theatre we have? Look at "Daniel Webster"—the MacLeish play (SCRATCH). We broke our ass trying to find that—we never did. And, notwithstanding whatever the other problems of the play were, we were sunk primarily by the fact that the leading character in the play was not good enough. There is no actor in the United States that can play that Orson Welles part, that Edward G. Robinson part—that kind of thunder-from-the-mountain man. There's nobody. Who is there? There's George Scott—that's who there is. And that's why George Scott is so terrific because there is no one else like him. There used to be Spencer Tracy, there used to be Van Heflin, there used to be a lot. When you couldn't get Heflin you got Joe Cotten, you know, and down the line. And the ladies. Where are the ladies? I mean the genteel, cultured ladies. There are no genteel, cultured ladies. Julie Andrews...

GH: There was Hal Prince's NIGHT MUSIC.

OSTROW: Well, the Prince show was a lot of ladies—and I've never understood Hal's position vis-a-vis women anyway—how he casts them, I mean. It seems to me that he always casts women in a very personal way. That may be good for his shows, but I don't relate to that.

GH: How does your method differ from his?

OSTROW: Well, I see women more emotionally than he does. I sense that from the women that he casts. They don't seem to be very emotional. They seem to be very bright and very cynical but not very feminine.

GH: Has an actor ever really fooled you at an audition?

OSTROW: Good question. No. I don't think I've ever been fooled. I think I've been disappointed but never totally fooled—and I've never really expected much from actors. I always find when there's a great talent that it's a marvelous present, you know, and that comes across on stage. There are very few actors who ever improve on stage. I mean, there's one who dazzles me and that's John Rubinstein. I never expected him to improve as much as he did.

GH: Are there any ways in which actors have hurt themselves or helped themselves—from the first audition to the call back?

OSTROW: I would think a big mistake would be to change the material that you originally auditioned with. That would be a big mistake, unless you are asked to. You call an actor back the second time one, because you genuinely think he can do the part. The other is because you want the variety to pick from so that you can slowly narrow the gap because, obviously, you don't have enough time to spend finding out adequately what their talent is and you have to hone in on half a dozen people, out of the vast number that you see, so that it becomes a kind of tiddly-winks game until you get down to the last six. And then you just concentrate on them and try to put them through as much as you think is necessary. But I don't think that anybody has ever really improved or diminished from the first impression I had of them.

GH: And it's true when they are on the stage?

OSTROW: I think so. There are very few surprises when you get on stage with them. I mean, I've yet to take an actor and say, "Well, I don't know how terrific he'll be." and he goes on stage and he brings down the house. I've never seen that happen. It's usually the other way, when you say, "Gee, I think he's marvelous." and he doesn't do as well as you hoped to.

GH: Is there any other way to do this rotten business except a cold, brutal audition?

OSTROW: No, it's a good way. I'll tell you what it does. It charges the actor with the responsibility of dealing with a terrible, awful situation—like a rainy, Wednesday matinee. There's no difference. Or, if you will, an opening night, which is even more important. So—they— coming into this cavern of a theatre, see four guys...I always turn the lights on. I prefer them to see us and for us to see them. Though, a lot of people like to sit in the dark and just have names—you know, voices coming out.

GH: Do you think it helps?

OSTROW: I don't know. It helps me. It helps me because there are a lot of people around you. I want to see what everybody else thinks at the same time, too, so that I can sense whether or not I'm the only one that's being seduced.

GH: So you are checking the reactions of the director and the casting director.

OSTROW: Of course.

GH: Do the people that you are surrounded with usually respond—as one—when something exciting comes along?

OSTROW: I think so, yes. If you don't then you've got a problem with your show. And that's happened. I mean, Stephen Schwartz during PIPPIN was just impossible. I mean, and it turned out to be an impossible collaboration. Luckily there were enough of us and too few of him to make any difference. But, I tell you, I've been in a show, my first show, where everybody reacted differently to what the part should be. I was too inexperienced to know, but had I been experienced I would have realized that that was the death knell of the show— because nobody had a point of view. Everybody had their own point of view, there wasn't any central point of view. While on 1776 every one of us—Stone, Edwards, Peter, myself—the minute that an actor came out on stage we knew he was right. It was like one voice. And I had the same relationship with Fosse on PIPPIN. It was like one guy speaking. Fosse had so much to do with the creation of the show, it was enough for me to gamble on.

GH: And so, it serves as an audition, then, of the working relationships as well as the actors?

OSTROW: Which is part of the reason that I mentioned at the beginning about learning the show. Because you can see where your problems are within the staff, as well as within the show.

GH: So at the audition, then, the show becomes a reality for the first time.

OSTROW: I think so. And, of course, if the director and the producer are opposed, I mean, my feeling is that you ought to give it another five minutes and then cancel the show—or fire the director. I mean, if you find that, let's say, two or three times you just don't see the parts together—then what in the world are you going to do a show for? I mean, you are all going to just pull at each other. Here's where all of the questions get settled. The whole sense of writing gets settled because usually you audition while you are re-writing. So that— when you choose to pick a girl who has the subtleties of a Jill Clayburgh as opposed to the directness of Nancy Andrews, obviously the re-writes have to be pastoral as opposed to black and white. So these are very important decisions that are made here.

GH: So the actors don't know it but they are helping create the show when they are out doing their thing?

OSTROW: Absolutely, absolutely.

GH: That's very interesting.

OSTROW: Well, it's very real for me. God! It's the best time during a show.

GH: Any advice to actors—as we wrap this up?

OSTROW: I never have advice for actors because they never follow it.

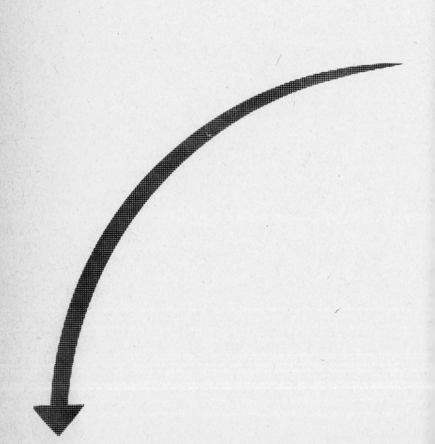

"Auditions. They are unavoidable."

Harold (Hal) Prince

A PRODUCER/DIRECTOR TALKS ABOUT AUDITIONING

GH: I can start out by telling you something that you might know or not. When you were doing COMPANY William Schallert auditioned for you. I was in his agent's office right after the audition. And he came back to the office and he did a number about his treatment at the audition.

PRINCE: Which was nice or bad?

GH: No, I think it was better than if he had gotten the part.

PRINCE: Isn't that nice?

GH: He had been treated so well. It was about twenty minutes worth of how beautiful the audition was and how wonderful and in the end he didn't get it but it didn't seem to matter.

PRINCE: That's terrific.

GH: Do you try to do that all the time? Is that a policy?

PRINCE: Well, I think it's not a policy. This is reflex action. My casting director is a girl named Joanna Merlin and she was picked the following way—and it will answer your question rather indirectly. I said, what would make a casting director, rather than—who are the available casting directors? When Shirley Rich left this office a lot of people saw a very good job and so I started to get letters and requests for interviews. Instead, I did a couple of those interviews and I didn't like the whole hide-bound, slightly cynical, slightly weary approach. Actors can get you down. I'm not arguing they can get you down. But it's very important to me because of the way I work that I have a fairly up, optimistic, jovial collaboration, when I do a show. And the collaborators include not only the authors and me but the actors as well. So, it has to be fun. And the pressure of doing a show is terrible—both in front of the footlights and behind them. So, I need patience and I need to be supported and I need all those things as well as to generate some excitement, and so on. That means I have to like actors and I do like them. So that the problems that they tend to impose, curiously enough they impose on stage management, on casting directors, on designers, costume designers, on all sorts of people. And I try as best I can to mediate and as often as I can to stay outside and let people cope with those problems themselves. Now, that means, I thought, I don't want a wise, philosophical, experienced casting director. I want what? I want someone who loves actors, someone who understands the problem of actors looking for work—and auditions—which means patience. Someone who roots for the actor, wants every actor to get that job. You can always tell a good casting director by how impatient they are with the director for not casting who they want him to. You know what I mean? They get very impatient with me—my casting directors—because I won't hire the one they have their trust in and their hope for. That's a quality. And then I thought—a Jewish mother. So, where do I find a young, Jewish mother who understands all those things and my mind went immediately to Joanna Merlin who had played the eldest daughter in the original company of FIDDLER ON THE ROOF— who was an actress, a beautiful actress, about whom I had the following facts. She is married, she has children, she has responsibility and being an actress in the theatre it's very difficult for a mother and a wife and I thought this would be part-time-day-time work when the kids are at school and might appeal to her. So I phoned her. She'd never done any of this before. I'll cut through the rest of it. She is dazzling at it.

GH: I know.

PRINCE: And it talked exactly to her needs and mine. Now, I think auditioning is potentially a humiliating experience. As a human being who finds it very difficult when the captain asks him at a restaurant what his name is — not because I expect to be recognized — I simply find identifying myself difficult. And, maybe that's why I'm in the theatre because people who have difficulty communicating that way resort to fantasy and I think resort to various means whereby they can identify themselves to other people, other than by saying their names. So, I recognize the potential humiliation of an audition—the probability of rejection terrifies me. In Neil Simon's play THE PRISONER OF SECOND AVENUE when the man came home and said, "I just lost my job." — I had a heart attack in the fourth row of the orchestra because to me that was it. I just was so upset at that rejection. So all those things make me quite compassionate. The atmosphere must be, from my point of view, supportive, friendly, as informal as possible. It must also not be misleading. The actor must not leave the auditorium thinking he got the job because you were so nice to him — because you did the equivalent of applauding him no matter what you thought of him. He must not be misled that way. That's as dishonest and, in a funny way, damaging as treating him badly. So you are treading a thin line. You want the actor to get a sense of whether you think he's right. If you can possibly let him know, right then and there, that you are not going to use him, it's doing him a favor. And if you can let him know why because generally the why is type, age, his voice and a preconceived notion as a director of what you are looking for, which he doesn't fit, it's doing him a favor to let him know so he won't go home and worry about it. Just as it's doing him a favor to let him know he did well and that you are very seriously considering him.

GH: What's the best audition you've ever seen?

PRINCE: Oh, I don't know. The best audition would be a composite of lots of auditions. Lots of people audition well. The people who audition well come out, stand still, read the lines as they appear on paper—they don't ad-lib changes, they don't improvise, they don't swallow their lines into their sleeves because they object to being there in the first place. I don't know of another way of getting a job in the theatre. I don't know of a better scheme than auditions, unless you've already seen the actor and you know the actor's range. But even actors you know and love you don't necessarily know their ranges and they may have to come in and audition. And Bill Schallert's a good example of this. He's an actor of great experience but I didn't know his range and he willingly came in and auditioned.

GH: Do you respect that?

PRINCE: I do respect it. I honor it. What else can you do? I think you ought to be open and direct and stop worrying and complicating the uncomplicated. It seems to me that the actor should not improvise, should not shuffle on and begrudge the act of auditioning but he also should not try to produce a scene, a finished scene for you. He should not move around the stage all over the place. He should also not do that stuff in the name of Actor's Studio thinking, which is make you sit there while he takes three minutes to get himself ready: shaking his wrists free, walking around, pacing, looking upstage and then suddenly turning on you and giving you a performance. He should be audacious. He should stand still, read the lines clearly so you hear them but also take a position with respect to the character. It may be wrong—and that's my job, to direct. After all, no one expects a finished performance but he should be willing to do something. Not to say to you, "This is six weeks before we open somewhere and I'm just showing you that I have a voice and I am a person—but I'm not showing you that I have an attitude about the role or the willingness to take a chance with it today to give you some notion of what I would do." People are afraid of showing you results too early and it's not fair. They should do what they can do and not hide behind "I'm a lousy auditioner." Some of the best actresses and actors are lousy auditioners and it's just a shame that that should be so because it makes it more difficult. But some of the best actors are wonderful auditioners—audacious and outgoing and they should make use of that and not complicate unnecessarily an onerous but unavoidable encounter—namely the audition.

GH: Do you consider it a personal process or an impersonal one?

PRINCE: I think it's impersonal realistically and unavoidably personal.

GH: O.K. I've heard rumors about Hermione Gingold's audition for A LITTLE NIGHT MUSIC.

PRINCE: It's a fact.

GH: Could you tell me what it was?

PRINCE: It's only pertinent in that I did not want to see her and she came to the audition—made the appointment because I was in Europe— I arrived and said, "I don't want to see her." I didn't want to see her. "What's she doing here?" Well, the message we got was—surely he won't refuse to give five minutes to someone who wants to audition. And I loved her the minute she came out onstage, she was perfect. It only proves how important auditions are. How you can't go by what you've seen somebody do before, necessarily. Another thing is—Bobby Griffith taught me years ago—that you must recognize that actors grow and you must see them again. You may not have liked them five years ago, they may be very different now; much better, more experienced and what you are looking for. A story of George Abbott comes to mind and then I think I must stop. It's that Brando finally appeared in STREETCAR and Abbott said to Griffith, "That young actor, I read in the program he was in I REMEMBER MAMA, I read this and I read this. Why have we never seen him? I thought we had the best casting." And Griffith said, "You've seen him fifty times, Mr. Abbott, and you've turned him down every time." Which is a way of illustrating how inferior auditions can be.

GH: *Do you like them?*

PRINCE: Who?

GH: *Auditions.*

PRINCE: Auditions. They are unavoidable.

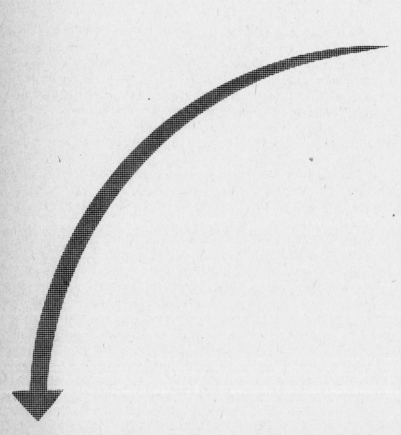

"We're sitting there praying for them to be good. . . just hoping they'll make it. Not out of charity but for many reasons — one of which is purely selfish."

Richard Rodgers

A COMPOSER/PRODUCER TALKS ABOUT AUDITIONING

GH: Do you like to go to auditions?

RODGERS: Yes, I do. I enjoy them. It's like digging for gold...and there's always the chance that you'll find some. You may have to "bend over" as the saying goes.

GH: (laughter) Do you remember any particularly spectacular auditions?

RODGERS: The most surprising was in a show that I did with George Abbott and—it was an audition in the theatre—out came a strange-looking girl. She wasn't pretty. And the pianist was in the pit and this girl crossed over from the wings to give her music to the pianist and did a fake trip over herself. It doesn't sound funny but it was. And then she sang and she was very funny and very good and when she'd finished we said, "Just a moment." and George and I talked to each other—and both of us realized there was no part in the show for her—and we decided then and there that one had to be written in. And we had John Cecil Holm who was the author of the book (of BEST FOOT FORWARD) write a part in for her. And this was a little girl nobody had ever heard of—but you've heard of her since—it was Nancy Walker.

GH: And that was just as a result of that audition?

RODGERS: Oh, yes, sure. She's had a whole career from that audition. So, you see, the performer can find gold, too, as we did. She was very funny in the show—and had a whole career—is still having it.

GH: Do you feel sympathy for performers at an audition?

RODGERS: Oh, yes, yes. I feel a great deal. I know what these kids suffer and they have to get out and stare out into that black void—with what they think is three or four or five hostile characters who don't expect to find anything good—and they are nervous.

GH: That's interesting, because I know actors look at the auditioners like that—as if they are hostile. But, indeed, that isn't true, is it?

RODGERS: We're sitting there praying for them to be good...just hoping they'll make it. Not out of charity but for many reasons—one of which is purely selfish. You're looking for talent and you find it. But then you do feel a great deal of sympathy for the kid who's obviously nervous and after you've had enough experience you can tell when the kid is nervous. You can tell by the hands. If the hands are at the side you can tell because they're not really still—they move a little—and the movement is nervousness. You can tell by the quality of the voice. I can tell by the way they breathe.

GH: How so?

RODGERS: Well, if a kid is breathing badly—breathing in the wrong place, taking a breath where one doesn't belong. The lack of breath is what does it, and what causes the lack of breath is nerves.

GH: Do you try to look past it?

RODGERS: You try to look past it and you also try to cure it...and that's almost hopeless. Oh, time and time again I've tried making jokes...you say to the girl, "Are you nervous?" when you know damn well she is—and some of them have a certain amount of bravado and say, "No."—most of them admit they are—and you have a certain number of jokes that usually work. I say, "You have nothing to be nervous about, we haven't shot a girl in two weeks." And it doesn't help. The joke doesn't help. There's no joke writer for auditions. Very often I've said, "You're nervous."—not asked the question but simply said, "You're nervous. Go take a walk around the block. Just go for a little walk and come back and you'll be better."

GH: Does that work?

RODGERS: That is inclined to work a little more because this isn't some guy in the dark trying to make jokes. This is somebody who is making an act of sympathy, saying, "You're not doing well because..." —without putting it into words—"You're not doing well because you're nervous and if you get a breath of air and realize you're safe, you'll do better." It often works.

GH: Any other cures?

RODGERS: No, in the sum and substance of the thing there is no cure. It's like your wife saying to you, "Now, don't worry." You're gonna worry. And you can say to a kid, "Don't be nervous." and the kid's going to be nervous because this is built in. The ones who aren't nervous I find are inclined to be a little too pushy.

GH: Does that turn you off?

RODGERS: No. It doesn't, again, because of experience. You have to think over that. You say, "This kid's pushing too hard because she's afraid."

GH: Does it take you long when somebody starts singing a song, to know whether that person is going to be useful to you?

RODGERS: Yes, it may take two full bars!

GH: You can tell that soon?

RODGERS: You can tell a great deal before they start to sing...in the walk itself, which may be overconfident, but mostly you can tell by the performance itself and you can tell pretty quickly—and you don't do anything about it. Never in my life have I ever stopped anybody. Never have I said, "That's enough." I couldn't do that to a human being. Here's a kid who's come over from Staten Island—she's scared to death—and you're going to shut her off in eight bars? Not me. If she can come over from Staten Island I can sit on my tail and listen to her for two or three or four minutes. What we try to avoid is a full operatic aria...because you don't need that.

GH: Would you suggest then to people that they not take too long with an audition?

RODGERS: No, I don't—the pianist does.

GH: If you were giving advice to somebody would you suggest that they be careful how long the song is?

RODGERS: Yes, I would. I would.

GH: Anything else about choice of material you could suggest?

RODGERS: The person who's auditioning should try and use something that will be appropriate. Some kid with very little vocal equipment who tries to do something from one of the operas is only hurting herself—but people don't know that, you see. The singing teachers aren't necessarily equipped to tell them what to sing. Singing teachers don't understand auditions very well—a great many of them don't, some of them do. But the person who's auditioning usually knows what part it's for and to do a rock and roll number for a part in a Romberg operetta isn't going to be much help.

GH: Would you suggest that singers have two or three types of songs fully up and ready to go?

RODGERS: Yes. Yes. Very often the kid will come out and say, "Do you want me to do the strong one first?" Or, "Do you want me to do the vocal one first?" And it makes very good sense. And this may mean that the kid doesn't know what the part is—and it may be very helpful to get the strong one in before the sentimental one.

GH: For your shows, the singing audition always comes first?

RODGERS: Yes. Oh, yes. We hear them vocally and then, if it's very hopeful, we let them have a script, take the script into the wings where it's quiet and have the stage manager explain what the part is about— what the scene is about—and then come back and read. But when you've reached that stage in the audition, you've progressed very far because most kids knock themselves out of the box with those first few bars.

GH: They do?

RODGERS: Yes, sure. And it's part of your job to tell—like a doctor who doesn't have to put you through a full physical examination to find out that you have neuritis in your arm.

GH: Would you say it's part of an actor's job to learn how to audition?

RODGERS: Oh, sure it is. What the actor doesn't understand—or maybe his nerves don't allow him to understand—is that we are just as anxious for him to be good as he is himself...I was in California one time—when we were casting a show and an opera singer was doing a night club job in Vegas and my wife and I took the train to Las Vegas to hear this woman perform in a hotel restaurant. That's going a little out of your way. But this is the kind of thing you are willing and anxious to do. And it turned out that with the microphone her voice sounded great. When we got her in the theatre her voice sounded terrible. Because she didn't have the help of the microphone—and I was plain stupid about it. We shouldn't have taken her on the strength of that audition. But she was a big name and we didn't feel we could ask her to sing again because she knew we were in the audience...and we took her and she contributed handsomely to the failure of the show.

GH: Anything you can say about the actor's attitude—when they come to an audition?

RODGERS: No, there isn't much I can tell you about their attitude because—for the most part, the attitude's inside. They may be hostile but they don't let us see it out front. But I can't imagine a beginner, standing up on that stage, with a thousand watt bulb for lighting—or even with the balcony rail lights on, which we try to do because it's a better light and makes them look better—but I can't imagine an actor standing up there and singing out into this black cavern—what Oscar (Hammerstein) called a big black giant...in one of the songs—without having some kind of deep emotional attitude. It may be hostile but they are not going to let me know it. And they may be nervous but they are going to try to hide it. Of course, the more they try the worse it gets.

GH: Was there ever an audition that was so moving that it's very memorable to you?

RODGERS: Yes. She was a darling woman. She played Bloody Mary in SOUTH PACIFIC. She's dead now. Juanita Hall. Juanita Hall was moving.

GH: Yes?

RODGERS: In those days we used to have a yearly matinee and invited all sorts of unknowns to perform. And in the audience we invited all the agents, all the producers, all the directors—and had a packed house for the matinee—and brought our people who weren't known, who weren't heard of at all.

GH: This was a venture of yours?

RODGERS: Yes. Oh, yes. We did it for years. Johnny Fearnley used to run them for us. And one day this wonderful black lady came out and sang. She was enchanting. And when we got around to doing SOUTH PACIFIC we sent for her and gave her the part of Bloody Mary.

GH: Just like that.

RODGERS: Just like that. Oh, those shows used to work. You have a full house...full of people who are anxious for these kids, who are unknown people, to succeed. Because the agents want clients, the producers want talent—and so do the directors and so do the song writers. We're very anxious to find talent.

GH: Yet you hear actors say things like, "They liked me." or "They didn't like me."

RODGERS: Well, I know what they mean. "They liked me" means anything from "You've got the part." to "Come back on Tuesday and read for us now that you've sung." or "Go off in the wings and take a look at the book." to "Thank you very much." And "Thank you very much" means you haven't made it. They know all these things. And if they don't know it as they go in they learn it from other people with more experience. I haven't been to many other people's auditions, so I don't know how they treat their actors. But I know I try to be as helpful as I can—polite—and we don't talk while the actors are performing—while they are auditioning and we never laugh. If somebody says something funny we don't laugh out in front.

GH: You don't.

RODGERS: No. The actor may think we are laughing at him.

GH: Ah. So you really do what you can for his comfort?

RODGERS: Well, sure, sure. And there are all the obvious reasons for it. You don't like hurting people and you want as good a performance as you can get.

GH: Do you ever try surprising a performer during an audition? Just throw him something to see how he handles it?

RODGERS: Not for that reason but very often we will ask the performer to change the key to find out if he's equipped to do it in a higher key or a lower key—or to do it with more power—or do it more softly. To see if he's equipped to get into our frame—oh, we do that a lot.

GH: One final question.

RODGERS: Anything you want.

GH: Anything you could say to actors who are starting out who are going to face I don't know how many weeks or months or years of people saying, "Thank you." and "Don't call us, we'll call you." and all the other euphemisms. Do you have anything to say to anybody like that?

RODGERS: Only what I've suggested—that the actor should try and bear in mind, when he steps out to audition, that those people out front are just as anxious for him to make good as he is. This has to be true of everybody. You can't look at an eighteen year old boy, stepping out to do an audition, and say, "I hope he's lousy." Why are you there? Why is he there? So he can be good and you can find talent. So, you make it as easy for him as possible.

GH: It gets so complicated, and yet it really is that simple, isn't it?

RODGERS: It's that simple. What have you got in mind? Why did you come here this morning? You came here to get a job. Well, who wants you to have a job. I do!

". . . you should never do songs written by the people out front because they have their own interpretive feelings about it and anything you do is going to deviate... You should always do a familiar song and yet it shouldn't be so familiar that it's one that four other actors have sung in the last hour."

Stephen Sondheim
A COMPOSER/LYRICIST TALKS ABOUT AUDITIONING

GH: Do you like to go to auditions?

SONDHEIM: No, I hate them.

GH: Why?

SONDHEIM: Because I always feel for the actors.

GH: Do you?

SONDHEIM: Yes. I feel very much what they are going through be-cause, you know, I audition songs for record companies and theatre party ladies and I know what it means to go through that where you're just—you know—parading naked without any of the rewards. It's an affront to your dignity, in my opinion. You're begging for something, you're asking for something. That's my projection when they are auditioning for us. I feel that somehow they are demeaning themselves. Although it is entirely my projection, that's not a realistic appraisal.

GH: Well, so many of them feel that way, though.

SONDHEIM: Well, I understand it. On the other hand I have no bet-ter solution. I don't know what else to do. There doesn't seem to me to be any other possible alternative in casting a play. You can't cast it through pictures and reputation. But I hate it. It's like fraternity initiation. Barbaric system—but, as I say,—I have no alternative.

GH: Do you do anything to try to put them at ease?

SONDHEIM: Yes. Actually, you know, I don't have an awful lot to say on the subject because I don't do an awful lot of it—it's Hal Prince who really does it. I mean, Hal's the one who talks to them and says, "Thank you." I do specific musical things like asking them to change keys or to change tone or to forget the phrasing and just sing loud—depending on what we're looking for. So that's always secondary. Hal's the one who puts them at ease or not and he's very good at it. He treats them very well and makes them as comfortable as possible and I've seen him reduce the tension and nervousness of many, many performers. Particularly if he's really interested in somebody—from their previous work—and just wants everybody else to see them at their best, including himself. And then occasionally he will work with them—actually right there on the spot. He'll give them some small set of instructions to re-read the scene. And he does it not only to help the actor—but to find out for himself whether this is an actor he can work with, whether the actor responds. It's not so much that the actor should do exactly what he says perfectly—just that the actor should make some change towards what Hal has asked the actor to do—as opposed to just doing it the same way again—because that means either a recalcitrant or inflexible or unversatile actor...In auditions, I think you want to see something about the actor's intelligence, about whether he listens and then, not so much about his skill—though that's part of it—but essentially about how he is going to be to work with because, obviously, it's a collaborative effort. A performance is a collaboration between the director and the actor or the director of songs, so it's a collaboration and it's one of the things that you look for. Essentially, though, I don't really have an awful lot to say about auditions. The one thing I know, I've learned, particularly from Hal and Arthur Laurents, is that you cast primarily for quality and not for skill. And unless an actor is truly untalented, skill or interpretation, etc.,etc., can be taught. The thing that can't be taught is quality because that's what the actor brings—and it's the quality for a given part, you know. If you want a sense of breeding—as we did, for example, in casting Joanne in COMPANY—Elaine Stritch is the only actress I ever saw who combined all the qualities necessary for the part. A lot of ladies had comic timing, a kind of abrasive toughness and yet warmth—but if they did they didn't have breeding. Elaine's got breeding. We saw some fairly well-bred actresses but they didn't have the abrasiveness or the toughness...Now, those are qualities—those are not something you can ask an actress to act because breeding is something you bring to the stage.

GH: Would you say then that if the actor can give as much of himself as possible that's the best he can do at an audition?

SONDHEIM: Absolutely. And you don't even ask for that at an audition. You don't expect them to give the best. How can they? They're under very peculiar circumstances because no matter how you schedule them—you fall behind. Actors are always blaming the producers and the managing staff. They don't think that it may be an actor who's screwed it up by coming in half an hour late. And so the appointment is at two-thirty but the girl who was supposed to be there at two shows up at two-thirty and she's got a rehearsal at three so you have to put her on right away so someone has to wait fifteen minutes, and so on... Also, you want to give as much time to each actor as possible. We generally try on first auditions—unless it's somebody we specifically are interested in—to give like five or ten minutes to each performer. So, it's two or sometimes three every fifteen minutes.

GH: Have you ever had to stop somebody in the middle of a song?

SONDHEIM: Oh, all the time.

GH: Just for time's sake.

SONDHEIM: Well, yes, just for time. Actually, I shouldn't say all the time. But you usually know after sixteen bars whether somebody can sing or not.

GH: It takes that long?

SONDHEIM: Eight bars sometimes—and sometimes four and sometimes one. But, you also know that that actor has been rehearsing the song for a week or two usually, they have more often than not paid for and brought an accompanist, and to shove them off the stage after sixteen bars seems too cruel. On the other hand, and one of the things I know that David Craig teaches is, as soon as the actor comes on with a five-minute song you're dander is up, whether they can sing or not, because they are forcing you to listen to them. We always send out instructions—please sing a thirty-two bar chorus or a short form song. A lot of them absolutely ignore your instructions and they deserve exactly what they get.

GH: Has anybody ever been hired who ignored the instructions?

SONDHEIM: Oh, I'm sure, I'm sure. One of the favorite audition pieces for certain kinds of baritones, who are trying to show a certain comic style is, "Where Is The Life That Late I Led?"—well, that's a very long song and that's always a mistake. But actors like to do that and it's very annoying.

GH: Now, you mentioned lateness and you mentioned lengthy audition pieces. Any other pet peeves?

SONDHEIM: Sure. If you ask them please to bring a ballad or a romantic song and they come in singing...Blood, Sweat & Tears—it's really not a good sign. It means that usually they just ignore you—so it's a kind of contempt—or, it means they can't sing and they are going to try to get by on shouting when, obviously, you've asked for ballads because you want to hear the quality of the voice. It doesn't mean that you want Alfred Drake—it just means you want to hear the quality of the voice. Also, another thing about songs is you should never do songs written by the people out front because they have their own interpretive feelings about it and anything you do is going to deviate. I can't hear anybody sing a song of mine without thinking, "Jesus, why did she take the pause there?" Not to mention if, God forbid, they change one word of the lyric! It's never a good idea to do that and it's also not a good idea to do too obscure a song because then the auditioners tend to listen to the song and not the actor. That's very bad. You should always do a familiar song and yet it shouldn't be so familiar that it's one that four other actors have sung in the last hour. Many an actor has had terrible chagrin while waiting off-stage hearing two actors before him do the song he has prepared. So you try not to do the contemporary big piece—whatever is going around that season. Outside of that, no matter how much you may resent being kept waiting off-stage, or the way the audition was set up, or whatever, or the fact that you don't want to sing a ballad—whatever it is that is griping you, you should never let it show on stage because hostility shows immediately and it's always an unpleasant quality.

GH: How does it manifest itself?

SONDHEIM: It's the vibes. It's the look they give you over the footlights.

GH: Can you sense it when they walk on?

SONDHEIM: Yes. Absolutely—it's the way they come out and the way they either don't look or look out front. It's always apparent—just the way nervousness is always apparent—and nervousness is a touching and good quality. Everybody understands what nervousness is and nobody has ever held it against an actor. And with sensitive people like Hal, his first job when he sees that you are nervous is to make you relaxed so that we can see you at your best and not at your worst and he will take whatever amount of time or talk or whatever is necessary to do that. But Hal is very good with actors—he cares about them. I've seen actors very badly treated.

GH: What's the best audition you've ever seen?

SONDHEIM: Pamela Myers.

GH: Is that right?

SONDHEIM: Sure. She came on stage—I don't know where—but we'd never heard of her—she sang, she bowled us over with the first song—or rather, she made us scream with laughter with the first song, then made us cry with the second. There was no part for her in the show—nothing that suited her—and all we knew was that we wanted her in the show. So, there was a part—the part that she played—that was written but that wasn't at all the kind of girl we had in mind.

GH: Yes.

SONDHEIM: It was startling and marvelous—and we wanted to be the first people to present her on a stage.

GH: Do you remember what she sang?

SONDHEIM: Vividly. She sang "Shy" from MATTRESS—and, as I said, we screamed with laughter, not to mention impressed by the bigness of her voice, and then she sang "God Didn't Make Little Green Apples"—and, we were all crying—and that's...you know...it was the most exciting, startling audition I've ever seen. She showed every quality that a performer can have by judicious use—judicious choice of two songs. She showed a comic quality and she showed her emotional quality and she chose songs that showed off her voice—so that we could see that she had this huge voice and her musicality and her sense of rhythm because "Shy" has a beat to it and "God Didn't Make Little Green Apples" is one of those vaguely rubato, ad-lib songs and she had impeccable musical phrasing, a sense of lyric—both are lyric songs, that is to say they didn't have very much of an effect on lyrics as well as music. And she had that too, you know—she was just extraordinary and Hal literally turned to me and said, "If we could find a part for her in the show..." because we couldn't conceive that she could play Marta at that point, until we started to talk about it—"If we could find a part for her in the show would you write a song for her?" I said, "Absolutely."—it was as simple as that. I wrote "Another Hundred People" for Pam.

GH: And she just came to this audition?

SONDHEIM: That's right. Out of nowhere. I think it was an open call—I don't even think that she was sent by an agent. She was twenty-one years old. None of us had ever heard anything of her. She was appearing at the Upstairs at the Downstairs at the time but she was fresh out of Cincinnati and school.

GH: Any others?

SONDHEIM: Marilyn Cooper—same thing. Came out in an open call, an Equity call—WEST SIDE STORY—and we just knew we wanted her in the show. Arthur wrote the part for Marilyn because, again, like Pam it was a small figure who came out on stage, opened her mouth—and out came Ethel Merman. And there's a girl named Pat Wilson who played the second Mrs. Fiorello in FIORELLO!, who auditioned for us and that was the most elegant audition I've ever seen. I don't remember the song but it was like seeing Lena Horne in a night club... it was such a perfected and finished piece...that it, in itself, was startling and —satisfying. She didn't get the part—I can't even remember what show it was for but that was the other best audition I've ever seen.

GH: Let me just ask you this. When you have to go around and play for the Ladies' Clubs and go through that, do you have any way of dealing with the nerves?

SONDHEIM: Yes, I take a couple of drinks for it, sit down. I've done it for so many years and done it so many times—it was actually ANY-ONE CAN WHISTLE that taught me because I did over thirty auditions to raise the money—and by the time I was through with that I no longer had the real nerves. What happens is that I am nervous for about the first two minutes, and then I get into the music. I have, as a matter of fact, a piece of advice that Isobel Leonart gave me that was very good because she used to have to go up and give story conferences to Louis B. Mayer—she was a screenwriter. And she said that she pretended that she was Margaret Mead and that she was coming into a very strange village, with strange tribesmen with odd ways and she'd look around and she'd say, "Oh, I see, they like beads and shiny things..." or what-ever—and she was able to distance herself by just looking around the room and saying, "What an odd group of people." And that's what I do now, with theatre party ladies. I just look around the room and say, "Isn't that peculiar? What a strange group of people." And once you do that, you don't have anything to lose—just as you wouldn't have any dignity to lose in front of an African tribe. You're not threatened in any way...they don't know from ego or from taste or anything. I mean, you go in an African village and it's just all weird and peculiar but your inner confidence isn't threatened. If you pretend it's a strange tribe it can't be humiliating because you just can't get humiliated in an African village. You can get killed but you can't get humiliated. But I don't have a lot of trouble any more and I've just as recently as last year given an audition where the people just loathed what they heard—and—I find I only get angry about it now. I just think: Oh, for Christ's sakes, why are they taking my time? Why, indeed, am I taking theirs? If they don't like what I've got to offer, I don't like being here so why don't we just quit.

GH: Yes. But you've been able to sense that?

SONDHEIM: Oh, right away. You can get that in ten minutes—five minutes.

GH: The same way actors can sense if they're getting flop sweat?

SONDHEIM: Sure, sure. And I have occasionally seen an actor stop in the middle of an audition and say, "I just have a feeling I'm not right for this part and you don't think I'm right for this part "—and they are usually right. They just save us time.

GH: ...just...that feeling is strong enough?

SONDHEIM: Sure, sure, as long as they really feel it—as long as it's not just neurotic cop-out—but you can never be sure. Also, I just think that it's generally a good idea to continue and finish it anyway, just for practice. I think auditions need practice just as much as acting, or any art needs practice.   That's why David Craig teaches auditioning. It needs training and practice. It's its own little art. And, as you must know, there are some actors who give superb readings and then you call them back a second time—Hal's very sensitive about this, he gets a little suspicious if anybody is too good. And he calls them back a second time to see if there is any change or whether it's going to be one of those performances that's perfect on the first day of rehearsal and never grows. And many an actor has lost a job in a Hal Prince show by that inability to grow—because there are some people who really have the reading down cold but have nowhere to go because they are not giving of themselves. Whereas Arthur Laurents always told me that the worst single reader he ever saw was Kim Stanley. He said, even during re-hearsals he felt, "This can't be Kim Stanley—this perfectly awful, ter-rible, incompetent dumb actress." And he said, it got to opening night in Philadelphia and then he saw Kim Stanley on the stage and he knew he was in the presence of one of the greatest actresses alive—but—she's incapable of reading, she's incapable of giving until she has worked through a performance over and over and over and over again until she's really confident of what she's doing—until she's tried everything. But during rehearsals he was in despair. You know, why is she copping out on me? Why does it have to be my play that she's no good in? And, of course, she was wonderful.

GH. You talked a little bit there about call backs. Is there anything that you like to see or that you don't like to see when somebody comes back again—and do you like to hear the same song again?

SONDHEIM: Oh, well, no. Quite often I'll ask them to bring back a specific kind of song. If you say to somebody, "Do you have a comic patter number?" and they haven't rehearsed one—then you can't very well expect them to do it then. So I suggest a number. I remember when we cast Beth Howland. We were trying to find an Amy for COMPANY and I said, "Do you have any song that has a lot of words in it, that you have to spit out and get very clear, get the diction out—like Gilbert and Sullivan and so on." She said, "No." I said, "Would you go home and learn 'Tonight at Eight' from SHE LOVES ME"—which she did. She sang "Tonight at Eight" and got the job right away. And that was the only thing we needed to see—whether she could do that. She had all the other qualities—she read the scene, yes, and she went home and Hal knew the song I had written for the character, which is not the song that's in the play now, but it was the same kind of song—with a rush of hysterical words and it had to be very clearly projected. And Beth is not a singer per se, she doesn't primarily have a voice —so I wanted to see what the delivery was like if she had a lot of words to deal with.

GH: I was wondering about Alexis Smith and FOLLIES.

SONDHEIM: Well, Hal saw her out on the coast and thought she was wonderful.

GH: First time?

SONDHEIM: Yes. And the only thing he didn't know was whether she could handle the song "Could I Leave You?" because he knew it was a difficult, almost aria, requiring a great deal. So—he just asked me to send the song to her, which I did—and then David Craig worked with her on it. And she learned it, came to New York, sang it for us and got the job. It's as simple as that. But there was a specific requirement there: which is we had to have somebody who could sing that song—and it's a hard song.

GH: And that's what David helped her with.

SONDHEIM: Yes. He worked with her. In fact, since David's moved to California, we often send people to him, if there is somebody we are interested in and ask him to work with them a little bit. Again, it's to give them confidence, particularly if they are doing their first musical. To give them confidence and find out what their strengths and weaknesses are. We get a report from him, but he works with them...he likes almost everybody he works with—and coaches them and then they come east—so they have some grounding when they get here.

GH: And Gingold for A LITTLE NIGHT MUSIC?

SONDHEIM: What we didn't know about her was that she had the kind of dignity, and that's what she showed us. I mean, she's a lady who's done a lot of work—so one has seen her. We didn't know about the fact that she could do something non-camp—and she was anxious to prove it to us and she insisted on auditioning—nobody wanted her to audition. And by sheer chuztpah—because she wanted to play the part—she read the script and she came in and she auditioned—and she auditioned beautifully and that was it.

GH: And did she do a song for you?

SONDHEIM: Yes, she did a little song and she said at the beginning, "You know, although I've been in many musicals I don't have much of a voice." And she then proceeded to do a song and she didn't have much of a voice—she had style but we knew that anyway. Nobody expected her to have much of a voice and she didn't and she doesn't but that's not why she has made a career in musicals, it's not her voice.

GH: Everybody has to musically audition for you who is in one of your shows? There is no star acceptance on name value, is that correct?

SONDHEIM: That's correct because you are doing a musical and everybody has got a singing part. I knew in advance that Desiree would be hard to cast so I didn't plan on giving her much to sing but I knew that she was going to have to sing something—so you've got to have somebody who can carry a tune. Glynis Johns is much more musical than any of us had any right to expect in a lady who is also going to be terrific in the part. She's very, very musical. Her sense of phrasing is as good as anybody's in the show. I'm not talking about the instrument, I'm talking about her phrasing. She's an instinctive phraser, musically. That is a gift. That has nothing to do with learning. She has what Frank Sinatra has and Mabel Mercer has...and a few others: Judy Garland, Streisand—an instinctive sense of phrasing—musicality—it has nothing to do with the strength of her vocal chords, it has to do with the musicality. There are many, many singers who have superb vocal chords and no musical instinct at all. And—her instincts are perfect. You don't have to tell her anything about phrasing, it's so natural to her.

GH: What did she sing for her audition—do you remember?

SONDHEIM: Yes. She sang a British music-hall song and she also sang a ballad.

GH: And you told her to do two things?

SONDHEIM: That was a general request to everybody that they should bring something romantic, because I knew that the style of the score would be romantic, and I suggested either Rodgers and Hammerstein or Friml or Romberg. I said, "Please do not sing Rodgers and Hart and please do not sing Rock. Sing something romantic." And...then I said, "Try to prepare a patter number of some sort."

GH: This was...?

SONDHEIM: General instructions to everybody. Usually you ask for two songs. That also makes the actor feel better—if they know it isn't all dependent on one song. They know they can work on two, it gives them some freedom.

GH: Does what they wear make any difference?

SONDHEIM: Yes, according to David it does a lot. It's best , I think, if you wear something that's vaguely suggestive of the part. The best way to audition for Fredrik, in our show, is to wear a suit or a vest or something with a tie—you know, not blue jeans and open-necked shirt. It just helps when you are reading the scene—to give some semblance of the character—and it shouldn't be anything too outrageous. Because, again, narcissism shows on a stage very, very quickly. It should be something quiet—the idea is to see the performer's face and body—and there's no point in trying to fool...if you're a girl with bad legs, you're a girl with bad legs: show the bad legs because, you are not going to fool anybody. The costume designer is going to know what your legs look like before she is going to design the costumes. So there is no point in pretending that you have good legs. If you don't have good legs—show that you've got bad legs and then let the people out front make up their minds as to whether good legs are important for the part or not—because if you don't have good legs, you don't have them and that's all there is to it. If you are not six feet—don't come on wearing

Adler elevators. Everybody knows they are Adler elevators. And if it's important that the man has to be six feet in his stocking-feet there's no way you can fool anybody out front—etc., etc., etc. So, if I were an actor I would dress very simply.

GH: Let me ask you one last question. Have you ever been fooled— for better or for worse?

SONDHEIM: No. If one thinks one is going to be fooled, what happens is that Hal has a gimlet eye—he goes right up on stage and talks to the actor. And we are talking and Hal will say, "Does she look under thirty to you?" and I'll say, "Yes, she looks twenty-four." And he will say, "She looks forty to me." Hal will say, "I don't know...I'll go up and talk to her." He goes up on stage and says pleasantries to the actress and comes back and says, "She's thirty-five." It doesn't matter what make-up she's wearing...but, again, there's no point in trying to fool people. Nobody's going to give you the part on the basis of being fooled— that's the point. You can never fool an auditioner because they are not going to let themselves be fooled. You might fool them on the first audition—but you are not going to fool them when you are sitting in an office signing the contract. So, there's no point in fooling, that's all there is to it.

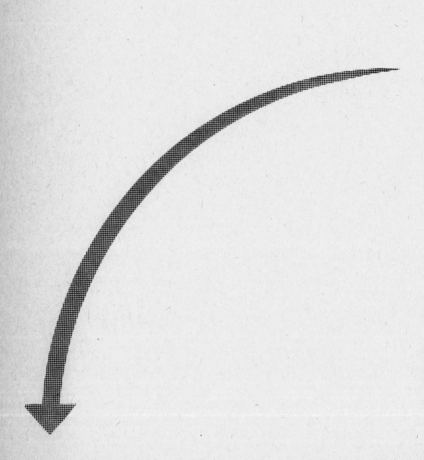

"*I always tell them: 'Don't try to express yourself. Express the character, we'll see you.'*"

Harold Clurman
A DIRECTOR/CRITIC/AUTHOR
TALKS ABOUT AUDITIONING

GH: Do you have any pet peeves at auditions?

CLURMAN: Yes. I understand the cause of the things that make me angry—well, not angry but, as you say, peeved is a better word. I don't like the kind of actor who has been told or instructed by his professors or teachers, or whatever, to show their contempt for the whole process and be as mute and as inexpressive as possible, by which they say, "The hell with you and the whole thing." Well, that annoys me because in that case they should refuse to read.

GH: Yes.

CLURMAN: The actor should try to make an effort to give some idea, at least, of intelligence to what's happening in a scene or indicate some line of characterization of thought, or something of the sort. If he undertakes to do a reading he should use it to the best possible advantage—for himself.

GH: Often I've seen pseudo Studio actors come in and do just what you are describing—the mumbling or the hostility or whatever...

CLURMAN: Well, I have no direct association with the Studio. I was called in to do the Playwrights Unit. I don't approve of many of the things that go on there. I approve of the idea of the Studio— only because it's a place for people to get a work-out of some kind. I don't want it to cease functioning. But, nevertheless, some of the things that they get from it—maybe it's an accent, maybe it's a distortion of what's been told to them—but I don't think it's due to deliberate instructions they are given—but they extract from their instructions what suits their temperament or suits their laziness or ignorance and perpetuate a false Studio idea. I don't blame it on Mr. Strasberg or anybody else particularly but I do think that a lot of these actors come away with a very false idea of the realities of the theatre.

GH: What's the best audition you've ever seen?

CLURMAN: English actors generally audition very well because they know how to read. A lot of good American actors don't read well. The worst readers I can tell you more easily than the best. There's Marlon Brando.

GH: The worst?

CLURMAN: Oh, a terrible reader. Also, Alfred Lunt. Those two are two of the best actors of our time. But that doesn't mean that I approve of actors reading as they do. In the first case, Mr. Lunt didn't have to read well. It was a first rehearsal when I heard him read. He didn't have to read well because he is Alfred Lunt and he was already known as a very fine actor. I don't know how he read when he was a beginner. In the case of Marlon—Marlon always had difficulty—exposing himself. It's a strain for him to give himself. If you read my book you'll see a long passage in which I describe my directing him in a play called TRUCK LINE CAFE, at the beginning of his career. It was his second part on Broadway, his first adult part. We had a big emotional scene and I almost had to kill him in order to make him speak loud enough to be heard beyond the 8th or 5th row. So I went to an extreme and perhaps unjustified means to get him to speak normally....at first Brando was a sort of hippie type in New York, but when he got to be successful all the kids, all the younger actors, began to dress miserably—in his fashion. One day I said to a boy who was working under me, "Why do you dress the way you do?" and he said, "Well, Marlon Brando dresses that way." And I said, "Do you have Marlon Brando's talent?" He thought that dressing badly was the thing that made one Marlon Brando! I used to kid Marlon. I used to ask him, "Who's your tailor?"

GH: Do interviews show you anything about actors?

CLURMAN: Yes, they show me a good deal. If you have sufficient time and question them you can get a good deal from them. As a matter of fact, you can almost learn as much sometimes from an interview as you can from a reading. I proved it to myself many times. Recently I had people come in and I interviewed them for a class I give at night in New York. I just asked them where they came from and what their training had been and so forth, that's all. And then I assigned them scenes and they were always perfectly cast—not just physically. People say, "You should be a casting director."—which I am in my own way—because I've actively sensed from the interview what they were like and what they would be capable of doing. You have to have a human sense, not just a theatrical sense. It has to do with being able to judge people in a room as to what they are really like. If you can do that in a room you ought to be able to do that for an actor on the stage or in an interview.

GH: Have you ever had an actor present an image which you've bought which wasn't really the actor?

CLURMAN: Very rarely. I've been able to guess almost every time—including—and this sounds like boasting but it's a fact: and the best example is Odets. Clifford Odets came to me as an actor. He always thought he was a good actor. In fact, he thought he was a marvelous actor. He thought he was a marvelous everything—a baseball player or anything. And when he failed he said, "Well, if I had worked at it I could be the greatest..."—that was his nature. I took him into the Group after I had interviewed him but every time I saw him on the stage—once or twice—he was not very good. He was never a good actor. When I accepted him into the Group somebody asked me, "Why are you taking him in? Is he a good actor?" "No." "Then, why are you taking him in?" I said, "He's talented." They said, "What for?" and I said, "I don't know but he's talented." I liked him, personally, but...he didn't show much as an actor, so I gave him very tiny parts—and he asked, "When are you going to give me a good part?" So, finally, I said, "You'll get something to do soon. We'll give you some good parts." I used to compliment him a good deal. I used to take walks with him and talk to him. One day somebody said, "You know you are hanging around with him more than anybody else, or at least, you seek his company. You've picked him among all the actors...and most of them are much better actors. You compliment him, why is that?" And then I said, "He's very talented." And they said, "What for?" and I said, "I don't know." Well, I found out later what he was talented for.

GH: I've had actors say to me: I want to come on and present a kind of leading-man image. What about that?

CLURMAN: Well, that's the worst thing they could possibly do. They become obnoxious. They mustn't present any personal image, they must present the character and we'll see what they are.

GH: The actor or themselves?

CLURMAN: The character. You always see what they are. They can't hide it.

GH: Have you seen people try?

CLURMAN: Oh, sure, all the time. In life and everywhere else. I've seen them try but they can't hide. I always tell them: "Don't try to express yourself. Express the character, we'll see you." Self-expression is not the idea. The actor should present a character as far as he knows it. Naturally, at the first reading the actor can't present the whole character. He doesn't know enough about it. First of all, the director should insist that the actor read the play. He should be given 48 hours, at least, to read the play. I saw some readings in England. I stopped in and a friend was casting some play, I don't know what it was, and they gave the actors a little passage to read—you know, not having read the play—and they said, "Read this passage outside." and I wanted to hit the director right in the face because every actor there, no matter who, could communicate nothing whatsoever because they didn't know what the hell they were reading. It was terrible. You couldn't see anything. The actors should have said, "I can't read...because I don't know who this person is, I don't know where he comes in the scene, I don't know what the situation is. Are you trying to find out whether I went to school and can read properly? Or do you just want to hear my voice?" Even the voice isn't completely expressive, unless there's a situation.

GH: So cold readings have no validity as far as you're concerned?

CLURMAN: No.

GH: *I guess one of the big bugaboos on interviews and auditions seems to be with nerves—actors' nerves.*

CLURMAN: Oh, well, sometimes if you see they are too nervous you say, "Calm down."

GH: *Do you have any tricks to try to calm them down?*

CLURMAN: Yes, sometimes I ask about themselves, or ask them a few questions about something else. Or, "Why are you nervous? I'm not going to judge you."

GH: *Are you in fact judging?*

CLURMAN: I only judge as far as I have a right to. Of course, the whole system of readings is bad. There's no question about it, it's a lousy system. Never did I ask any of the Group Theatre actors to read. I chose them for keeps, not for the show. And I would say 90% turned out to be outstandingly talented.

GH: *Your choice was based on what?*

CLURMAN: On contact...talking to them, listening to them and asking questions.

GH: *So vibes have a lot to do with it.*

CLURMAN: That's the whole thing—vibes! In good readings you see that they are very professional, which you might know from getting their history and so on. People engaged in radio read very well. They've had a lot of experience at it, but then they generally don't progress much beyond the reading. After three weeks they are doing just what they were doing at their first reading.

GH: *Are you wary of a very good reading?*

CLURMAN: Naturally, it's better to have a good reading than a bad one. But sometimes I say, "Do this as if you are flirting or suggest some special action and see what happens." But, generally I leave them be.

GH: Do you prefer to see actors' instincts at work?

CLURMAN: Yes. Actors ask me about that in classes—I say, "Don't do too much. Don't try to give a full interpretation because if you do you may move in a wrong direction from the director's concept—you may throw him off, especially if he's an inexperienced director. He's looking for one thing and while you may be giving an excellent reading and an excellent characterization, if he's looking for something else, he won't see that you may be able to do what he considers the proper one. Give him just a sketch, a good sketch of what you see. But don't try to do it completely, as if to say: "That's it, that's the part." Just use your intelligence and give the director some idea of what you feel about the part.

GH: How can an actor free himself?

CLURMAN: There's an exercise that's very often used. An actor will walk across a stage, and you watch them, and they think you are judging somehow their walk and then you say to them, "All right, go back. Multiply 27 by 7 and then walk." —and they walk and you say, "Which time did you feel better, easier, less self-conscious?" "The second time." "Do you know why? Because you were thinking about something except acting." And there's an exercise where you tense yourself completely. You tense yourself almost until you are ready to fall down and break—and all through your body, every part, rigid. When you relax the contrast is so great that you immediately feel less tense.

GH: Do you like to go to auditions?

CLURMAN: No.

GH: Why?

CLURMAN: Because I think it's a bad system. I think as little of auditions as the actors do...except that they are necessary under the circumstances of our theatre.

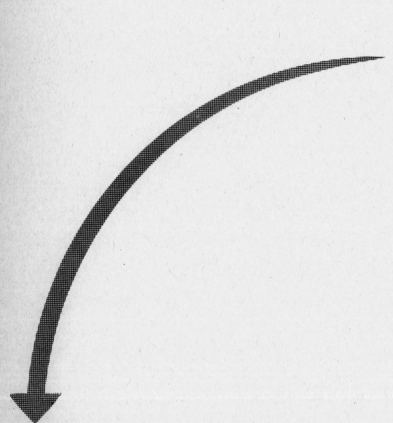

"I generally respond to a rich audition, an audacious audition."

"Remember, no one ever said it was going to be easy."

Gordon Davidson
THE ARTISTIC DIRECTOR OF THE
MARK TAPER FORUM TALKS ABOUT AUDITIONING

DAVIDSON: I find auditions frustrating, and I feel guilty that I should be running them better, and I don't, and I guess the reason is we're often squeezed by quantity, numbers of people to see, and because every play requires a different kind of audition in a way. I remember when I auditioned CATONSVILLE, I did very little reading from the play script. Instead I did a lot of talking with the actors because I was much more interested in where their heads were and where they were coming from and where their spirit was, assuming I knew something about them as actors. If I didn't know anything, I had to deal with that also. It was tricky because I could easily be fooled. That is, actors "acting" commitment rather than having an understanding of the material which transcended feeling. With CATONSVILLE, there were actors who were good actors but always seemed to be actors and I was looking for people who could appear not to be acting because there was a certain natural quality. Yet I didn't want too studied an approach because it was a theatrical poetic piece. So that was a tricky set of auditions and very time consuming, but also very interesting. When we've auditioned, as you know, HAMLET or HENRY IV the basic skills simply have to be there: speaking the verse, or handling the imagery...a sense of period of style. It's very hard to get past that in order to then make some other evaluations. I love it when an actor brings a lot into an audition even if there is a risk they over-do it. By bringing a lot I mean that they've thought about the part, that they've made some decisions, choices about the character and the scene that they go with those choices. Then if I respond at all, I'll often throw them a change...

GH: Arbitrarily?

209

DAVIDSON: Arbitrarily.   Simply because they've done so much preparation I've got to know what else is cooking in there, and you sometimes find people locked into their choices and it's a little hard to make them unlock it.   Now that's partly due to the tension of the audition, but sometimes it has something to do with the instrument itself.   So I generally respond to a rich audition, an audacious audition. I don't like to see actors using the audition time for preparation. I have the feeling one tends to waste audition time on both sides of the table. At least I do.   I mean maybe we talk a little too long and don't get on with it.   Maybe it should be more business-like, but I'm very aware it's a tough process; and the typical musical audition where you come in, do it, and get off may be just as revealing as spending twenty minutes. It's such a human thing that it's very hard to just dismiss people without spending time.   I also basically believe that you know in just the first few minutes of the audition...I really do...

GH: How many minutes?

DAVIDSON: I have a feeling within a minute of the audition that you know whether you're in the presence of talent or not.   You may not know whether you want to cast the person, but you know if there's an actor that's interesting and exciting.   But very often we are just too embarassed or inhibited to cut it off because we feel the actor is giving something and they might as well have a chance to go through with it. Now sometimes, because of the particular audition piece, there might be something at the end that you will never have seen in the beginning. Now that's the nature of the choice, the material.   I mean it might be a big emotional moment, or you might say, "Oh I see what he was doing at the beginning—it looked like he wasn't even acting at the beginning and look what he's come to."   But that kind of care and preparation of the audition is usually not given.   I wish actors would prepare much more.   They simply don't.   They tend to do it off the cuff.   And it's disaster in Shakespeare, as you well know.   Total disaster.   They can wing it more with other material but one would wish for much more care.

GH: Do cold readings do anything for you?

DAVIDSON: Sometimes too much preparation brings too many screens and you want to get to the person and the talent, so through a cold reading you discover some more about the instrument, how he (she) thinks, what he looks at...how he deals with those impulses. So I suppose a thorough audition would include a number of these things: a cold reading, some prepared things, some improvisation...I suppose that would be the most interesting audition.

GH: What about interviews?

DAVIDSON: Well, if you know the person...then it's still good to try to establish a line of communication, so you can see exactly what's happening...Let's take an extreme example...I offer Laurence Olivier a role. I still would want to sit down and have a conversation with him about the role and the play and points of view on it...for his sake as well as mine. "Take a meeting, as they say."

GH: Something has to happen between you and the person before you could ever sign him?

DAVIDSON: Yes.

GH: Any hints to actors?

DAVIDSON: One is to prepare. Two is to not be afraid. Again not every director is responsive so the actor has to be ready to make choices. I guess risk is the key word...

GH: Can you think of the best audition you ever saw?

DAVIDSON: My personal best audition was Anthony Zerbe's audition way back in 1966. I heard about this wonderful, useful young character actor who was trying to make himself known to me. So we had a meeting and chatted and then Tony stood up and did a medley, the way a singer would do a medley—of every style of acting and writing available in the English language. I mean he just packed it all in. In seven-and-a-half minutes or something he had done Shaw, Shakespeare, Cummings, Beckett...I don't remember how many more. He just segued in an incredible virtuoso display...Now it might have put other people off, but I guess what you finally respond to is talent. And here was both talent and energy and a sense of daring, a little reckless, and genuine and yet theatrical. And he knew what he was doing. How can you resist it?

GH: Do you like auditions?

DAVIDSON: No, because I don't feel I do them well enough. I generally feel pressed for time. I have had good auditions and fun in certain auditions, but most auditions are a drag.

GH: During the audition do you empathise with actors' nerves, with some of those problems they bring in?

DAVIDSON: I try. We all try to be as polite and sensitive as possible. But I don't think one tends to invest the same kind of energy in an audition relationship between an actor and a director, let's say, as one does when you have a cast. But the director/auditionee relationship is one of judge, and no matter how nice you are...it's accept or reject. The relationship I try to create in a rehearsal, and I think other good directors do, is not about pass or fail, not judgmental, about work. It's not good or bad, it's work. So much today, and something else tomorrow.

GH: So you think it's important in an audition to keep a judgmental distance? So it's a test, really?

DAVIDSON: It is! I know there's two theories about tests. Progressive education and all that versus the Old School...but finally you have to test. One way or another, it's "you've got the job or thank you next time." You can make the circumstances better, a little better, make the people feel that at least they had a chance to do their best, which many auditionees don't always feel. "Oh I wish I could have"... "He didn't quite give me enough time, etc." You try to do your best... create that circumstance. But once given the opportunity to do his best, the actor performs his lonely task and you sit there saying I like it or I don't. Remember, no one ever said it was going to be easy.

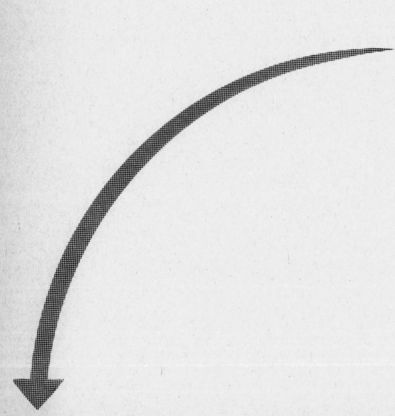

"*Anything in this world is easier than going to an audition. Maybe the gas chamber, or the electric chair are more painful than auditioning . . . but I'm not sure.*"

Robert Greenwald
A PRODUCER/DIRECTOR TALKS ABOUT AUDITIONING

GREENWALD: The worst thing in an audition, as far as I'm concerned, is neutrality because you've seen thousands of people who are just neutral. But if something special happens, even if it's totally wrong for what I'm looking for, at that particular time, either I'll remember them for later—which often happens—or I'll make suggestions to them to try something else. There are all kinds of other elements: timing, you're the first one, the last one during the day. All that crap, I think, does have some kind of an effect. What I get a little bugged at is when actors ask you the same question over and over again. Or I ask, "Do you know anything about this play?" and they say, "No." and I know it's because they want to hear me talk. I don't object to that, but it would be so much wiser if they were to ask questions that I haven't been getting all day. I have some of my own ideas but what I want to see in an audition, generally, is what they have to bring. I want to see what their attack on it is, even if it's totally opposite of what I've been thinking of. Then, I'll either suggest they go in my direction or I'll say, "That's interesting." and pursue that line of thought.

GH: *You did something, at one audition, which was to take a line from a greek tragedy and tell them "Sing it." and it scared them. What did you hope to gain by doing that?*

GREENWALD: Several things. One of them was: to see how free they were because I wanted a cast of people who were willing to take chances. They had to be able to take emotional risks and be uncomfortable. I had some of them stand on the table as if they were

215

drunk and telling their friends—just to see if they could break down the image of what it means to perform a classic. Some people would get up on the table, be drunk, and still would talk in the phony classical mode. It was incredible. But others would get an idea as to what I was trying and would go with that direction and would loosen up their approach to it—which I wanted.

GH: What's the best audition you've ever seen?

GREENWALD: Bill Devane for RANCHMAN. He took the play which is about Caryl Chessman, a guy being executed and he was absolutely outrageous. He was tough and really felt the crowds surrounding him and you felt him fighting for his life and he did it all in a short period of time. I mean, he didn't say, "Look, I need more time, I need to prepare, I need to get into it." He just did it—full out.

GH: Do you have any pet peeves? Things that actors do at auditions that turn you off?

GREENWALD: Yes. Unprepared—which a lot of people are. It's incredible. You don't get it as much here as you do in New York.

GH: You mean they are more prepared on the West coast than the East?

GREENWALD: Yes. And, when I was doing musicals and rock and roll shows: "I didn't have my music ready." and "I thought I'd just come in and we could rap a little bit." I don't give a damn about rapping. I just want to see the work. There would be all kinds of explanations and on top of it people would be late. I am absolutely wild about people who are late for auditions. If it happens twice in a row, ninety-nine out of a hundred times I will not hire that person—because I hate people who are late for rehearsals. It drives me crazy. Then there are people who try to audition you...

GH: How do you deal with that?

GREENWALD: I usually won't answer the questions. I'll say, "We'll find that out in rehearsal." I try not to be nasty because I know it's coming from anxiety but it's such a turn off.

GH: Do you know fairly soon into a reading whether you are interested or not?

GREENWALD: Yes. Within a minute. I don't know, that may sound outrageous to people. Occasionally, I find something out as it goes on. But when it gets down to the final two or three choices and they are close, then I don't know right away, but in the initial stage I'll know very quickly.

GH: How about cold readings?

GREENWALD: Well, that's what we do in New York all the time and I'm used to it. Usually we wouldn't even give the actor a complete script, just a couple of pages to look over. I don't know that I've seen any big difference in giving them a script and a week to look at it. Of course a piece like the Shepard piece, (TOOTH OF CRIME), for instance, you have to read the script in advance and you have to think about it and develop an attack on it. It's music, it's rhythms, you know...and I think there if you just gave somebody a speech they'd go crazy.

GH: And also you're going to want to see what choices they make best.

GREENWALD: .Yes, based on reading the play and thinking about what that play can be. I thought it would be very interesting to see, having read the play, what they came up with. The more I worked on it the more I thought the key to it had to be rhythms, the varying rhythms, because it was about rock and roll. So the rhythm of early rock, of hard rock, of acid rock—I mean, how they could get some of that in their speeches. Now, they were not going to make the same choices as me but if they had an inkling that it's about musical fields, that could only come about by reading the whole script and then coming in and trying it.

GH: What about interviews, just straight interviews?

GREENWALD: The only thing they tell me is about the very uptight, method actors and I try to stay away from them. You know, when they start asking you all those intention/motivation questions. First of all they are not actors that can take some chances, which I prefer. Second of all, there's a chance they are going to continue to hock you about all that method stuff, which is their work not my work, basically, although certainly we all get into it. You can tell by talking to a person if he is quiet and shy, a little held back, physically weak, whatever, but you can't tell—can they play Richard III? I talk afterwards, after they've auditioned, I talk a little bit if I'm interested. Then I want to find out about them.

GH: What about pictures and resumes?

GREENWALD: I never look at pictures. The resume—it's only interesting to me to see if they've done certain kinds of work and to see what people we know in common. It's the easiest way to begin a conversation because I get so bored talking about the play, I'd rather talk about how they worked with Joe Chaikin or with somebody I know in such and such a play.

GH: You take notes on performances that you see?

GREENWALD: Yes, I'm starting to keep that because I find it helpful. Of people I'm really interested in.

GH: Any instance of a really good audition that you were not able to use in something .which you were casting but that you went back to later on?

GREENWALD: Let me think a second. Oh, yes! Melissa Murphy auditioned for HELP! and a year later I called her for WOMEN OF TRACHIS.

GH: Had you kept a note on her?

GREENWALD: I kept it in my mind, yes. I remembered this girl I'd really been interested in and I liked a lot. It's funny, because it was a good audition for *HELP!* but she was a little tense. A year later, she'd been going to this teacher and taking some kind of voice—movement thing—she's totally loose and relaxed now. I mean, I was very glad that I called her back to see her because she was excellent and further along towards what I needed at this particular moment, which is a kind of openness.

GH: Do you audition any differently for movies and television as opposed to theatre?

GREENWALD: In general, I would say that less is more to an extraordinary degree in auditioning for film or television, and stage actors must learn to trust themselves not to do too much, to put it in their face and their eyes and let that speak for them.

GH: Any advice to actors going on auditions?

GREENWALD: Yes. Try to find another profession. Anything in this world is easier than going to an audition. Maybe the gas chamber, or the electric chair are more painful than auditioning...but I'm not sure. You can see why I'm not an actor.

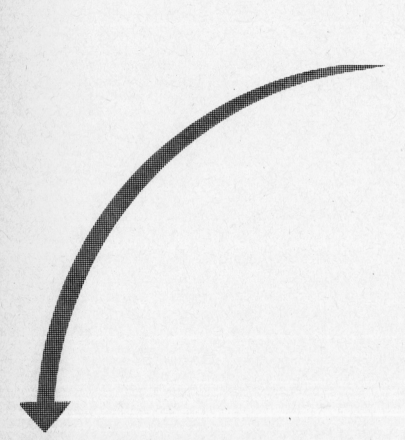

"... a lot of actors — especially young actors — come in defensive and surly and ungiving, putting it onto the interviewer to do all the talking and all the doing while they sit there and don't do anything."

Edward Parone
A DIRECTOR TALKS ABOUT AUDITIONING

PARONE: I always am impressed when people come in "as themselves" and do not try to impress you with the role that they think they are reading for, or the role that they are up for. Paula Kelly was an example and Barbara Colby was an example. Both were examples of simply being themselves. They weren't "coming on". I mean, I'm sure there are a lot of interview situations which are very cut, dried, and closed, and uptight—at the other end. But I don't think it's a good idea to anticipate that, or go along with that. I mean, try everything you can to be as natural and open yourself—no matter what the other person is doing.

GH: In other words, don't come down to their level.

PARONE: Yes, exactly. Don't be at their level.

GH: If a beginner goes on an interview—how do they handle that? They have no credits, they don't have those things to talk about that experienced actors have...

PARONE: Well, there's rarely anybody who doesn't have some experience. I mean, they wouldn't be really coming in to see anybody without some—school or college, or whatever—and I think it's best just to state that: that they've not had any professional experience, or whatever, but that they have done certain things in school and these are the things they are interested in. It also matters whether they are studying or not because then you can sense that at least they are serious about it, they are going out of their way to study, whether they are working or not. That is sometimes a help.

GH: Any other way you can tell whether somebody is serious about their work?

PARONE: I think you can just tell by the way they talk about it, whether they are really interested in what they are doing. I mean, a lot of people come in paranoiac, defensive, because of the situation—they don't like to feel that they are begging for a job. They are not begging; in fact, they are there as an equal—to inquire about a job. And the other person, the interviewer, is there to see whether a job can be offered. Finally it has to turn out to be an equal situation. But frequently, a lot of actors—especially young actors—come in defensive and surly and un-giving, putting it onto the interviewer to do all the talking and all of the doing while they sit there and don't do anything.

GH: Do you expect someone to come in and generate a conversation?

PARONE: Not exactly to generate a conversation but, I mean, if asked a question I expect them to be willing to give enough of themselves to answer the question fully and as openly as possible...I mean, everybody's been in the position of going for a job interview. And, admittedly, it's not easy for actors because they get rejected so often—more than they are accepted—but if you look at it as a rejection of yourself then, I think, you are in trouble.

GH: What is it then?

PARONE: It isn't rejection, it is simply a case of a relationship not happening at that moment. Usually, it has nothing to do with the actor. If you have done everything you can to prepare for it—and you are what you are—then you are not being rejected because of that.

GH: What are some of the things that an actor can do to prepare?

PARONE: For an interview—best not to anticipate rejection. And not be anxious because anxiety is worrying about something which has not happened yet. And if in fact you are thrown out on your ear then you might say, "Well, screw you!" but until you are, there's no reason to assume that you are going to be. You never know at what point in the interview something will happen that makes the interviewer catch fire. You never know. It could be instinct, it could be some little thing in the middle or at the end as you say, "Goodbye." It could be at any time, something will catch fire, and I think you only get it from being free and open with the other person. And dignify it in the sense that you know your own worth: that's what you are offering.

GH: Have you seen experienced actors under these same kind of pressures?

PARONE: I've seen experienced actors who were very easy and friendly and nice in interviews—and others who for whatever reasons are defensive and feel they shouldn't have to be interviewed, or shouldn't have to read, or whatever.

GH: Do you feel most actors should be prepared to read?

PARONE: Yes.

GH: Because that's a kind of status symbol, you know. If you don't have to read you are considered more of a star.

PARONE: Yes, right.

GH: Is that breaking down?

PARONE: I think it's breaking down a lot. I mean, I know some— I wish I could think of some examples offhand of people who were perfectly willing to read—very experienced people. And I think you should be prepared to do anything that's asked—short of humiliating yourself...I mean, anything directly to do with getting the job. If you want the job. I don't think you should go unless you really think that you want the job, or that you can do it...or that you are willing to put yourself out to get it.

GH: So would you say that enthusiasm was a vital quality?

PARONE: Yes. Enthusiasm for the project.

GH: What are your pet hates?

PARONE: Don't over-hello yourself. Listen to what's being said to you. Try to—just follow simple instructions about what people want you to do. If you are reading a play, don't sit at the table. Go to the middle of the room or go as far away as you can, because it's for a play and not a television show or a movie where they want you up close. Prepare. Make a choice—or a choice of what you have to read. Prepare that and come in and do it. Don't change your mind in mid-stream and don't change your mind as a result of a few words that are said before you go on to read. It's not necessary to flatter the interviewers.

GH: Is there anything anybody does that particularly bugs you?

PARONE: That kind of flattery. It just drives me crazy. "I've so wanted to meet you. I've so admired your work..." Or, "I'm a cousin of bla-bla." or "We met at so-and-so's house." I mean, don't use any social connections or relatives or friends of friends who might know the people involved. Come in as yourself. Solo. Alone—just your talent. That's all you need. And put your bags, briefcases, goodies, shopping bags, everything at a place convenient to make a fast exit. Say, "Goodbye " politely and get out. So that they can talk about you after you've gone—right away. While it's still hot.

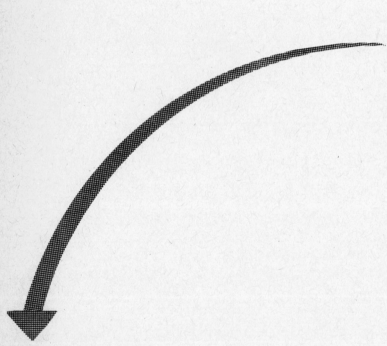

"I have very good vibes on hostility, and react very negatively to it — and I think it's one of the most destructive things actors do for themselves."

Rosemarie Tichelor

"Never apologize."

Michael Fender

Rosemarie Tichelor
Michael Fender
TWO CASTING DIRECTORS TALK ABOUT AUDITIONING

TICHELOR: Actors always think they want to psyche out the director or the casting director—know what they want and be that. And they can't know that because the director often doesn't know what he wants until he sees it. And so if they try to be someone else or come on with a certain manner that will impress, or will charm, I think it's a dead end street. And the alternative, which is the most difficult thing in the world, is to know who you are and be yourself.

GH: How can an actor find out who he is?

TICHELOR: I think one way is to learn very early how to deal with his tension, in terms of an audition, and his anxiety. I mean, just withdrawal or hostility, won't do anything. The actor has to know that the talking means very little, I think, and that he's going to be judged by that reading and so he can't fall into the trap that that's his friend. I think the important thing to do is to always take a moment for preparation. And an actor infuriates me and infuriates producers—and it happens a great deal—when you've given him scenes to look at, or you've told him what to prepare, and he walks in and he didn't have this, he didn't have that. And I think what it does, it puts in the casting director's mind, and certainly in the producer's mind, a sense of...lack of interest. Impressions—I mean, that's what so much of it is based on: that impression. I mean, the whole thing is based on that impression and often a casting director can say if it's a pattern or not, and that information is circulated very quickly.

GH: The good ones get around too, don't you think?

TICHELOR: Yes. Oh, the good ones always get around.

GH: Any other pet peeves? You said lack of preparation is one.

TICHELOR: Preparation is one. Hostility is another. I have very good vibes on hostility, and react very negatively to it—and I think it's one of the most destructive things actors do for themselves. I mean, I understand where it comes from, but they have to find ways of dealing with it productively. And when they deal with it by verbally attacking the producer or the director, they are just ruining their career. And it's the hardest thing to find use for that tension and anger. It comes from being always on the brink of someone saying, "You're not good."

GH: And yet we are not really saying that, are we?

TICHELOR: We're not saying that but that's the interpretation, you see. There's several reasons why an actor doesn't get a role, having nothing to do with talent. But I think that's the problem for the actor: that he naturally thinks that it's him and it's his lack of talent, or his lack of being good. He has to realize all the other reasons why he doesn't get it. I think if he could know that it could help him. Part of his problem is not being a complete judge of himself. Actors who have learned that are much healthier people.

GH: Do you think the word gets around from a good audition, even if an actor is wrong for the part?

TICHELOR: Yes. I keep notes on everything I see. On the way they work, on the way the actor thinks. I'm interested in an actor who thinks. I'm interested in an ease with verse without a kind of strong technical enunciation and without, on the other hand, everything naturalistic. And a fullness, and color, a fullness of choices and different colors. And the personal quality coming through. Using yourself in your work, which I find especially lacking with young actors in certain areas—they are often overtrained and they haven't incorporated themselves into what they've learned.

GH: What about cold readings?

TICHELOR: I always like to call back or give someone a half hour, or an hour, or a day, preferably, to read. I don't find a cold reading productive. I really don't. I mean, it doesn't hurt. You learn something else but you don't know really how much you are learning. I mean, if I know the actor's work, if I've seen the actor on stage many times and he's thrown into a cold reading and he messes it up, then I'll say to a director, "That doesn't mean anything. Don't listen to that—give him more time. He can do it."

GH: How long does it take you, do you think, to realize that an actor is somebody who might be useful or interesting?

TICHELOR: I see a lot of two-three minute auditions. My first impression takes me immediately and then I watch and listen and look for specific things, to see if I see that too. And then I draw back because I want to know—am I seeing an interesting person or quality that's shining through—and how much more is there?

GH: Any advice or suggestions to actors about going on interviews?

TICHELOR: If it's a specific reading—and I know what the director is looking for—I will give certain advice. I would like to tell women not to wear clothes that completely disguise their bodies—which they may feel they have to do, but it's not going to fool anybody. The director's going to want to see them again. And, just be yourself, which is the hardest thing.

FENDER: Prepared audition speeches are like choosing a dress to wear. You'd think it would be a marvelous thing—they could dress themselves properly, you know, and so often they don't. I think there should be courses given in "how to audition" in the universities, the schools.

GH: Like the one that Michael Shurtleff gives?

FENDER: Yes. He says, "Think of the auditioner as an enemy."

GH: Is there anything that auditionees and, let's say, especially young auditionees do that bothers you personally?

FENDER: Never apologize. Also, actors are a pain who do not bring resumes to auditions, I think. They don't realize how important that is—after they've gone—just to remember who they are. It's the calling card.

GH: And picture.

FENDER: And picture, yes. And so many don't, you know.

TICHELOR: You know, I'd like to give some instructions for directors and producers more than for actors.

GH: On how to conduct auditions?

FENDER: We have a tendency to be very courteous here—and we are probably courteous to a fault because they begin to think of us as friends and buddies, you see. Which can work both ways. It can help you in solving the producer's problem because you have the actor's confidence—but, at the same time, if they don't get the job then they wonder where your loyalties are.

TICHELOR: A pet peeve of mine is the rudeness with which actors are treated in production offices by directors and producers—the dismissal, the "Wham-bam, thank you, ma'am." That is destined to bring out the hostility and the lack of courage and the lack of confidence in an actor.

GH: Is there any other way to do this audition business?

TICHELOR: I don't think so.

FENDER: I was an actor once myself and I recall that I think if you've been doing a lot of auditions, it's easier—and if you are working when you audition, it's easier. The strongest advice is probably really to be sure you should be in the theatre.

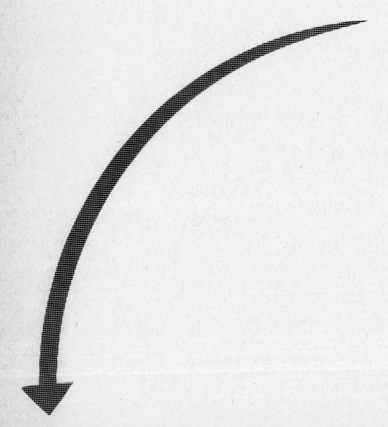

"...I don't think they (the actors) should be so brilliant that their own vulnerability is covered up."

Eric Christmas
A DIRECTOR TALKS ABOUT AUDITIONING

GH: Do you have any specific do's or don'ts for actors concerning auditions?

CHRISTMAS: Well, I think do's first of all—I am concerned at the moment with casting a season of Shakespeare and I think that it's advisable to look at the plays and to consider what you might reasonably be cast for. In other words, don't go for the great roles, unless you really feel that you are ready and are capable of playing them. But there are some wonderful roles inside all the plays, some of them very small, some of them not so small but subsidiary roles that you might in fact be cast in. And, this sounds silly I suppose, but I really think people should read the plays.

GH: Do you find a lot of people who don't?

CHRISTMAS: Yes, the ring speech—Viola's ring speech turns up endlessly and I suppose one in ten girls has really read the play and is really living the situation as it exists inside the play—and they do something, most of them do something that is nothing whatever to do with Viola's predicament. You know, they turn it into a —into a kind of an aria, really, and it doesn't relate to what's around. And don't worry about the natural hang-ups, such as fluffing or—showing nerves, you know. I think it's much more stimulating when someone is vulnerable and shows that they are both human and shows also that there is more to them than what is happening at the moment.

GH: Now, as an actor, what do you know that other actors who haven't auditioned people...don't know?

CHRISTMAS: Well, I think, first of all it's totally unnecessary to explain...so many people explain all kinds of things...the cold—the state of health—they were up all night—they are not quite sure of the lines—the plot. You know, all these things. Maybe sometimes a few words are essential if it's an obscure piece but no apology or explanation is needed really. It's the person you go for and it is the person who eventually will be the essence of the role, even if the characterization is obscure and far removed from the person—it is what that person knows. O.K. I'm an actor now—it is who I am and what I am and what I feel and what I know and what is instinctive to me that will be the value inherent in the performance, even if that role is far removed from me as a person. This is something I never realized until recently. So, I think, what I am saying is: instead of assuming all kinds of masks and cloaks and props and attitudes, you really say—what have I got that I can bring...let's say I'm playing Shylock. Now, I don't cover myself with a kind of cloak of Shylock, I say: what can I bring to Shylock? What do I know? What do I respond to instinctively? I think it is that, the truth within oneself, that will be believed by an audience. Simplicity. I'm being very complicated in an attempt to say that simplicity is the answer, you know.

GH: (laughter) How about interviews? Do you see things in people from interviews?

CHRISTMAS: Yes, I do. In many cases I feel that those three or four minutes when they do their bit is the least important. What it does reveal is their ability to perform. Sometimes you get, as you know, a very exciting and stimulating and attractive person and it all disappears when they get up there. But I like to go from those two or three minutes to, not so much an interview, but a chat really, an attempt to break through the defenses that have gone up. I don't care who it is, there is a considerable layer of defense in everybody's work when they audition. Guthrie used to go to the extreme and used to apparently cast people entirely on instinct, even before an interview. A person would enter a door and he would say, "I want you for my Mark Antony." you know.

GH: He really did?

CHRISTMAS: On occasions he did and it became a terrible problem.

Sometimes it worked out, you know, but it went the other way as well. I tell you what I find particularly valuable is if someone does their piece, maybe very well, then if you can throw some suggestion to them, some direction to them. It can be arbitrary, it can be the simplest thing—saying, "Instead of sitting down there would you mind sitting over there?" or a little more subtle, a little more deep than that if you wish but—ask them to do something which they are not prepared to do and see what happens. And I feel very negative when nothing happens at all. You don't expect them to do what you've asked, or to even have understood what you asked, but you do expect some change, which means that, as a director, you will know that there is somewhere to go. There's a story—you may possibly know the story—the old lady auditioning for a role on Broadway and the director was sitting in about the seventh row of the stalls and he stood up and he dashed up on the stage and he said, "You're absolutely what we want. We've been searching—we've seen three hundred people. You are exactly what we want. Can you rehearse Monday?" And she said, "I'd love to but I only do auditions." And there is that type, there's the professional auditioner, you know.

GH: Are there any things that specifically turn you off—that actors do at auditions?

CHRISTMAS: Well, there is a list—coming back to Shakespeare— there is a list of pieces that don't exactly turn one off but you hear them so often and you wish they wouldn't do them. Launce and his dog turns up all the time. Mad Constance, we see many of those. The ring speech, as I mentioned...Oh, yes. And...I get a little closed in when I see something that is so pat and so prepared and so well worked out— that is, again, the kind of professional audition, because you want to go beyond that.

GH: How about speech? Doing Shakespeare.

CHRISTMAS: I don't have any particular theory of speech other than the ability to convey, with clarity, the thoughts and the feelings that are inherent in the text. Now that can be done in many, many ways. I sound English because I was over thirty before I left England...but I don't believe in English patterns of speech necessarily. The English, of course, are such respecters of consonants that I think that that is the value that the English can bring to the American speech. Whereas the American actor tends to rely on the vowels. So that I think the value of English speech is not diction or certainly not elocution but the energy in the consonants. You see, speech...it's not so much speech, it's thought and so often actors have not really thought about what they are saying...either that or their thoughts are so obtuse and so contradictory...again, simplicity, you know. The simple line—there's no one answer—there's no one simple way but whatever way is decided upon, even if it is convoluted psychologically, it should have a simple line. I thought one of the great things about the Brook DREAM—no matter what one might feel about moments of interpretation—that the line through that text was very simple, wasn't it? And—getting rid of, you see, getting rid of—that's the great training now. If ever I was in a position to form a school—I do a lot of so-called teaching, I put on plays and I suppose that's a form of teaching—but if I ever was in a position to formulate a school I would really make it a kind of "shedding" school. You know.

GH: Let me ask you this. As an actor do you prepare when you audition?

CHRISTMAS: Not really, no.

GH: Some people have exercises...

CHRISTMAS: It depends on the role really. I'm very, very much concerned with energy; that and implication rather than statement. You know, if you have a cylinder of compressed gas and if the gauge is reading 2,000 pounds and if all you hear is a little Pssss! that's an incredible implication of energy. But if a thing goes BANG! You know, it's dissipated—and I try to imply energy and have it under control—because that's one of the endless paradoxes, isn't it, the control through implication? It's all there—Fred Astaire was a perfect example, I think, in his work. You just felt that he had given you about one tenth—not that he had withheld it from you but it was open-ended, you know, and on he could go. And again, coming back to the auditions, some of the kids are—are hitting ceilings. Maybe they've nowhere else to go but— I don't think it's that as much as having worked it out and this is it, you know. It's very hard for me to be succinct over this.

GH: No, I understand what you said "having worked it out." In other words, there's the possibility of exploring.

CHRISTMAS: Yes, absolutely, exactly! Not totally, because otherwise you are in terrible trouble. You must have a frame...you must have stepping stones, a pattern, somewhere but I think then you can go from that. Yes, precisely. And I try to make those discoveries or to have them upon me through instinct as I work, and that takes the place of a lot of so-called nerves—certainly the destructive kind of nerves. So really it's existing outside you. You know, if there was a mouse in this room now we would be reacting to the mouse, we would be concerned with the mouse, but the life and the reality is the mouse, you see, and we are incidental to that—it's outside, you know, and it's a spontaneous expression of energy that is outside ourselves. Sometimes it's inside too much, certainly when it's intellectualized, and thank God I'm not an intellectual—I don't think people should be stupid but I don't think they should be so brilliant that their own vulnerability is covered up.

GH: So, vulnerability would be a decided asset?

CHRISTMAS: Oh, I think, absolutely! So I think, to sum up, the most valuable advice to anybody going to audition is to give yourself and to share and to realize that, wonderful as the theatre is, there's a tremendous world around and if you join that world and contribute your little bit to it—in other words, get outside yourself, the world's not going to end if you don't get the deal, you know?

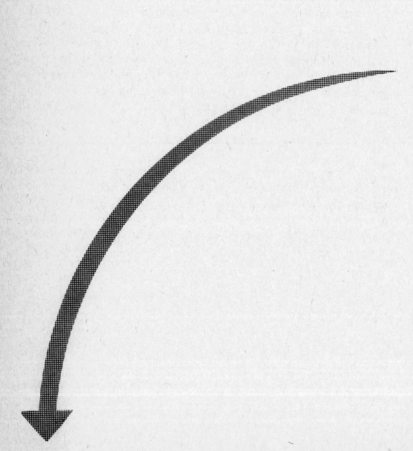

"In films I really just look for faces and intelligence more than for talent."

James Bridges

A WRITER/DIRECTOR TALKS ABOUT AUDITIONING

*GH: What is the difference, for you, when you are auditioning some-
one for a film as opposed to the theatre?*

BRIDGES: In the theatre, I'd like to have seen them somewhere
onstage. And in films I really just look for faces and intelligence more
than for talent.

GH: Do cold readings have any value for you?

BRIDGES: Yes, they have some value. In films it's been more
successful to give somebody a scene and let them go away and think
about it and come back. There have been some very funny things
that have happened. Well, one actress, Nira Barab, wanted very much
to be in THE BABYMAKER. She took the scene in front of the
fireplace away and came back. (She was working intensely with Strasberg at that time.) And the producer, Richard Goldstein, very straight,
rather dearly old-fashioned with the pipe and the tweeds, sat behind
his desk. And Nira came in and she was terribly nervous and very
method-y and said that she had to "prepare" whereupon she sank
down out of sight behind the desk and lay flat out on the floor. And
I just sat there on the couch watching and he kind of leaned up over
his desk and put his pipe down and didn't know what was happening.
And she was there for about five minutes—just collapsed. And then
she began to improvise and I picked up and began to improvise with
her, back and forth, and I read with her and then she began to say the
lines of the thing and played the scene very well. I've found that in
both films and theatre, if I read with them, myself, particularly in films,
I can have more of a response.

GH: Do you try to play the scene with them, eye contact and all that?

BRIDGES: Yes. In the theatre, I like to get as far away from them as possible and see how their voices project and see the total thing. Whereas in a film I like to get as close to them as possible. I almost never move away from anybody reading for a film. We sit around a table, very close and just deal with them that way.

GH: How about interviews? Do they tell you a lot?

BRIDGES: Yes, I can tell in an interview whether I want to work with someone.

GH: Do you identify with actors auditioning?

BRIDGES: Oh, terribly, sure. God, I used to be an actor myself and I know it so well, sitting out in the hall and then coming in.

GH: When an actor comes in that you have not seen before, are there any things you consciously or unconsciously look for?

BRIDGES: Consciously, I think, I look for a sense of humor. And I have this awful thing about nose jobs and hair so I never cast somebody who's done things to their face, because I'm always aware that there's another person there, somebody that you have to deal with. And the same thing with hair. And I've shocked a couple of girls on interviews, who've come in with wigs: And I've said, "What does it look like under all that hair? What is your real hair like?" And too much energy almost always turns me off because I used to do that myself so I know what it is. You know, you bounce in in your tennis shoes and your tweed jacket flung over your shoulder and it's almost as if you had put a straw hat on the back of your head and you do your interview—or do your reading. And you can get parts like that. But I'm always suspicious of those readings.

GH: Any other pet peeves?

BRIDGES: Actors phoning my house, which has happened recently a lot.

GH: Are there any things that actors do—psychologically or verbally, that serves as a kind of smokescreen between you and them?

BRIDGES: Well, an actor who comes in and is defensive and is hostile—which obviously comes from some sort of insecurity.

GH: You said earlier you know what the actor's going through because you were an actor. Can you describe what those feelings were for you?

BRIDGES: Yes, you have this vanity, this extraordinary vanity. You feel that you are absolutely the right one for this and that no one else should have it. It seemed like I could play anything. And that whole period waiting outside was just very strange with all the other people sitting there. I would figure out who was up for the same part that I was up for and I began to cast the play in the outside room. I never really knew very many actors. And then I'd walk into this hall and from then on it was kind of blank. I never remembered what I said and I never really remembered how I acted, except I knew that there was an enormous amount of energy involved. I can remember almost everything about all those outside waiting times when I was very sensitive to the coffee and the pages and the people and my shoes. And when the door opened—I never can remember what happened inside. You turn on this thing—or I did. And I always found it false. And I never remembered how it went...it's this thing of wanting to please and on the other side there is somebody judging you. And being in the judge's seat is equally hard because—I think I've found myself blushing more and turning red, on the other side, than I did when I was there. It was all kind of sunshiny when I was on the other side. But I was very young. But now I see all these people coming in and I can spot it when it's really good. There's no doubt. And sometimes it has nothing to do with reading or the way they dressed or the way they look—you just spot that something there. It's magic. But I can never remember what happened on the other side of that door.

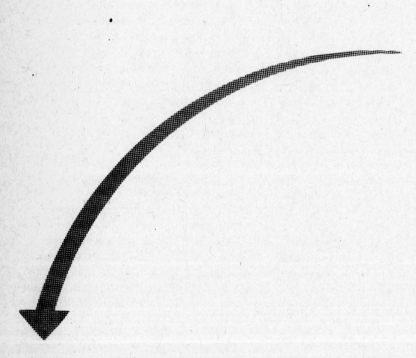

"If you are there, you are there to get the job, you are there to try to get the work, therefore you handle yourself in a certain way but you do not handle yourself in a way which is belying your basic reality about yourself..."

Milton Katselas
A DIRECTOR TALKS ABOUT AUDITIONING

GH: Is there anything you look for in an interview situation, in terms of attitude from an actor?

KATSELAS: Generally what I look for is somebody who is more like a human being than an actor. In other words, he is not coming on with his actor things, or he's not acting during the interview. That he is a human being in the interview and talks to me and has some humor about himself, and has some humor even about the interview and is non-actorish. So I look at him as a human being. And it's very difficult in five minutes or ten minutes, twenty minutes, whatever the interview happens to be, to try to make an appraisal of the actor. But you are not really trying to appraise—which is one of the things I immediately make known in the interview—I'm not trying to appraise his talent.

GH: What are you trying to do?

KATSELAS: I'm just trying to meet him and find out who he is and what his voice sounds like and what his face is like and his hair and his eyes and is he intelligent and does he seem to be the kind of guy that one could get along with and could work with—and is he right for what you are looking for, just in a physical way. A lot of people come in and try to do a lot of things in an interview. And I don't mean they shouldn't do things, that's fine if they have ideas of what they do. But I think they should do them from the point of view of being real, of being a person. It's like saying, "Here I am," you know.

243

GH: What are some of the fronts or defenses you've seen actors use when they come in to talk to you?

KATSELAS: Well, there are some actors that come in who resent interviews and therefore they come in with a certain hostility. Then you try to get to the person and talk to them and they'll know that you are there and you want him to be there and you realize that it is a difficult thing, this set up, but that's the way it is until somebody invents another way.

GH: O.K. Now what do you look for?

KATSELAS: Well now, if it's possible I will read him. What I am looking for in that first reading is the sense that I can believe the thoughts that I've had about the part and the thoughts that the writer has put forth about the part. Usually, I translate those thoughts of the writer into my own thoughts, and my own feelings. What I try to look for is to determine whether the actor satisfies those kind of private thoughts that I have about the part and those thoughts that the playwright seems to put forward. Stanley Kowalski is a certain kind of a rough, tough guy who has a certain kind of sexuality—let's put it on that basis. In other words, I'll isolate certain parts of the character and say, in this production that guy must satisfy those needs. And if he does, terrific. Then I go the next step, and have him back to read again, this time possibly with the producer.

GH: What do you look for, when he comes back for a reading?

KATSELAS: Well, I would say the second time, I'm going to look a lot more closely at his acting ability. I mean, how does he handle himself? Does he talk and listen with the other person? See, it's never strictly one thing. It's like, I'm looking at him to see if he has the emotional risability for a part. I will work with him or assign him that scene to read that's a very emotional scene. If, on the other hand, I think he's a very emotional actor—does he have the charm that's necessary for this part? Then I will give him a certain scene and see how he executes it. So, usually, the second and the third reading is simply trying to get to specifics about actors.

GH: You are a great one for pushing the responsibility on the actor.

KATSELAS: Yes, well, I try to do that all the time because eventually the responsibility is going to be in the hands of the actor more than the director. He's not the one on opening night that has to deal with the nerves and confront himself in such and such a part. Now, when that occurs, when that actor is up there he's up there alone, with whatever assistance he is getting from his partners and so on. As you know from my teaching, too much of acting is put on an effect basis. That is, we wait until we're called or we wait for a director—we can work well with good directors. If the picture is good, we will be good, or whatever. You know, being the effect of the project. And I'm always trying to get the actor to be more and more cause, taking the responsibility in relation to the part and in relation to their work. So I try to increase that responsiblity right from the first step all the way down and in a gradient kind of way, because that's the way it works.

GH: Improvisations. What do you look for when you have somebody in to improvise?

KATSELAS: I might want to see if somebody can, with their imagination and their work, make something out of nothing. I'll give them an improvisation which is meaningless and not dramatic at all and see out of that if they can be very natural and very easy and not try to push and be dramatic and be an actor, but just be simple and real. In another improvisation I may try to test the actor's belief, to give him something very difficult to believe in and to test and see if, with that difficult thing to believe in, he can execute it. Now people who have studied all the time will tell you that that's not the way to do an improvisation, you are setting it up improperly, and so on. Well, that's not the point. The point is, an improvisation is something like a test. You want to take certain aspects of the actor—just as choreographers test to see the elevation. To see the leap, they will give the person a certain test. To see if a person can soft-shoe, they will do a tap, they will do a certain test—they will play certain music and so on. So the same thing applies here. I may want to find out just how intimate the actor can be and is willing to be. Sometimes maybe having selected one of the people already, I will bring in actors that I'm thinking about and see how they match up and how intimate they are willing to be with each other very quickly. So, improvisation is used as a test. It also will tell me something about the actor's training— has he done improvisations and is he capable of it under this kind of difficult circumstance. I want to see how he functions under duress.

GH: Do you have a kind of visceral reaction when somebody walks in the door?

KATSELAS: Yes, I have a very strong reaction immediately and I have, on occasions, made a decision to take somebody immediately. If, on the other hand, they are stars or people unwilling to read, or whatever, then I base it entirely on what I've seen in their work and then that reading that I have with them. We did that with Eileen Heckart, with BUTTERFLIES and in the past I did it with Joan Hackett. We were stuck, we were already in rehearsal for a play—and this was before she'd even done anything, this was, like, in '62. And she walked into the room and I said to the playwright, "That's it." And then she read. But I was convinced before she even read because she read pretty good but not all that great—and we took her. And the same thing happened when I did ZOO STORY with George Maharis. He walked in and said two words and I said, "That's it." So I do have those reactions. The girl that's in 40 CARATS, the young girl Deborah Raffin, I just saw her, you know, in a hall and I said, "Where are you going?" and she was going up to have an interview with me. But I knew when I saw her in the hall that that was the kind of girl that could play the young daughter in 40 CARATS. I still put her through all the readings, but I had that immediate reaction. And in the back of my mind it was, "That's the girl." With Blythe Danner I just saw her in a play off-Broadway and I knew that was the girl but I still brought her in to read twice and then had her read for the producer and for Keir—because Keir in summer stock had casting approval.

GH: Then it's the presence that the actor brings in.

KATSELAS: Yes. I mean, the character in the piece is a human being and the more I try to get what is called in engineering terms a mock-up of that character, of what he is, of what his make-up is, what he looks like, how he moves and relates it, to some degree, to my experience—so that I have a reality on that character, an affinity for that character, and when that takes place—and I start thinking about actors, or an actor walks in the room, there is to some degree the appraisal of that actor in relation to that mock-up that I have. And this is what all the actors call "the picture" that the director has of the actor but, at the same time, I am much more interested in the qualities that I come to agreeing about in this mock-up, in this idea of the part, than I am about the specific look. There is a specific look but each actor that walks in, does he convey those feelings, those thoughts and ideals about the part—not just the physical image?

GH: Any last word of advice to actors?

KATSELAS: Well, I think that the most important thing for an actor is—is dignity, that an actor has a sense of dignity. And by dignity I don't mean pride, I don't mean false hope, I don't mean hostility. I mean a sense of the fact that he is in a profession which has been one of the most highly thought of professions in the history of man. Perhaps one has difficulty getting a credit card—but it's not that kind of dignity that I'm talking about. I'm talking about the dignity in the sense that one is able to communicate, as an artist, to mankind ideals, messages, feelings and ways of approaching even one's life. Each and every person that has ever attended any theatrical or movie adventure for any length of time has gotten some kind of information, even out of a comedy, or out of a Western, they've gotten some kind of information that they've been able to apply to their lives, to some degree. And the actor is the source of that. Sure material is, but we could have theatre without material, that is, actors could just get up, as they did in primitive times, and dance. Now this is not putting the writers down but it is a fact that the source point of theatre and of movies is actors. And therefore when an actor goes on an interview he doesn't have to be a beggar. He doesn't have to be anybody who is saying, "I've got to have this," no matter how broke he is. He must be willing to be himself at that interview, not to fake, not to pretend and not to try to sell a big thing but to be himself and to come with a certain dignity and not to be talked out of that dignity because he has to read, and improvise and meet, which the actor considers an indignity. Therefore, if he considers that an indignity, he really basically doesn't believe that he has dignity, because you cannot wipe away something with one interview. The only way that you can wipe it away is how the actor behaves and handles himself. That can be an indignity. But if the actor handles himself with dignity and with presence and with being there he cannot lose because if it's not this thing then it will be something else. When I say he comes as himself—some people think that means they can behave any way and without responsibility in an interview. If you are there, you are there to get the job, you are there to try to get the work, therefore you handle yourself in a certain way but you do not handle yourself in a way which is belying your basic reality about yourself, your basic belief about yourself. You are not there to sell yourself in a way that is cheap and that you cannot personally live with. But if you can live with it then you do whatever you want to do and you do it with dignity and with a sense of yourself and of being there and, as I say, if that's done there is no price for any of this stuff. The only price, really, I guess, would be success. Because you have got to win, you cannot lose if you come that way.

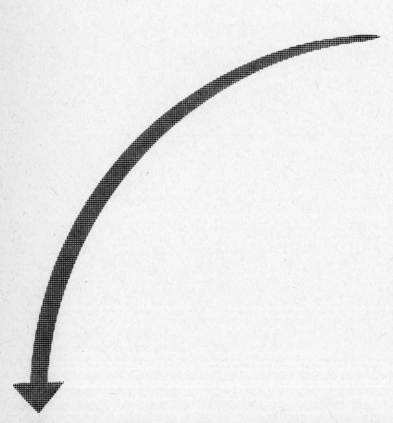

"*I think a new actor or actress should audition for everything they can, right or wrong . . . you learn a lot in auditions if the people you are auditioning for want to give a little too.*"

George Eckstein

A PRODUCER TALKS ABOUT AUDITIONING

GH: Can you remember the best audition you've ever seen?

ECKSTEIN: Well, every once in a while it happens, someone comes in—a girl about three or four years ago did that in a *Name of the Game* I was doing. I had seen her at a theatre, she was in the audience and someone told me she was an actress. She had a very interesting look and I thought gave a brilliant reading. She played the lead in the show. The first piece of film she'd ever done and she was beautiful—her name was Laurie Prange. And I think she will be important when the material and she coincide.

GH: She read well, obviously. Was there anything else that she did?

ECKSTEIN: It was the quality. The girl herself, what she was projecting as far as vulnerability, intelligence, sensitivity, those things were apparent. And we felt whatever she lacked in shading or experience could be directed.

GH: Are those things that you look for always?

ECKSTEIN: Yes, I think so. You know that the character has to have certain qualities, whether it's vulnerability or invulnerability or intelligence, some sort of character depth, humor. Those are basic qualities and you assume—particularly in the person who is an experienced, trained actor, that with a competent director you will get the shadings and the detail filled in

GH: How about interviews?

251

ECKSTEIN: Interviews are terrible.

GH: You don't learn much from them?

ECKSTEIN: Oh, yes, I learn a lot, but I don't like interviews. I don't think any actor does. I think they like readings better because it gives them something to hold on to. I mean, they know they are in there for a specific reason and not just to sit there being judged. But it's very unnerving for both parties. I don't think actors generally realize that both readings and auditions are really as unnerving for both parties.

GH: Have you had an actor put you at ease?

ECKSTEIN: Yes, that happens. Obviously, some people are much more adept and have much more poise in these situations than others. And sometimes some people are so uptight that whatever their real personality is does not get a chance to emerge and you are always conscious of the fact that unless you are able to put them at ease you may be judging them unfairly. Not allowing them a good shot at it, whatever it is.

GH: Do you usually go through interviews and then auditions or do you just go straight into the readings?

ECKSTEIN: It varies. Very often in television because you are working under severe time limitations, you go with a known quantity, and obviously it results in unfairness, in not allowing new people, young people particularly, to be seen, or to have the opportunity to have film. But there's a great deal of money involved and every hour's delay is a question of $1,000 or so. So you go with people who you don't think are going to harm you. And in that case, very often, there aren't auditions because you know what you are dealing with.

GH: Is there anything that actors do on interviews or auditions that you don't like?

ECKSTEIN: For me, someone who comes in and consciously tries to make an impression, whether it's over-pushiness or over-phoniness. I think that's about it. Because that's a mask between the person that you are looking for, which is what that person normally would project.

And sometimes you assume that's what the person normally projects—phoniness, and you try to terminate the interview as quickly as possible. Also, after an audition you'll meet somebody at a party—see them in a situation where they're not relating to you as a potential employer and suddenly there's an entire personality change, almost always for the worse. It's funny but I guess for a lot of actors acting is a mask and they have to put on some different personality in order to do it. That's why, I suppose, it's more difficult for so many actors to play anything resembling themselves.

GH: It goes back to vulnerability, which is such a valuable side to show.

ECKSTEIN: It's essential.

GH: Is there any way an actor can predict what you want?

ECKSTEIN: I think they could do a little research. Sometimes the instructions given to them by their agent or the casting director or the producer/director who summoned them on this interview, may not be complete enough. I think they should ask what kind of part is it that I'm coming to read for. Don't be put off by "Oh, what's the difference." They should really find out what kind of character's involved. I mean, a girl who comes in, or a man, the only tool he has is foreknowledge of what he's being judged on. If he's being judged by his masculinity then he should know that. We had one actress come in yesterday saying she doesn't think she's right for the part, didn't want to read, liked the script very much, and I believe that, and felt that she just wasn't able to play it. And that decision was greatly respected by all of us. And that's a refreshing change of pace. It saves her time, saves our time. And she wasn't then forced into a position of reading something she felt was alien to her and possibly giving a bad reading, which might jeopardize her chances for future employment, besides losing this particular part.

GH: It also shows a certain amount of intelligence and judgement on her part.

ECKSTEIN: I think that happens. I am sure that has happened more times than I like to think about, in the past, when an actor has come in, or actress, read for a role for which he or she was particularly wrong and because they were that wrong it has colored my opinion of them in the future.

GH: Can you remember any particular cases of somebody who has given a terrific audition and didn't get that job but later on you remembered them?

ECKSTEIN: Oh, I can't even tell you how many times that has happened.

GH: So the audition has value whether you get that job or not.

ECKSTEIN: I think a new actor or actress should audition for everything they can, right or wrong. If this sounds contradictory to what I've just said, it isn't. Because, for their sake, it's a tremendous experience. When I was an actor for a brief, a forgettable period of my life, just getting the audition, getting the reading was a big plus—because I felt that I was banking that experience and every successive reading became a lot easier. Also, you learn a lot in auditions if the people you are auditioning for want to give a little too.

GH: Did you ask questions when you went out as an actor?

ECKSTEIN: Yes, I think so, or I left myself open to comment, let me put it that way. It's funny how very seemingly banal suggestions or directorial comment can suddenly open your eyes, where a couple of years of schooling never did. I remember I read for a play in New York, and the director at the time said, "All right, now read it again and forget that it's a comedy." And suddenly I thought, "Oh, my God, all these years I'm doing this wrong!"

GH: Any words of advice as a finale, to actors?

ECKSTEIN: Just be persistent—but not too persistent. Be persistent in terms of the field but not too persistent in terms of me personally.

GH: That's a fine line to draw, though, isn't it?

ECKSTEIN: Yes. Some people, no matter how persistent they are

are not offensive, there's something in their personality that acts as a governor. They will not intrude upon your sensitivity. They just have that kind of empathy for another person's problems and are just unable to be rude. However, some actors don't know where that line is.

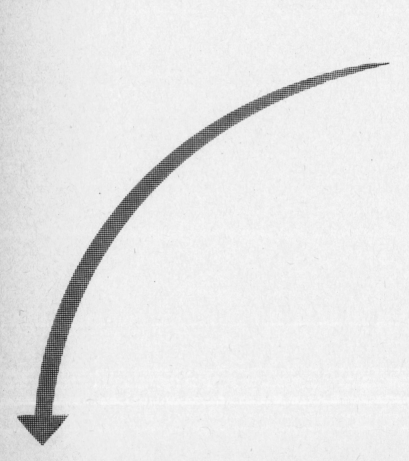

"The key is to bring a little love. You know, you bring a little love for the work. If you really love the work it shows."

Darryl Hickman

A PRODUCER TALKS ABOUT AUDITIONING

HICKMAN: I remember one day an actor came in and Larry Auerbach (director of *Love of Life*) said, "Now, is there anything you'd like me to tell you about the scene?" And the actor said, "No!" I mean, he was nervous. I mean—so overtly, "Leave me alone!" and so a director, who is extending his own self to an actor—I mean there's no way that they're going to communicate after that moment. So, the actor has to come to the point where he is willing, openly and vulnerably to lay out his work and to be judged positively and negatively without having a sense of resentment about it. That's very important.

GH: Now, if an actor feels this problem, how might he do something about it?

HICKMAN: Well, in my own case the first thing I did was go to Milton Katselas. I said, "I have problems reading and auditioning." and he said, "Well, let's see you do it." And I did an audition and he said, "You're right. You do have a problem and let's investigate." So he said, "First of all, how do you feel about auditioning? Do you like to do it?" And I said, "Well, I don't think I really do." And he said, "Why?" and I said, "Because it makes me kind of angry." And he said, "Well, I see that." So once I recognized that then my next step was to choose—do I want to audition or not?—and if I did want to do it then I had to give up the anger and resentment of doing it. Once I made that choice then it was easy for me really to eliminate it and auditioning became fun. I came to the point where I really liked to audition—especially musical auditioning.

GH: Can you describe to me how it feels when you like to audition?

HICKMAN: Well, I think the key to it for me was that I gave up any sense of needing approbation. I simply went in, did what I did, and gave up any sense of feedback—or need for feedback.

GH: Even the job?

HICKMAN: Even the job. What I had to ultimately do was to do the moment and leave it there—and walk away from it and whether the job came or the job didn't come, it was not important. I had to give up that need for the response. And once I gave up the need for the response I got all kinds of wonderful response. In those last few years when I was working, I got very good feedback on auditioning—and I got to be very good at it. I had fun. And the key was to take the pressure off myself—either I got the job or I didn't get the job but once I finished, I walked out and it was over.

GH: In the good phase, that latter phase, what kind of preparation did you do before you went to an audition?

HICKMAN: I remember one audition I did where—it was very interesting—it was for an off-Broadway play—and I went in and I was really wrong for the role but the play interested me and I prepared very carefully for the audition—days—I worked—oh, I learned the lines and I blocked it and I worked on beats for the scene and worked very hard on it. I went in and I was very good—and they called me up and they said, "Listen, we want to take you to lunch." So, they took me to Sardi's and they said, "You're not right for this part but it was such a sensational audition that we wanted to have lunch with you." I got an audition and I got a lunch. So, I mean, you don't know. The thing is to find a way to enjoy it and if you can do that you've got it licked.

GH: Now, sitting on this side of the table, what are some of the "do's" you might say, for actors coming in to audition—for you?

HICKMAN: Be there. To me, acting is more being than doing. The ability to bring yourself into a room is rare—and most of us don't do it in the living room. And I find that most actors don't do it in the reading or auditioning process. They bring a facsimile of themselves—sometimes based on the idea that they are playing a character—so they come in with an attitude about what the character is or what the scene is about. And the primary thing that I respond to in watching is: do I sense a presence in the room that is unique, that is interesting, that is human, that has varieties of colors. If I see that, I don't care whether the scene is read well or not because any decent actor can't read a scene wonderfully the first time they read it—they just can't do it.

GH: How does an actor develop that presence?

HICKMAN: He lives—and allows his life to seep more and more and more into himself and his instrument, his physical presence, his voice and so on.

GH: Is there anything metaphysical involved?

HICKMAN: I think it's a consciousness evolution. I think the more intellectual emotional, spiritual awareness one has—the more one is able to be there, rather than the facsimile of presence. And I think the presence is primary condition for the actor, both in an audition and on the stage. It is for me.

GH: If you are auditioning somebody for a "soap", what is the process?

HICKMAN: Well, most of the auditions that I sit in on are called by the casting department and they are usually given the script ahead of time, which they usually know pretty well. And they come in simply to read the script—for two or three minutes.

GH: What do you look for?

HICKMAN: I personally look for: a) that presence, b) are they generally in look, in feel, something like what we feel we need for the character, I then look very carefully to see if the actor is able to really look and listen to the other actor. That's extremely important to me and I find generally they don't really look or really listen to, what the other actor is doing or saying. To work, I think, to forget a plan that we may have for the scene or what the character is—and to work moment to moment, with the other actor, is the key to good reading.

GH: You think cold readings then are a good idea?

HICKMAN: I think not bad—particularly if you have the presence that I'm talking about and are able to trust and work moment to moment.

GH: What do you learn from a cold reading?

HICKMAN: I learn if the actor is able to be there and really look and really listen to the other actor. If they are able to—see, I think most actors, at best, are able to be themselves. I think very, very rarely does an actor characterize, or know how to play a character. And I think the primary goal of most actors, particularly in television and films, is to be themselves as-fully as possible. In a soap opera you don't have time to write characters anyway—you have a general notion, and you are looking for a presence that electronically transmits from your set. The actor has it or he doesn't have it—and the needs of craft, to me, are secondary to that presence.

GH: Actors so often use the phrase, "They didn't like me." or "They liked me." which puts the whole game on a very kind of personal basis. Do you think that's what it is?

HICKMAN: I think, and if you'll go back to my own case, you ask that actor, "Well, did you like them?" And I think that's the key. The key is to bring in a little love. You know, you bring a little love for the work. If you really love the work, it shows. And if you want to transmit that work, transmit that love to those who may be watching, including the audience. Your primary concern would be to give them something, rather than to evaluate what you are going to get back. And that's the key, I think. Whether they like you or don't like you is irrelevant. It's how much you liked them.

GH: Do you think you can tell as much on an interview as you can from an audition?

HICKMAN: I can usually tell in about ten seconds whether the actor is there or isn't there. I can usually tell by the way they walk in the room—and the minute they've said their first two or three lines I've probably made an evaluation of whether their level of work is consistent with what I'm looking for.

GH: Well, what about nerves?

HICKMAN: The presence comes through the nerves. The nerves are all part of the presence. Because we are all scared to death all the time anyway. We are all facing a future which is at best uncertain and none of us know from whence we came—or where we are going...and we are terrified, all the time. We just walk around like it's fine.

GH: Well, the audition then, or the interview, is kind of a capsulized version of that life/death motif?

HICKMAN: Yes, and the chances are whatever the play's about, it's about somebody in trouble anyway—or it isn't a very good play—so, if you are in trouble you might as well let yourself be in trouble. It reads better than pretending it's cool.

GH: How does a television audition differ from the stage audition?

HICKMAN: One thing that is different, particularly for soaps, is that it's understated in the way that this conversation is understated. You and I could not communicate on the same dynamic in a large theatre and get across what we wanted to get across, if we didn't have this microphone sitting right here between us. There's an intimacy in this conversation. In the theatre you've got to be intimate for a thousand seats. It's a whole different thing. And soap opera, particularly, is more intimate and conversational. I guess one of the signs of it is a certain amount of lack of even vocal projection. The more easy and intimate it is the better it works.

GH: It seems to me, there's an energy process, though, no matter what the medium—that has to continue. And some actors, when they get down to that more intimate medium—lose the energy.

HICKMAN: They do. Yes. I think the first thing you do is to allow the real energy that is there in you to be there. That's preferable to trying to manipulate it. Once you get very well crafted then maybe you can say, "Now I'm going to bring some energy here and put a little there and take a little out there—or do a little dynamic here." That takes real knowledge of the craft. Not very many actors have that kind of knowledge. One thing, one pitfall here—and I see this happen for our soap auditions—is that actors come in who've been around long enough to know that the kind of intimacy that I'm talking about works pretty good for soap—and they come in and they act intimate—they act natural—and it comes out artificial.

GH: What are the symptoms?

HICKMAN: One of the symptoms is monotony. They have a tendency to restrain everything—the emotional peaks and valleys—and flatten it all out as though it's everyday conversation. And we don't talk that way in regular conversation. There are peaks and valleys and ups and downs and ins and outs, even if the dynamic is more intimate. And the minute an actor starts to act natural or, for my money, act anything or attitudinize the flow of that living energy is usually diverted somehow—and that reads to me.

GH: What's the best audition you've ever seen?

HICKMAN: Ah—in the year or two that I've been here I have seen one actor audition really well and he came back the second time and auditioned again, just as well, and we said, "We would like to hire you for this part." and he said, "I'm not interested in doing a soap." And we got very angry and said, "Well, why were you wasting our time?" He had come in, he was very open, we just felt immediately there was a willingness to communicate. First of all to send his own energy, which was very positive and very definite, very specific, almost aggressively so—but it was flat out what it was. There was a sense of humor—humor about himself. He had a little exchange with the director, he didn't push—I forget exactly what he said but it indicated that he may be wonderful, he may be lousy—let's see what he was going to be today. And it was immediately winning because he put us at our ease. He made us feel comfortable, so therefore we wouldn't have to be nervous about him and we got relaxed and he was very relaxed. Then he moved at his own pace and did it in his own time—and he really looked at the girl he was talking to and he really listened to what she was saying to him. I couldn't tell you what the scene was about, I didn't even listen to the words—and he walked out and we all said, "He's terrific." And we called him back and he came back and he said "Well, here I am again we'll see how it goes today." Sense of humor, put us again at our ease—did it just as well as he did the first time—only different, it was a little bit different the second time. It was again moment to moment. He happens to be a fairly well-crafted actor.

GH: Who?

HICKMAN: Chris Sarandan is his name. It's the one audition that stands out in the year or two I've been watching that really had all of that that I would recommend and it was apparently not only noticeable to me, it was quite noticeable to everybody else.

GH: Do you find that when that audition is right most people on this side of the table know it?

HICKMAN: Yes. They don't know why they know it but they know it, they know it. It just leaps out...

GH: What's the best audition you've ever given?

HICKMAN: I auditioned once to do one of the Woody Allen plays. I had like forty-five minutes. I sat in the corner, I read the play—it was crazy—and I went in and it was a love scene, or something, and they had this stage manager that I was supposed to be in love with. And I said, well, it's all crazy anyway, and I had a wonderful time. I put my arms around him and I kissed him and I made love to him and he got all embarrassed—and then I went with that and I jumped around and danced around him and I just had a marvelous time. And I left...total satisfaction—and I didn't even know whether it was any good or what it was—and they called up and they said, "Can you get out of the run that you're in, in stock?" and I couldn't—so, I guess there was somebody else they had in mind, too, but it apparently worked okay. But it was good because I felt good. I felt like I had done something—I had made a statement of some kind that was specific, that was honest and an expression of something that I might do on the stage.

GH: Can you put yourself in touch with how you felt while you were doing it?

HICKMAN: Totally free. And totally willing to listen to the next moment and go with it—no matter what craziness came to me—and I was crazy. And they laughed up a storm.

GH: Any final word of advice for young actors auditioning?

HICKMAN: Have a good time.

GH: Back to humor again.

HICKMAN: Oh, yeah. If we can't enjoy acting I think we ought to go be—something else. There's always going to be nerves and anxiety and a certain amount of concern about being approved or disapproved...I mean, you can't do away with all that. But, unless you are willing to go there and do it with a kind of joie de vivre and a kind of abandon and relaxation, what good is it? So, you become a star—you're a boring star.

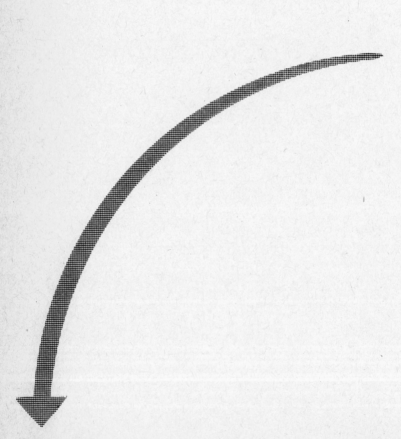

"I like a cold reader in comedy because I can immediately tell if he's got an inventiveness in him."

Jerry Paris
A DIRECTOR TALKS ABOUT AUDITIONING

PARIS: One of the things I did all the time as a director, when I became a director, was walk my actors—everybody that read—I'd walk them to the car, practically, for the first two or three years, out of my own insecurity. And people used to break up. Studio people would say, "What are you doing? Walking all the way to the thing, you are late, you are going to miss the next two guys." But I always felt a terrible need for them when they didn't get the part, when they read well, to pacify them and build them up, which in the long run isn't too good because they start calling you when you don't come around. One shocking thing happened on a film I made. There was some boy—a young guy who was marvelous but the studio head didn't like him. He kept saying he wasn't clean-cut enough, and the actor had heard about this so he came for the interview the third time on the sound stage and he had rented a tuxedo, with tails and everything, full dress with the top hat. He was there to be Mister Neat. And he got the part. That was really a shocking thing, to me. But gutsy. Another shocking thing is undressing. I never had anything to do with that. But a girl did it to me once, in casting. She just took her dress off. It was one of those dresses which just unbuttoned in the front and said, "There!" And I wasn't looking for that kind of girl, or that kind of a thing. I do comedy, I don't do X-rated pictures, usually, and she just figured she'd turn me on a little. And I was in an office and we were reading her, with Jerry Lewis and she just did it. And I had my lunch, I had a brown bag, you know, and I couldn't believe it. I couldn't eat my lunch, or anything.

GH: Did she get the part?

PARIS: No, she didn't.

GH: Are there other things that actors do that bother you, when they come in to see you?

PARIS: Yes, sometimes they try to win my love through false things; that we are old friends because they did a walk on. Also, I do a thing that's a bad habit. I will get very excited about someone and enthused, and then I might drop them after I've been so enthused about them and used them in a part. I can't hide that either, it's hard for me. Carl Reiner does this too, by the way. We get terribly excited and then— zoom! We also show that and don't use them again. And that kind of lets them down so suddenly. It's not always fair to the actor. Maybe something happened that he didn't come through in a role or a scene for that moment, you know. But it's hard for me to hold my feelings in. It's better if you can be a little more aloof about it, a little more reserved. And I'm not with actors. Like today, I was casting a little bit part, but I get involved with it and enthused about it. I think I sent two or three people out thinking they are going to do it.

GH: Is that good?

PARIS: I think it's good at first, and then as I'm talking to you I think that it possibly isn't good because in the long run it hurts them more. They get their hopes up then they are not going to do it. Maybe it's better if I was a little more reserved and I didn't show my feelings and then they didn't know if they got it and if they didn't get it they didn't think they were with a dishonest director.

GH: It's very personal for you, casting.

PARIS: Terrible! In comedy, especially.

GH: Do cold readings do anything for you?

PARIS: Yes, it helps. It helps a lot. It's a terrible thing to do, but... to get a person's timing on humor, it's very good to do a cold reading to see how fast they grab that. If they take it home and study it you are not really sure if the actor in rehearsal can grab things quickly and invent things quickly. Dick Van Dyke is the greatest cold reader in the business, so is Carl Reiner, because they have the type of mind that picks up—immediately, the first line of a scene, they know what the scene's about and then—they are more inventive in rehearsal, usually. The person who takes it home and just get it all plotted out in comedy usually has it set that way, and a set bag of tricks. I like a cold reader in comedy because I can immediately tell if he's got an inventiveness in him.

GH: Do you like improvisations?

PARIS: Yes, we do that a lot. We throw the thing away and say the scene's about and then they come up with funnier things and sometimes we use those funnier things.

GH: Give me one last piece of advice for actors.

PARIS: Just use your personality honestly, be yourself. That's really very important. Try not to be something else because then you won't deliver as your real self and we need you. That doesn't mean typecasting. The young actors today, they are so much better than way back. There were so few good actors. I mean, there were the great ones; the Cary Grants and the Jimmy Stewarts, but there were a lot of just pretty boys and today it takes so much more than that, and most young actors are really great. Be yourself because the scripts are better, and we need your personalities the way they are.

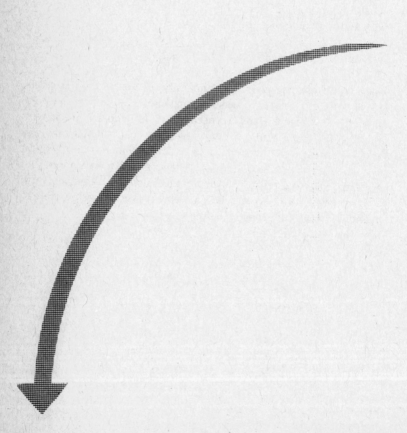

". . . you are dealing — dramatically speaking — with someone's life."

Renee Valenti
FORMER VICE PRESIDENT OF COLUMBIA PICTURES
A MOTION PICTURE PRODUCER
TALKS ABOUT AUDITIONING

VALENTI: Actors are under the impression that the minute you find somebody terribly talented you are going to make them a star. And it doesn't happen that way because then in turn I have to sell them to the producer, or the director, or both and what I see, they may not see. What they see, I may not see and it's a fight. But more often I'm fighting the actor who is not quite sure he wants to do television. He knows he wants to do theatre, knows he wants to do films, but he's not quite sure that he wants to do television.

GH: *Really!*

VALENTI: Yes. And I'm talking about finding a star for a series. The main objection, especially with New York actors...and I'm from New York, you know, is that since there is very little television in New York, the actors have deluded themselves into thinking that anything but theatre or films is denigrating to their art. That's a very old-hat thing.

GH: *I'm surprised that it still goes on.*

VALENTI: It does. A prime example is David Birney, who was doing productions at Lincoln Center. Then he got a very good deal on a daytime show. He did a couple of years of that and was very successful and then decided that he didn't want to live in California, and wasn't quite sure that television was where it should be for him. We then had to sit down four or five times, and I talked to him about what exposure means to an actor. Not selling short theatre at all—but

271

one night on television the audience that watches the actor, he'll never get in a theatre in ten years. If a show does not do well—20 million people are watching. Now those figures stagger you, but that's a show that's not doing well that 20 million people will watch. And that show will not sustain on the air because there are not enough viewers. You try to get that across to the actor, you try to get across to the actor that whether the series is successful or not, it can make him. I use as an example: Burt Reynolds. The series that I produced in New York: *Hawk*, one season. That's all. But it sure as hell made Burt Reynolds. *Bridget Loves Bernie* did it for David Birney. I mean, it's extraordinary...that's one of the frustrations of my job. Another is fighting the producer and director constantly. For example: I was in London on *QB VII*, a six-hour movie for television. And I found a brilliant actor in London that nobody in America knew. And I was determined that this actor was going to be the co-starring lead in that picture. Now we had Ben Gazzara, Lee Remick, Leslie Caron, Jack Hawkins, Robert Stevens, Anthony Quayle—I mean, we had names coming out of our ears. The network did not want an unknown in that part. My company did not want an unknown in that part but I fought by transatlantic phone. I had seen a test this actor did for a film called *The Abdication*—I fell madly in love with him. I finally told the president of this company, John Mitchell, I said, "Look, I have a year left on my contract. You can tear it up if I'm not right about this man." I said, "You pay me a lot of money for my opinion and my talent." Well, we finally used him: Anthony Hopkins, and three weeks after we cast him in *QB VII* he won the Best Actor Award in England for Pierre in *War and Peace*.

GH: But you have to go out on a limb like that.

VALENTI: You sure do. So it's contrary to what most actors think, you know, "If Renee Valenti liked me I'd be working."

GH: Do you get feedback like that?

VALENTI: Oh, yes. If an actor has met me and he's done a scene for me and he doesn't get a job it's because Renee Valenti doesn't like him —because if she did, he'd be working. They can't conceive that there are 35,000 actors and, percentage wise, one percent parts...what am I talking about? Less...a half of one percent parts over a season. They just don't know this side of it.

GH: It's not an easy position to be in really, is it?

VALENTI: No. If you take it seriously, as I do, it's very hard. You know that you are dealing—dramatically speaking—with someone's life. And if you put the right person in the right vehicle it can change their life. Like Billy Dee Williams in *Brian's Song*. Nobody knew him. Jimmy Caan had been around for years and no one really even knew him until *Brian's Song*.

GH: What do you base these opinions on? I mean, if somebody walks in the door. Is it from the minute they walk in? You get a sense of them then?

VALENTI: Yes, yes. That happens when I meet them, for the first time—almost the minute they walk in.

GH: Can you describe what that quality is that somebody might have that somebody else would not have?

VALENTI: It's very difficult to put into words. I've always used a very cliche term like, for me—a light bulb goes on.

GH: Are you seeing something in one person maybe that you don't see in another?

VALENTI: Oh, yes. Oh, absolutely. And it's not necessarily how they carry themselves and it's certainly not what they say—but it's what happens when they are saying it.

GH: Do they communicate with you more, perhaps?

VALENTI: It could be somebody who's totally uncommunicative.

GH: Really?

VALENTI: Totally. What I try to do is not talk to actors about acting, because that puts them on the defensive, and it means they have to prove themselves the minute they sit down. So I talk to them about motorcycles, tennis, swimming, sex, anything but acting.

GH: *Does that put them at ease?*

VALENTI: Yes. You hear them heave a sigh of relief. It's, "Oh, boy, she's not saying: 'what have you done lately?' " Because, "What do I do when I answer: "Well, I haven't done anything yet.'?" Then it's over—and you can't put them in that position. So from the conversation, I then decide whether I want them to do a scene, because I can't see everybody do scenes. So I make a choice and in making a choice sometimes I go too far over in one direction. For example: those actors who are extremely shy, I never know what they have going on inside. Not taking a chance and not wanting to miss, I will often give them an audition faster than anyone else. The ones that come on strong are easier to read and it's easier to know if they have something going or not.

GH: *Is there anything in this initial interview stage, that actors do that turns you off?*

VALENTI: Yes. An overly patronizing attitude. And hostility turns me off. I'm tired of hostility. There was a time when I could understand it, but it turns me off now. I've decided that, yes you can be bitter, yes you can be unhappy, you can be sad, you can have any of those emotions—but you don't have to be hostile when there's an open door. There was an actor here one day who was doing a scene. I knew him to be a good actor because I had seen him in a play in a little theatre. Now, after each scene I give my opinion. I don't say, "Thank you very much."—I give my opinion: right, wrong, or whatever, it's my opinion. And in the long run I think it's far more helpful to the actors than just saying, "Thank you very much." and they walk out and never know what the hell they did. An actor was here, doing a scene, and after it was over I said, "I'm very disappointed in you. Really. Because that was just lazy. You are better than that and I resent your wasting my time." There was a pillow on the chair and he picked it up and threw it across the room at me. And I said, "You know it's much easier not to say anything. And if I didn't care, I wouldn't. But I do care that you may leave this office and go to another studio and do the same scene. It doesn't do you justice. Well, wouldn't it be easier for me not to say anything?" and we went on. Later that day, I got a handwritten card from the actor. I still keep it.

GH: (reading the card) It says, "It's just that I've never been tucked in, you know? I appreciate your extended hand. Thank you." That's terrific.

VALENTI: That card means a lot to me because in spite of his hostility, I was still very honest with the boy. He left, he thought about it, and he sent the card.

GH: And learned something in the process.

VALENRI: Yes, yes. It's such an interesting business.

GH: We are constantly playing the human game, aren't we?

VALENTI: Yes, yes.

GH: O.K. you get into a reading. What do you look for when somebody is doing a scene for you? Is it possible to generalize on that?

VALENTI: Well, I will never have an actor do a cold reading. I don't believe in it.

GH: It doesn't have value for you?

VALENTI: No. Some directors double cross me, and say, "Oh, you don't mind doing a cold reading." And the actor, being scared to death that if he says "no" he doesn't have a shot, says "yes" and very often kills himself. But that's the exception to the rule. Wherever possible, I give the actor the entire script so that he knows what he's doing. Then I expect him to be able to give me in that reading the essence of the character, so that I know he understands the character. I don't care if the reading is not gang-busters. But if he has the essence of the character and the reading is fairly good I know that with time and work he can get it. That's on a specific. I also look for his relating to the person he is reading with. Now that's a little harder because often actors are reading with a casting director and we are not known to be that good at all! But, when actors are good they will relate to you, whether you are good or bad, and I look for that.

GH: Humor?

VALENTI: Yes. Where it's called for. But if the actor is coming in to read for a comedy, humor should not be strained, unless it's a schtick part. Also, there is a look for the role. I love off-beat kind of casting where the look totally defies. I love that kind of casting. And I like to take somebody who looks like a Mafia hood and have him do comedy. That's what made Sheldon Leonard work—that's what made so many comedians work in films. But it's nothing new, we just haven't done it for a long time. For example: when I did the pilot of *Hawk*, I don't think Gene Hackman ever played a heavier murderer. We cast him in the pilot and he played the psychotic killer. He wore steel-rimmed glasses and he was sensational. You know, normally he just played nice parts. I like that kind of casting.

GH: Is there a difference between television casting and feature films?

VALENTI: Not so much today between television and film because most of the actors that are going into film have been weaned on television. There is a difference, though, in my opinion, between theatre and film and television. In a theatre you can get away with an older man playing a younger role because, except for the first eight rows, it can work. Also, in the theatre you take a lot more time with make-up than we do—out of necessity—and a lot more can be done. For example, you are more likely to use a 25 year old, brilliant actor, playing an old man. We do it very seldom. Sure, Dustin Hoffman did it in his movie (*Little Big Man*) and I thought it was sensational. But that's very rare. If it wasn't Dustin Hoffman they wouldn't do it. And yet I go to little theatres around town and I see young actors playing old men—and it works. I mean, it works if their attitude and everything else is right.

GH: Do you cover a lot of theatres?

VALENTI: Yes. Sure. Monday, Tuesday, Wednesday, Thursday—I'll cover anything, any place. Friday, Saturday and Sunday belong to my family. And that's the way I break it up.

GH: That's a very heavy schedule.

VALENTI: Yes.

GH: How do you feel about actors?

VALENTI: I love them. I absolutely adore them.

GH: Do you empathize with their nerves when they come in to see you or they are reading with you?

VALENTI: Totally, totally. I think if you ask enough actors how they feel when they walk into my office as compared to a lot of other offices they will bear that out. Without sounding Pollyanna, I believe in dignity. And I don't think that actors are afforded dignity. I adore them and I find that my friends are all in the business. For years I've tried to be chic and I've tried to say, "Oh, no. I don't socialize with people in the business." And I find that people outside the business bore me.

GH: Any capsulized piece of advice you could give to a beginner?

VALENTI: Yes. Don't try to reach beyond what you are capable of doing. Be very sure of what you are doing. Be the best at it you can be because that initial audition is very, very important. It can be a key. And although people say, "Oh, we are just looking for some kind of feeling." It's not so. Don't be over-anxious and jump in before you are ready. Over-anxiety is really the biggest problem with young unknowns.

GH: Really?

VALENTI: Yes. They are afraid that if they don't do it now they are never going to get the opportunity.

GH: Not true?

VALENTI: No.

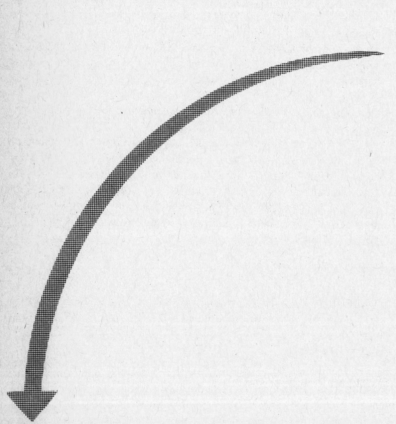

"Well, the only thing you can say to a young actor of any
kind is this: if they want to be actors then they just stay on
it. They persist and they take lessons and they study and
they live it and they work it . . . You've got to act every day."

Joseph Barbera

THE PRESIDENT OF HANNA-BARBERA CORPORATION TALKS ABOUT AUDITIONING

GH: When actors come to audition for you they are doing mostly audio, right?

BARBERA: Mainly, at this point, it's audio. Yes, in other words, we look for a character. Like for instance, we are doing eleven shows this year and in at least eight of them we have a dog. Now when we have a dog we have to try to give the dog a personality. Now, what is it this time? One dog we had had a crazy laugh and he became a big star. Another one is a coward, you see? Now, another one we made an eager beaver. So we have to find a person who can interpret a dog. Now that is murder.

GH: How do you go about finding somebody for that?

BARBERA: Well, first of all we call in the people that we know that have done it and try them first. But if people we've used for years have given us about all they've got, it is wide open here. We are looking constantly, and people send us tapes. Constantly sending us tapes. And a lot of people send us imitations in dialects, which we rarely use. We don't use Italian dialects, Jewish dialects, Polish dialects, because there's too many organizations that will destroy us.

GH: What do you want to hear on a tape like that?

BARBERA: What a person does best. That's the best way to start. Now, if they do imitations, O.K. Southern girl, Southern fellow, oakie girl—because they may be a certain quality that we haven't heard before. You talk about Tennessie Ernie, Andy Griffith, they have

279

quality...so we look for that.

GH: Do all the tapes get listened to?

BARBERA: We try to listen to all of them. Now I know some people will say, "Well, I never heard from them". Well, it could be because there's nothing in it. But the one thing everybody must understand is that we need the voices just as much as people would like to have the job. You see, it isn't that we have a few that we want to use over and over because even the networks don't want us to do that.

GH: When somebody comes in here to audition for you—what is the process, then?

BARBERA: We'll take a script that we've done and we'll say, "Just read this." Now, "Can you give us a hillbilly? O.K. Can you give us a teenage voice? O.K. Can you give us an old voice?" Let me explain why we do that. We have a cost problem. Most of our talent does more than one voice in a show. We have people that do three to six voices in a show. You see? Now they get paid—let's say the more voices they do, the more they get paid. It also saves us time.

GH: You need somebody who's technically very facile, don't you?

BARBERA: Yes. Then, of course, why do we use experienced people? It's because we have a time element. There are no giant rehearsals. You never get a script two weeks ahead of time and rehearse it and study and come in and read it and go back. You get the script a half hour before we start, usually. Then we do one run-through with everybody sitting around a table.

GH: O.K. let's say an actor needs a distinctive voice, he needs to be able to read quickly, cold and so on. Anything else they need to make a good impression here?

BARBERA: What he needs to do—and everybody agrees with me, is to get himself in here. He has to be listened to and he has to have a tape. If he's persistent enough we'll finally get to him, I'll tell you that. I'll tell you, I went through years myself of sending in cartoons and samples which were always rejected. I have more rejection slips, I tell you, from magazines and people, including a letter from Walt Disney. He said that "When I come to New York I will call you and talk to you personally." That was when he was first starting and he was very nice about it. But I never heard from him. He never called me, which happens to be the luckiest break that I ever had. Otherwise, I might have vanished into that giant studio and that would have been the end of that.

GH: Any advice to a young actor starting out who would like to get involved in this voice over business?

BARBERA: Well, the only thing you can say to a young actor of any kind is this: if they want to be actors then they just stay on it. They persist, and they take lessons and they study and they live it and they work it. You see, you just can't say, "I want to be an actor." and then stay there, and wait to become an actor. You've got to be working at it, you've got to be studying at it so that when the time comes you've got to be able to do something on a stage in front of people professionally. You've got to act every day. Get a tape recorder, read things, listen to yourself, go to little theatres, join little theatres. That's the thing you've got to do, you've got to work at it. And that was a long piece of advice...but that's the only way, really.

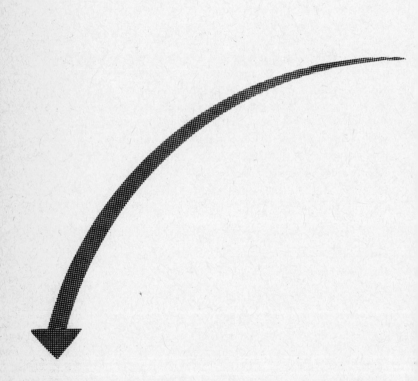

"I've also had people come in that walk in as though they have a bus to catch. They walk in and it's...'Let's get it over with'—like they are going to the dentist's office...They hardly get through with their speech and they are up out of the chair and next to the door—I think that comes, too, from a lot of rejections."

Mel Kane
A COMMERCIAL PRODUCER
TALKS ABOUT AUDITIONING

KANE: Ours are mostly entertaining commercials. That's our theory—it's entertain and get your message across. You don't have to show the hammer and the head and the inside of somebody's stomach to sell the product. Anyhow, getting back to casting. One thing that I watch when a person comes in is whether they are neat and clean and courteous. I've had people walk in that looked like they came from skid row. It shows to us kind of a lack of concern. I've had actors doing their bit for us and I look at their clothes and their nails and if they come in and they haven't shaved—well, it's subtle, but you feel like if that's the way they go on an interview, who's going to take a chance on giving them the job. Suppose they walk in on the set that way or suppose they don't bother even to wake up on time on the day you are going to shoot. There's a certain feeling of being with it and on the ball when they walk in—caring. Another thing, I won't wait for people that aren't on time. I think it's good training for the actors. Even though they would say, "Well, wait a minute. I go on calls and I sit out in the hall for an hour before they get to me." That's really beside the point and that's another point I want to make here. Some of them act that way when they come in—with like a chip on their shoulder, "You make me sit out in the hall there for 45 mintues." And it usually isn't our fault that that's happening. It's usually the actors that preceded them that take up too much time. One thing, too, I've found that turns us off on people—some people will come in and they will try and be very cute and very funny and have all kinds of little anecdotes about the business, about what they read in the paper today. Or make remarks about my hair or my suit...and what they are doing is holding progress up for that day. In other words, they are the ones that are causing the others to wait—who may have got there and are sitting there for an hour and are complaining about it later. And I've had some bad situations along those lines

GH: Like what?

KANE: Oh, I can give you a specific example. What we do here is tape commercial auditions on a closed-circuit tape with a small Sony. We have a camera on them and I had a director here standing by the camera and one man came in and handed me a composite, 8 x 10 glossy, and I said, "Who is your agent?" and he said, "Well, that's going to take a little imagination." So I let that go and I was walking over to the machine and he says, "Say, who Marcels your hair for you?" Now I was really irritated. So I got to the machine and I started to turn it on and I looked at him and I said, "Do you know something? You're not right for me and you're not right for this commercial so let's not waste our time." And he came over to me and shook his finger at me and said, "You think you are God, don't you? You think because you are an agency producer you have all the power in the world. You don't think I'm human, do you?" and I said, "No, I don't. And you'd better get out of this office right now." So he stormed out. But there is a sense that these people are rejected a lot. They are on interviews all the time and nine times out of ten they are rejected and they come in steeled for that and it's quite obvious. Another thing that turns us off on people along those lines—I had it happen the other day in a casting session. We'd been looking at person after person and we were trying to give everybody that walks in a fair shake. A lot of agencies when they walk in the door will say, "No, you are not right." We don't do that, we go all the way with them. We know they took a bus to get here and maybe cancelled an appointment or got a babysitter—we do the whole job with them. I've never yet told somebody by looking at them, "You are not the type." Never. We are very courteous along those lines. But one thing that bothers us is when we are taping, many actors say, "Can I see that back?" when they have finished and I will have to say, "No." And then they will think I am a real hardnose. And the reason I say "no" is first of all, if they see it back they are not going to like it, they are going to want to do it again. They don't know what our motives are for taping it. Then they think that they are not getting a fair shake, that we are sloppy by doing it once and not working on it. But we know right away that he's right or he's not right. But there are actors that say, "Can I see that?" and more often than not I'll say, "No." because we don't have the time, there are people waiting. We try to move the people through. That's something that could turn us off on a person. One thing that professionals do that we like a lot—and it always seems to be the ones that do a lot of commercials. They'll come in and we'll introduce them and they'll shake hands, then they ask questions about the commercial so they fully understand the commercial and they really listen. And then they go, they do their thing and you can say, "That's fine, that's all we need right now. Thanks for coming." They'll get up and say good-bye and walk out. That's nice and professionals do that. It's the non-professionals that will come in and try and be cute or tell you what happened on the way here on the bus, or, if you are giving them direction, they are shaking their head, yes, but they are not really listening. I've had situations with some actors where if you give them the slightest bit of encouragement, if you make a statement like, "Gee, that was good," fifteen minutes later your phone is ringing. They have gone back to their agent and told the agent you flipped out over them. And the agent says that if you want him you'd better come now because he's got three or four other things pending right now. So, oftentimes we won't say, "That was good. Fine. Terrific." And they walk away, again, feeling kind of rejected. Once an actor said, "Why do you always leave us with the feeling that there is a chance that we might get the commercial? You never really say, but we always go home and wait by the telephone and think there is a chance." And my answer to that was, "If we tell you, no, on the spot, we really don't want to hurt your feelings and we are not always really sure, ourselves, because we have to work in teams, and it's not one person's decision. After you leave we discuss it, with the art director, the copywriter and myself. We can't really say—'Yes, you've got it.' So we always have to leave the door open as far as not saying to him, 'I'm sorry, you are not right.' " It could be possible later. And I've seen it happen where in my mind I'm shaking my head after they leave and I'm saying, no, I don't think you can act at all—or he doesn't have the right look and an art director will disagree with me and he'll say, "Gee, he's exactly what I had in mind." And then we'll have to arbitrate it and maybe call in a third party. So we never really say yes or no before they leave. I might say, if I feel we are all enthusiastic—and I can usually tell—"What is your availability for June 5th?"

That would be the day we are shooting. And they'll say, "I'm in the clear as far as I know." That might be an indication to them that we are really interested. Oftentimes that is an indication. If I feel that the art director and copywriter are interested, or if I am, I'll go that far as to say, "What is your availability?' We don't want to get too interested in him if he's doing a series that week. Although, that's supposed to be screened out before they ever come to us. That's another bit of the information I give the casting girl. I say, "Do they have any conflicts?" In other words, "Have they ever worked for another bank commercial before?" Or, make sure they are available to shoot the day we are shooting, otherwise there is no point in them even coming up on this job. One of the other points that I feel turns us off, too, I've found that non-professional people that come in, treat this like it's an acting class, or that they are going to learn a lot from it.

GH: How do they do that?

KANE: With some people, and this is rather subtle, it's almost a feeling that they are picking your brains, that they have never really done this before—it's kind of a lark, and they have an attitude of, "Who needs to act to be in a commercial?" And we especially find that with pretty girls. In Hollywood there are a lot of great bodies and they think that's all that's necessary to become another glamour queen. Girls that get into the business because of glamour, have never thought of going to acting school. They figure, who needs to act for a 30 second commercial? And yet the people who became somebody from commercials did it on acting ability. Another thing we like, too, is people who come in who are very honest, they are not trying to impress us with past achievements. Actually, we never even read a resume. It doesn't mean a thing here, to us. Neither does a composite, other than a record of who their agent is, a reminder. I've also had people come in that walk in as though they have a bus to catch. They walk in and it's—what is it? let's get it over with—like they are going to the dentist's office. You want to say to them, "Look, if you want to go, be my guest, I hate to hold you up." They hardly get through with their speech and they are up out of the chair and next to the door—and I think that comes, too, from a lot of rejection. That's the unhappy part of this business and this is one reason I've never wanted any of my kids in the business. It really does something to these people, they go from one call to the next and they are constantly rejected and it begins to show, unless they have been successful at it. But I do have people come in and they give you the feeling that they resent being there, and you can't wait for them to leave. It's like they have a grudge, they treat the commercial as though—and this is another point I wanted to make, as a don't. They give the attitude when they come in that it's a real comedown to do a commercial. And yet most of your big people in the acting field now are trying to get into commercials. Our New York office did a whole set of Polaroid commercials with Laurence Olivier—and this is the kind of competition they've got, so they've got to be very professional.

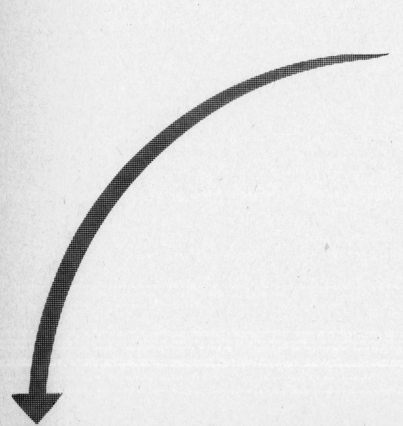

*"There's no spontaneous things happening during an audition
...except fear."*

John Biroc
PROFESSOR,
CALIFORNIA STATE NORTHRIDGE UNIVERSITY
A COLLEGE PROFESSOR TALKS ABOUT AUDITIONING

BIROC: The main problem I find with auditions is that they tend to be very unhumanistic. It seems to me rather ludicrous that in an actual show we go through all these techniques for relaxation for the actor because everybody knows in directing that an actor cannot perform well unless he is relaxed. Yet when we audition for some reason we are stuck in some traditional mode that prevents us from allowing the actor to relax. The way I auditioned actors for one show was to get them together, relax them first, then get them into groups of twenty. Kid with them, break the ice, a few jokes and then get them to play some theatre games which tended to add to the cohesion. It tended to free them.

GH: *What's an example of some of the games you played?*

BIROC: At first group activities. The whole group would do it, not an individual yet because I didn't want to put anyone on the spot. Games—they all became animals. And as they became animals, they had to start inter-relating with each other. And this gave me a chance to see who could subserviate his own ego to having the whole group function, which is very important to the types of shows I do because that makes it primarily an ensemble. Games like standing around in a circle and everybody closes their eyes and everybody begins to clap a different rhythm and they have to all get on the same rhythm as soon as possible. And this, too, shows me which ones will tend to try to dominate the group and which ones are able to hear the central beat of the whole group and be able to find it and go along with it.

And so a lot of the exercises are tell-tale, you find out a lot about the kids as you go...different kinds of exercises where you have maybe five or six at a time cross the floor. First they walk through mud, then over a picket fence or something, then through a tunnel, then over barbed wire, then come to the end. And do it a second time and motivate it. Show me why you're doing it. This again is to see what kind of imaginations they have, to see if they're traditionally oriented or if they really can bring some imagination into their work. I then go further into individuals, and eventually I narrow it down. But I don't get to the individual until everybody feels secure within the group. Because if an individual is forced to get up with people he doesn't know...again you're tightening up right away. Then it can be a number of things. It depends on what kind of a show I'm doing. Because at that point I'll change the audition depending on whether it's a traditional piece or improvisational piece. Sometimes if I'm doing a totally improvisational show after seeing the movement, the imagination that can be brought to their work, listen to their voices a while, I can tell that these are the kinds of people I want. If I'm doing a more traditional work, then I would have them get up and read. Because then I have gotten to a point where I can see how they move. I have heard their voices somewhat, imagination, and now if they can read and they can understand what the author is trying to say, fine. Or what I like them to do is to prepare something before they come in rather than cold readings. Because in cold readings I have found, for example when I act, I do a hell of a good cold reading, my cold reading is fantastic. But after that it's all downhill. A lot of people do that. A lot of people cannot cold read. I had a kid I taught one time that had some difficulty with perception. And he would stagger through the words. Now if we relied on cold readings, he would be out. But once he sat down and figured it out and was able to go over it a few times he was dynamite. So I don't put that much stock into cold readings. Usually when I get a group of people together, the group tells me what is necessary for that particular audition. So I can drop an exercise on them and suddenly realize that at this point because of where they're going right now, this other exercise would really be appropriate, I could really find out a lot. So just with the exercises I have in my head, we can go from one to another. I really feel good about that because I enjoy going into an audition very vulnerable. Because that's just exactly what the actors are, too. We're all vulnerable together. So we can find things out. Sometimes I'll jump into an exercise with them to trigger certain ideas.

Later on I might do an exercise called first impulse. As you follow your impulses, the group has to relate. The whole group is relating to each other but it's total free-form movement, total free-form whatever but they can't speak. They can make sounds or noises or whatever, but no spoken words. The group follows. Things happen—it's just a total spontaneous thing. You have to sense where the group is going. And it's not a copy, but a falling into a pattern where the group is going. Every once in a while I might come in if I see that it's sort of dropping, I'll maybe point on the floor and go, "Ssssss." And all of a sudden you'll find everybody coming around and reacting to what I'm doing. Nobody knows what it is, of course, but they're all reacting to it. And people will possible pick it up, whatever it is, start playing catch with it. Playing keep-away with this imaginary thing. Somebody might drop it, and all of a sudden there is a feudal thing taking place for this thing. This really happened. And they picked it up and carried it around as if they were in a procession around the room and everybody was falling into place with this whole thing. It's a total spontaneous thing. I think what we also have to look for in auditions is a word I've been using: spontaneity. We like to see actors on the stage being spontaneous with the material. Giving us as directors ideas. But yet during the audition process we really don't do anything as far as spontaneity is concerned. There's no spontaneous things happening during an audition usually except fear. So you should see where the kids' heads are at, if they can be spontaneous, if they can play the moment. Very important in an actor. All these things we have talked about for years. Every director wants it on the stage, but the audition process doesn't have it. And it's got to.

GH: Is there anything in auditions that actors do that turns you off?

BIROC: Yes. Trying to force his or her ego too much so that they come on ultra-strong. I'm not talking about stage strength, because that's very important, but the thing of, "Hey, everybody else get out of my way. I'm here now." That bothers me tremendously, because I know I will have a difficult time in the ensemble with a person like that. I don't need anybody telling me how good they are. And it bothers me when they try to use me like that. And when anyone comes on ultra-strong, I tend to turn them off. Or somebody during an audition that tries to push everybody back somehow by dominating an exercise. Right away, that person is out. Because they can't subserviate themselves to the group.

GH: Would you advise other colleges to try this kind of extended audition as opposed to the more traditional auditions?

BIROC: Yes, you're not only learning more by it but you're also giving the kids more of an education and we at the university level are involved in educational theatre. One of our professors here said, "Well, it's good that they have the traditional, in front of the light audition." And I said, "Why?" '' Because that's the way it is on the outside." Well, my answer to that was that there was a lot of prejudice on the outside, a lot of bigotry on the outside, therefore do you have prejudice and bigotry at the university because it's on the outside? Of course not. You get them to feel secure with themselves primarily, and then they can face any kind of situation on the outside. I think what we have got to do at the university level is to get a more humanistic approach to the auditioning process. To get the kids to feel secure about auditioning. To get the kids to realize that auditions can be very exciting, a nice challenge. And I think that way they will be able to bring to an audition the best of their abilities and not let fear get in the way and put up blocks. I prefer a large room rather than a theatre to audition. Because if they can see their audience, if they can see the extent of what they have to do, if they're made to feel comfortable, relaxed, then they start opening up. If necessary, have callbacks on a big stage after that so you can measure their projection. But the first thing you really have to do is find out a little bit about where the people are at, get them to talk a little about themselves.

GH: Do you think besides this, it's important to acquaint them with what we call the harsh realities of the professional world and the professional audition? Or do you think it's more important to educate them to your way of thinking and feed that into the community?

BIROC: I think they can be alerted to what goes on in the harsh realities of the world, the old traditional types of auditions. But I don't think it's necessary to put them through that type of an audition in order to know that it exists.

"*I believe in the dignity of the moment.*"

John Ingle

**PROFESSOR, BEVERLY HILLS HIGH SCHOOL
A HIGH SCHOOL TEACHER
TALKS ABOUT AUDITIONING**

GH: What do you look for in an audition? What makes you sit up and take notice?

INGLE: The kind of dignity of the audition itself. The seriousness of purpose. Absolutely. And our kids, I know it sounds egotistical, but if you could sit in on these auditions, you would see that there is never any applause, there is never a clack, there is never a sound in the room. There is the business of auditioning.

GH: Do you create that atmosphere?

INGLE: Yes, you have to demand it. And nobody ever applauds. Sometimes we have 150 people sitting in.

GH: So the people who are auditioning also watch the other people who are auditioning?

INGLE: Yes, as a learning thing I think it's very important. It takes the mystery out of auditions. And I think it's tough. But educationally I feel it's really sound to do it this way. We just did GOD-SPELL last March, we auditioned probably 100 students. The audition consisted of the song "Day by Day", two very short songs, plus two of the parables. Those auditions were all done in the auditorium. We audition where the thing is going to be. We have the big theatre and the little theatre. And again it's a learning thing as far as I'm concerned. I would like, and I think it would be very healthy if parents of the high school level would come and sit in on these. Then there would not be the bitching and moaning about "my child didn't get the part." There is not favoritism because we have as many as six people auditioning on the staff. We are a group of people with rating sheets, and you are rated one to ten numerically on your singing ability from THE MIKADO, for instance, one to ten on your dancing ability, and one to ten on your acting. And that includes voice, style and presentation.

GH: So it's kind of an impersonal process?

INGLE: Absolutely. I use the term anonymity, so that you become anonymous when you get up to perform. You are friends with no one, you're not enemies, but I don't care about the scene you did yesterday in class or the role you did last month. You are anonymous, you are merely time-slot 2:05. And if you can go through that anonymity, and create a character, that's it...Also, projection, not only vocal projection but character projection, commanding the audience to listen and go with you. A certain amount of arrogance, as a defense...if I call it arrogance I really mean self-confidence. But arrogance is a little more obvious than self-confidence because self-confidence is kind of a nebulous thing to teach a kid. But it's the kind of thing where you say, "I have worked hard, by God you listen." I don't think that's a negative arrogance, I think that's a healthy arrogance. And it may not even be arrogance.

GH: Is there anything auditioners do in these auditions that bothers you?

INGLE: Yes, the lack of anonymity. "Here I am again folks, ready to come on strong...it's me again, it's Bill again, I'm here." So the kid comes up playing the sum total of every interpersonal relationship that has ever been between him and the instructors or him and the audience.

GH: So he's trying to use something other than the audition?

INGLE: Yes, sure...something other than the now.

GH: Do you get flack about favoritism?

INGLE: Sure. We are tested. We are offered goodies, not graft, you know, but it's kiss-up time.

GH: So you have to be firm.

INGLE: And open. Not only firm, but public.

GH: Suppose 50,000 high school kids are going to buy this book. What, in capsule form, would be your advice to them about auditions?

INGLE: From the very outset, starting with the concept that, "I enjoy this, yes, it is traumatic, but, yes I would rather be doing this than anything else. I mean, this is a very important moment, therefore I must enjoy it, I must work like hell to make it as perfect as I can make it within my present state. Which means, absolute preparation, vocal, musical, choreographic, characterization, text, whatever. Because if it's five minutes worth, by God, it's the best five minutes." Otherwise, I think it's insulting. It's insulting on the person auditioning you and hurtful for you.

GH: Do you like auditions?

INGLE: Yes, because good things happen in terms of learning things. If a person auditions badly, instead of being hostile to that kid, as adolescents in the audience can often be, you seek first to be supportive. And you can only really see this if you see a kid audition, say, for five, six shows, and be wretched on his first audition and get roles in his fifth or sixth audition purely through a slow process. So that's why I like them. Now, for instance, the forthcoming audition is for four days—the high point of the entire department. By 1:15 tomorrow afternoon in the Little Theatre there will be 200 people there. All people who are auditioning, every kid who's going to audition will be sitting there as this one boy starts at 1:15. But I believe in the dignity of the moment. From their standpoint as actors, from. my standpoint as a teacher/director—I don't want anyone to waste my time.

GH: Do you like actors?

INGLE: Very much, if they treat their craft seriously...

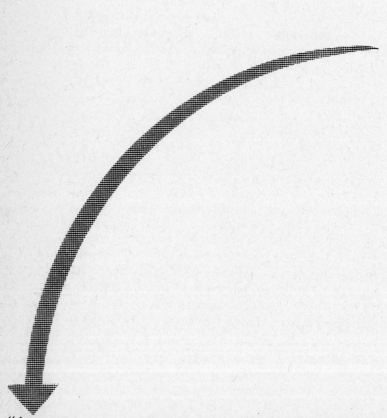

"*An actor must act. He must get up in front of people. He must communicate. An audition is another marvelous opportunity for him.*"

Omar Paxson
PROFESSOR, OCCIDENTAL COLLEGE
A COLLEGE PROFESSOR TALKS ABOUT AUDITIONING

GH: Do you like auditions?

PAXSON: Oh, I love them, I really do, because you get to see young kids trying to communicate something under pressure. We had a girl, Jane Murray who just auditioned for the Tyrone Guthrie Theatre. She went to the audition scared to death, and she started to do something dynamic with the people who were auditioning and they immediately sat up and took notice. And she's back there now with a full-year contract. She was able, from doing years of auditions here, to somehow catch their attention in ten minutes.

GH: How do you learn to handle the tension of that kind of experience?

PAXSON: Well, constant auditioning. Everybody here has to audition for everything. I think for Jane it was just getting up that courage, and every time she did it she was just as nervous as the time before. But she got a feeling of strength about the things she could do well, and what showed her talents. The problem is that most students don't feel confident that in a ten minute time period they can do something that is somehow going to communicate the basic spirit of what they are.

GH: Is that the bottom line?

PAXSON: It is for me because in ten minutes, if they have to do a

Shakespeare piece or a classical piece or a modern, they're not going to give me a full character. But if I can see a type of spirit or vitality coming out of the human being, and the person's handling their body in a decent way, and they have a vocal technique where they can project or throw their voice, that's all I want. How do I describe it? Is it a spirit, an intensity, a wanting to communicate himself?

GH: Is there a way that you know of that actors can develop the ability to communicate that energy and spirit you're talking about?

PAXSON: Somehow you have to be able to take all your talent and crystalize it and communicate within five or seven minutes what you can do. I think experience is the only teacher; and the only way to prevent audition fears is to absolutely know what you are doing, and to have rehearsed it until it is a part of you like a finger.

GH: What about choice of material?

PAXSON: The first thing that comes to mind is, is it used or is it different? Anything that has been used over twenty-five years, and you've heard used over and over is eliminated. I get tired of hearing the same thing over and over. Pretty soon you get a preconception about what you want to hear or perhaps what you think in your own bias you should hear. So we try to get them to open up. For instance we had a boy who was really working on auditions, took an independent study on auditions, and we spent an entire period finding material. I started out reading Aristophanes and when we ended up at the end of the term, his best material was from Aristophanes. It was absolutely marvelous. And nobody has ever used it. For his classical auditions that's what he chose. And a couple of minor characters from Shakespeare that no one ever does like Lance and Crab from TWO GENTLE-MEN OF VERONA. I never hear that. I've seen it performed. And sometimes rich but minor characters from plays that are fairly well known, I think that's very important. I get tired of hearing the potion scene from ROMEO AND JULIET. Or St. Joan's great speech in Act 5 of ST. JOAN. We try to put our students on to new material. The second thing we look for is what will fit their talent at this particular level. And the third thing is if they have a tremendous talent in one area to find material which is going to accentuate that great talent.

GH: Any pet peeves about actors?

PAXSON: Oh, yes. Actors who simply can't use the language. Now, if they can't use language, then why don't they just dance? Which is marvelous—we've had people audition who were bad with language and who really impressed us because they used pantomime sequences. Or they've danced, and they have had tremendous physical control and urgency of spirit through movement. If they cannot hold the language, if they cannot complete sounds, if their articulation is dreadful, that really is my pet peeve. Because if you are going to try to communicate, and language is one of the things you want to communicate with I want to hear it, and I want to hear sounds. So that's my pet peeve.

GH: Any others?

PAXSON: Personality things, like people coming to auditions and they're so frightened they all of a sudden project a chip on their shoulder. We're not ogres, we don't think they're ogres. They are precious talent, and I think that's important on the other side. To project that you really love the fact that this young kid's trying out. Then the other real pet peeve is this: learning lines is essential, and if you haven't done that, why even show up? That's laziness, procrastination, putting it off until the last minute. Another peeve is if somebody has to do something, and they become apologetic. You know, "I can't do this, I'm not very good at this." If they have to apologize for anything, they shouldn't be there. Because they are communicating themselves, and if they don't have enough pride in themselves, to really want to communicate what they are, then why waste anyone else's time? And so I think you have to build a sense of pride in the kid when he auditions. You have seven minutes to live...really live. But you have to be prepared to do it.

GH: Is there a better audition system than the one we know?

PAXSON: There's nothing wrong with an audition. I mean an actor's life is performing, this is part of it. I think it's healthy. If someone is a director, he directs. If he's a painter, he paints. A playwright has to have a half-a-dozen clunkers in his trunk because he has to learn. An actor must act. He must get up in front of people. He must communicate. An audition is another marvelous opportunity for him.

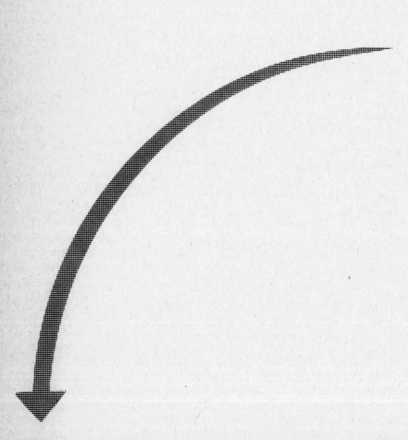

"The fact of the matter is that the overwhelming majority of actors are smarter than the overwhelming majority of the people who are interviewing."

Richard Dreyfuss

AN ACTOR TALKS ABOUT AUDITIONING

DREYFUSS: For the most part people on the other side of the desk, the people interviewing you—don't know how to interview actors. Because what you are trying to find—especially in a film—is some kind of personna that comes out of the person—as opposed to doing a good reading for the theatre. On film you are dealing with mythology, with a myth, with literally an aura that you can give off. Now, normally, when you go in for a film interview—or a television interview—they ask the same ritual questions: "What have you done? What film work have you done?" Like that. Now, what is not understood by the directors or the producers or the casting people number one, is the terror and the pleading that is going on inside anyone who wants a job. So when you ask those rote questions you get nothing at all, you simply get information. So, I've found as an actor, I would try to take over an interview in the sense of going beyond those questions. I would ask questions, I would deal with what is the common denominator between who is on that side of the desk and myself, which is the script or the work itself. I would ask questions about the script, I would give them my opinion about the script. I would let them see as much of Rick Dreyfuss as possible rather than just the information of my history—because what they see, normally, is just words. So what you try to do—and what I tried to do as an actor, always—was to not really be aggressive but at least to allow myself to show more than just that information.

GH: *Were you scared when you were doing this?*

DREYFUSS: No.

GH: *You mentioned that actors are afraid, begging and so on. I*

303

wonder if that applied to you.

DREYFUSS: When I say afraid—there's a judgement that an actor must live with on a constant basis—more than any other artist I know of. The process of rejection that goes on in interviews, you can't help it. So when an actor goes for an interview you know that 99% of the time he wants the job and he's in a supplicant position—so he's very often afraid to come out of himself and so he'll let the other person lead. And what I realized. when I was about 18 years old, was that that was very boring and not getting me anywhere. Anyone can say that they did HAMLET in the park and in Toronto—and who cares? What is important is the reading that you do—if you are there for a reading—and then to make sure that you are interesting. Because the actor's instrument is only himself and the more interesting your instrument is, not only are you going to be remembered but the more use you can be put to. That is what you are doing, that is what your job is. So when I was 18 years old I just started taking over interviews rather than responding to their lead. Not in terms of hostility. If I had been given the script beforehand, I would talk about the script, about the character. If I felt, for instance, that they were leaning away from a reading—they were looking like, "God, we are not going to read him."—I would go for a reading. I would say, "Let me work. Because my cold reading is better than anything I could say to you." If it was a general interview, I would ask them as many questions as they were asking me.

GH: *So you really made this your session as much as it was theirs, if not more.*

DREYFUSS: Yes, yes. Now, later on, in certain situations, I sat in on the other side of the table and I saw it from their point of view. I was involved in a film once where they were casting two major roles—the major roles of complex, well-written parts for women. And after the first two interviews I said to the producer and director, who had just been sitting there, and I said, "Excuse me, but you don't know what you are doing. You are not getting from these people what you want to get." And they said, "Why?" I said, "Because you are asking them things that allow them no showing. They can't expose anything about themselves to what you are asking, so let me handle the next interview." So the next girl came in and she had read the script—and I said, "Did you like it?" and no one had asked that before. And she said, "Yes." and I said, "Which character do you want to play?" and she named one character. "Do you like her? Do you like that person?" and she thought for a long time and then said, "No." and she told us why—what about the person she didn't like. And so we did one reading and then I said, "You played it as if you didn't like it. Now what you've got to do is find out how to love her because you can't play a character that you don't love." And so she did it again. And then I would ask questions like, "What characteristics do you like to play? What personality traits do you like to play?" Because I know that in myself there are certain behavioral traits, personality traits, or attitudes that I like playing. There are certain actors who like to play anger, certain actors who like to play joy. I like to play self-awareness, I've always known that I like to play a character who knows about himself or knows even that he doesn't know something. And I've always kind of imposed that on the characterizations that I've done. So I asked them these questions and we started getting more responses from them. So the interviews went from five minutes to twenty minutes to a half hour—so the casting took a lot longer but we got a better judge of what was going on.

GH: So from your experience, the interview tells you more in the film world and the reading tells you more in the theatre?

DREYFUSS: I've had strange experiences in the theatre. I used to come down here (to the Music Center in Los Angeles) and hang out—I'd say, "Well, what's going on, you know?" and finally one day they said, "Here, read for this thing." And I'm a good cold reader and so I read. What I did was—I didn't know I was being manipulative, but I was doing Duddy Kravitz. I realized that I had been manipulative in the sense that I didn't purposely come down here and purposely make friends with people like Mike Montel (former Mark Taper Casting Director), but whenever I was downtown I would always stop by the Taper and I would get to know the people down here so that they were forced to think of me for roles. Then, what happens is—in the theatre you can get away with playing parts that you couldn't on film. For instance, when I did MAJOR BARBARA I went into Mike Montel and I said, "Who is playing Bill Walker?" and he said, "Well, we have an offer out to someone but we don't think he is going to take it." And I said, "I want to read for it." and he said, "You're kidding." because Bill

Walker is always played by a big, tough, broad—well, I had an image of the character...so they let me read. And reading, in the theatre, is what is most important because, obviously, you don't have to suffer under the physical personna and the mythology of film—the face thing. Also I find that the more intelligent you can be at an interview, the better off you are—in general. There are some directors and producers who are intimidated by intelligence, which is one of the reasons why there is a mythology that actors are stupid. Because they have been told, trained through circumstance not to show their brains. I mean, I've been kicked out of studios for recommending changes in scripts. But, in the long run, if you are going to talk to a Gordon Davidson or a Mike Montel, or Gordon Hunt, or whoever, the more intelligent you are about the part or the play, it shows a good director, a good casting director, that you can contribute something to the rehearsal process other than the memorization of lines.

GH: Were you automatically a good cold reader? Or did you learn it?

DREYFUSS: Well, I'll tell you. You see, it wasn't automatic it's just that when I was growing up, 9, 10, 11 years old, the only way I could act was by going into the bathroom and doing plays—and I started to do that. Then on television you go up for a reading. You get the script, you read it in the lobby and then you go back and read. And I have a fast head.

GH: How about preparing an audition, if you get a script ahead of time? Did you do a lot of work on something like that?

DREYFUSS: No. My first instincts are always the best. I always have an immediate visual and visceral image of the character. And I go with my first instinct, the faster the better. It's more committed, it's more intense. If I start working on it I get all fouled up. That's what you do in rehearsal. That's when you step back and start analyzing and you allow yourself to be bad for two weeks. But on an interview, I'd much rather cold read than anything else. I've cold read to the extent that I have literally not read the sentence ahead of what I am saying. Because you get an instinct of what is going on in the scene and then you go. And even if you make the wrong choice in terms of the whole play, your choices are going to be interesting—at least that's the way I felt. I've found that the longer the interview, the better—always the longer the interview. Because you have to have enough time to relax and to be able to be seen as a person and not just as a supplicant. And I have a general rule, in terms of myself, that the interview is more important than the job. This has less to do with acting than it has to do with being a person. Because there is such a common level of abuse given to the people who are being interviewed. It's necessary, it's so important to turn around to the person who is interviewing you and tell them to go to hell.

GH: Do you think it's necessary?

DREYFUSS: Absolutely. You see, you have to let a creep know when he's being a creep. What happens to actors is that they are treated as talking pieces of meat who have no other privilege than to act. Memorize your lines, move where I tell you to and change the inflection in your voice when you are supposed to—and that's all! Because you have the brain of a turkey. And the fact of the matter is that the overwhelming majority of actors are smarter than the overwhelming majority of the people who are interviewing. So what happens is, after a while, you are being talked to as if you are not there—you are just the body sitting in the chair—you have to say, "Excuse me. I'd rather not do this job if this is what I have to go through." And there's a very specific reason why you do that. It's not just because you want to be a bad guy or a rebel—but very simply, an actor's instrument is himself and the more you give away in an interview, the less you have as an actor because your soul, your body is your instrument. So by the time they offer you a role that demands something of you, you've got nothing to give them. So you have to always take the risk. You may lose a job at Twentieth Century Fox or the Taper because you got into some argument but that protects your instrument. You are not giving yourself away, you are not letting yourself be abused and you are protecting what you have. Now I have, supposedly around town, I have a bad reputation because I get into arguments a lot. But I just always knew—however arrogant this may sound, that there was an inevitable making it at a certain point.

GH: So in those interviews you were really behaving as if that time was already there before it really was.

DREYFUSS: Yes, well, I was behaving the way I had to behave. But you see, I never abused them. I was never late. I was late once. John Rich yelled at me. I was 2 minutes late for some 3 camera show I was doing, when I was 17, and I was 2 minutes late back from lunch and he yelled at me like I've never been yelled at in my life, before or since then. The only thing I do is forget pencils, I always forget pencils. But I didn't act as though I was going to be a star, I acted as if I was a person and I knew then that if I sucked up for a job, that I was chipping away at whatever I was. And what I am is my own instrument...it doesn't make sense to be humble and to be begging and pleading because that means you are hurting your own work. And eventually if you do get the part you are not going to be open, you are not going to have enough resources to play the role.

GH: Can you remember what the best interview or audition you ever had was?

DREYFUSS: The best audition I ever had, that I can remember offhand, was for JULIUS CAESAR.

GH: Where?

DREYFUSS: For Joe Papp. It was interesting because I was making a name for myself, and I had reached the point, in my own mind, where—if it was any kind of naturalistic play in this country, if they don't know that I can do it, then forget it. And my agent at the time thought,"You don't have to read for anything, you're a big shot. You don't have to read. If you are not offered the part, forget it." But I had never done Shakespeare for anyone so I went and forced my way into Papp's office because I really wanted to play Cassius in CAESAR. So we were talking about the play and we were disagreeing constantly. And he said, "Would you be willing to read?" And I said, "Yes." And my agent turned around and I said, "Well, no one's ever seen me do Shakespeare. He has every right to hear me." And I said I would do it. And he said, "Would you be willing to read for me?" and I said, "No." and he said, "Why?" and I said, "Because you are the producer, not the director." And he said, "Well, we don't have a director yet." And I said, "Well, I don't take directions from producers. I have an enormous ego and I sublimate that ego to a director, only. And I won't let anyone else tell me what to do. The director tells me what to do." So we went back and forth and finally he rented a director.

GH: For the day you mean?

DREYFUSS: It was really funny because I had been doing Caesar in my bathroom. And I was taking a shower...and I was doing "I cannot tell, I..." and I got NERVOUS—I got nervous, I hadn't been nervous in three years. And I was petrified. I went down there PETRIFIED. And I walked into Papp's office and we were talking and I was trying to get rid of this nervousness. I was talking to Edward Call, the director, about the play and trying to get us talking about something. And Joe Papp broke in and said, "All right, let's cut this short. Let's have a reading." So we went down into this reading room and I knew the circumstances, I was auditioning for Papp but we had had this battle of wits, or ego or whatever you might call it. And so I just made Papp Brutus, as I did Cassius, and I was really good. As soon as I started then I relaxed and then I just dealt with him as Brutus and what happened, again, was I finished it and as soon as I finished it Papp said, "You got the job and he's not directing. Hah, hah!" And I knew, I knew, and I thought it was funny that he did it that way.

GH: You said you were in the shower and this fear came over you. Now you don't have anything to lose—speaking objectively—where does the fear come from?

DREYFUSS: I might not have gotten the job. You see, the idea that I'm a celebrity, that I've made a name for myself, that doesn't mean in my mind that anything has changed in terms of my talent. Whenever I really wanted a part I would get nervous because I wanted that part and I didn't want to lose it. And the thing I had to rely on was that somewhere inside of me, with all the insecurities, that I knew that I was a good actor.

GH: Do you have any specific way of dealing with that fear?

DREYFUSS: The best thing to do in any interview situation is never lie about where you are at that moment. If you are nervous, use it. You cannot be cool if you are nervous. And if you are nervous, then let yourself be nervous. I walked into Papp's office and the first thing I said was, "I'm nervous, I'm terrified." And I copped to it, because then you don't have to work against the lie that you are telling anyone and the lie that you are telling yourself. So if you are given the part of Hamlet to read, for a reading, and you are going to read: "Whether tis nobler in the mind..." like that—and you are nervous, then just be where you are and read it that way. Don't impose any kind of emotion on it. Because what they are looking for is whether you can be malleable, how you can be manipulated into different places. Because, let's face it, no matter what anyone says, it's a collaborative medium—an actor's contribution is immense—but it is colored by the contributions of the director or the writer. And if the director sees that an actor can't make switches that he finds necessary, that's bad. An actor has to be able to make adjustments. That doesn't mean that an actor gives in to a director—either in the rehearsal process or in an interview. Don't agree for agreement's sake, don't agree to get the job. But you should be able to have that respectful fight. The Utopian situation in the theatre is that fight. No one's ever going to have no arguments. As long as you can have the openness to argue with your director and then come to a common agreement, or a common compromise.. then if the director insists and he gives you reasons, then do it.

GH: Have you got one sentence to say to an actor about an audition or an interview?

DREYFUSS: Well, I would say—take a chance. The thing I would say to actors for the most part is—act. Most actors, not only in this town, but most actors are not actors, they are people who want to be famous. And they have no understanding that you can be an actor without being paid. The actors that call themselves actors only when they are working for money are people I despise, because the only way you can learn acting is to act, which means go to workshops and work your brains out. I'm just realizing that the last few years, when I became semi-notorious, have been the most harmful period of my acting career. Because I've become involved with everything but acting. Business deals, publicity—and my acting has suffered.

"Auditioning is an opportunity to go beyond where you are right now. It's an opportunity to extend yourself — to go outside of yourself a little bit, to become a little bit bigger than life."

Karen Morrow
AN ACTRESS TALKS ABOUT AUDITIONING

MORROW: Singing auditions to me are the best—and I do the best at those because—and I think it's important—because I know what I do best. For anybody who is auditioning I think, always lead with your strength. So that, automatically you are very comfortable and you know you've won. It is a contest. So, if you go with what you are strongest in then you've won, ahead of time, so you come in without the challenge and do what you do.

GH: Come in without the challenge?

MORROW: Yes. Come in with the thing that you have that can't be challenged, whatever it is lead with that—as that is the thing you are the most comfortable with. Comfort, comfort, comfort.

GH: How can you become comfortable?

MORROW: How? I become comfortable by wearing something that is not restricting. For instance, my agent used to say, "Wear three inch heels because your legs look thinner." I don't care!—at this point whether my legs look thinner—I will wear slacks now, cut very nicely with a waistband that is movable because my diaphragm expands—or something that won't show perspiration stains so that I have to keep my arms down. A hairdo that will not wilt the minute you walk out onstage—so that you don't have to worry about anything physical. I only have to do what comes from my toes and is absolutely unhampered by anything. Also, audition situations are very strange. You may audition in a barn, you may audition in somebody's living room, audition—as I have—over the phone.

GH: Over the phone?

MORROW: Yeah. That was early on—an agent asked me to sing for his wife over the phone and it was so exciting. I did a whole show number from BELLS ARE RINGING with the actions and everything over the phone...I got hired for a cruise, around New York. And here (in Los Angeles), even here, I didn't audition but I sang for Ron Moody and it was a terrible room. It was a terrible room and there was nothing to help—I was at the far end of the room under some sort of a light and they were all sitting at a table—which I think is absolutely rude. So, I made it my point to tell them that, and said I would prefer to have a chair—may I stand by the piano? Something that would make me feel comfortable. Even a prop. A chair, a proscenium to lean on—just something that makes you feel good so that you don't have to worry about, Oh, my gosh, do my hands look all right? So that you don't have to stand outside of yourself and watch you. There are fourteen people out there watching you—so you don't have to watch yourself. Do you know what I'm saying?

GH: Yes.

MORROW: Okay. That's how to be comfortable--use whatever you can.

GH: It's an exchange of energies, then?

MORROW: Oh! Oh, boy! Absolutely. If you can give away your energy, give it away for nothing—you have absolutely notning to lose—they will take it and they might give you something.

GH: Even if you are holding back a little?

MORROW: I don't...I can't do that. I can just show them all my energy and hope that they get caught up in it—and I hope that it's infectious and I think it is. This is why I always like auditioning, like it.

GH: Have you always liked it?

MORROW: Always. From the very beginning. The first audition

did I was reluctant going in the door but once I got in there there was no stopping me. Absolutely no stopping me. That was when I was a toothless teacher at age twenty-three—and fat and Polish...with eyeglasses. Anyway, people say, "Why do you like auditioning?" and I say, because to me it's like a job. Those people will go out of there having seen me perform, and they will spread the word. And then it will go on—and it's like doing a personal appearance for each organization. Word gets around very fast, very fast in the business.

GH: So you are auditioning not just for that specific job.

MORROW: Never! Never! Oh, that's interesting. Another thing—don't think too much about what they want—like dressing the part. Every time I dressed the part I came off badly. Very badly—and absolutely insignificant. I became one of the people lined up against the wall, even though I was in good company—because I was conforming...I was being somebody else. Be yourself because, ultimately, you can't keep changing. A girl whose name I forgot—she was Tammy Grimes' standby and I took over for her. She stood by for everybody—everybody. And I went to an audition and I said, "Hi! How are you?" and she said, "I'm fine. I don't know who to be today." So she had no personality...then, of course, she's never gone anywhere. She never was one person. So, in the long run I think you preserve your own identity.

GH: Or search for it—as we were talking about earlier.

MORROW: Yes. Leave yourself open. But that comes with a challenge, too. Always, again, lead with your strength and what you do. Then, have the director, if he's smart enough, or the producers or the choreographer, whoever it is, have them present the challenge after that and ask for what you can do differently. I don't believe in mystery. Somebody else might, I don't believe in mystery. Coming out and not saying anything to anybody and whispering to your accompanist. Anyhow, an audition is an opportunity—it's an opportunity to expose yourself and to take a chance. After that, after you feel very comfortable, I think, and after you know that you've won round one, then I think you've got to take chances because this is the same as in life. Unless you risk something you're never going to gain anything. Now there are some people who don't know how to handle risk. But you've got to go for broke, I think, and not be afraid. I don't know what's going to help you not be afraid—but just know that if you don't get the job, it's not a personal rejection. Never, ever, ever. If I didn't get the job, I'd say, "Well, I don't care. That must mean that I, Karen, was not the right type." Not that I wasn't good because I knew that I was unique. It has to do with the whim, or a particular idea of those people out there at the moment. What they really have in mind.

GH: Can you second guess them?

MORROW: You can try—but I don't think you can ever know if you really have or not. So all you can be is be true! If they see the truth people are caught up—maybe they don't realize it but they are caught up by that—sucked into the truth. And they will know and say, "I don't know why I like her but there's something about her." Well, it may be truth. So you don't come on and try to be what you think they want. It's the same in a relationship. You can never guess what is in somebody else's mind. You can only say what's on your mind. And if my song is on my mind at this moment then I'm being very honest and very true.

GH: Can you remember the best audition you ever did?

MORROW: Yes, as a matter of fact I think one of the best auditions I ever gave was, oddly enough, for THE GRASS HARP four years before I really played it. Yes, yes—because it was a set! I love auditioning in a theatre. To disarm, I love to disarm people.

GH: How?

MORROW: Ah...surprise! But not phony surprise like pulling out a flag or jumping out of a window. I immediately walk into a theatre and I look around and I see the set—and that was the ILLYA DARLING set and they were auditioning at that theatre, which I think was the Hellinger, for GRASS HARP. And I didn't want to have to think about the words and just stand there. So, I said, "I'm going to carry my music, if you don't mind, because I don't want to have to think about this." They'll never forget this, too, they told me about it. I jumped around, I used the set that was there. I got up on the steps and I sat on the thing and leaned against it and it helped me a great deal. The minute I walk in I look for help—I mean, you're on an empty, big stage. Then you've got to remember what to do with your hands and your feet and your toes and your nose and your hair. But that was probably one of the best auditions I gave. I've done a lot! The worst audition, I think...when I think back on bad auditions it has nothing to do with me. Absolutely nothing to do with me. It's the vibes from the people, again. It's not being treated with respect. There's one good thing about out here, in Hollywood, they make you feel wonderful! Absolutely so dignified and grateful that you are there in their office to read their script and they make you feel pretty and everything! They make me feel pretty. In New York there's not that much time and there's a lot of ego problems.

GH: How do you handle that when people are rude to you and not paying attention to you and so, consequently your audition is not good. Do you have a way of handling that?

MORROW: I'm trying to think of how I handled those. Again, I look for what I know is comfortable—that I can suck them in to my reality. I did that to Ron Moody. If they are not paying attention I jump up and down and wave my arms until they watch. That's what I did there and he was very conscious and very ashamed that he wasn't paying attention, you see. Oh! I think the worst thing that anybody can do is be belligerent, or be hostile. If you do indeed feel hostile and angry toward those people, you must not use that, you must immediately look for something that makes you feel good. Even if it's asking them for a sip of coffee—something that might make you feel good. And take that away from you because—boy, it shows! I mean, don't you know when an actor is belligerent? I know of one now... who goes to his agent and says,"...What are you doing for my career?" You don't want to do anything for his career. People don't want to be uncomfortable. They want someone who's going to carry the ball for them—because they're all scared to death. Writers, producers, directors—they are not sure they are doing the right thing. Nobody is sure. If you're tentative, if you're not so sure you can do the job then they are not going to be too sure you can do the job and it's going to show. I don't think anybody's that good that they can cover that up. Even nerves I think are difficult to cover up.

GH: Do you have them?

MORROW: No.

GH: You don't.

MORROW: No. I have that big perspiration under my arms...but that's not nerves so much as it's just the adrenalin and the excitement. I'll sing for anybody—just within reason, now.

GH: You've always felt like that?

MORROW: Always—more so—because now I'm at the point where I feel I have some sort of a reputation and there are some things that I just won't bother to sing for. When Glenn Jordan asked me to do OLIVER—asked me to come down and sing for Ron Moody, my stomach went "guuch!"—I shouldn't have to sing for them!!! And then I thought, wait a minute, Ron Moody has never heard you sing. Of course, he's going to direct the show—he should know. It's not an audition, you're hired, the offer has been made. And then I thought, I can't wait to go down there and show Ron Moody what he's got. And I mean that in all modesty because it has nothing to do with anything I've done—it's a gift that I've got—but, again, it was my strength. Now, when I got to the book I was very nervous—but I told him that. And I said, "Please ask me to do it again. Please ask me..." And he said, "All right, we'll do it this way." O.K. then I tried to do it. To listen, pull it in, then comes the challenge, listen to the challenge, ask the questions—don't be ashamed of asking the questions if there is anything you don't understand—and then try! And then just plain try—and even if you have your finger up your nose or something embarrassing like that, at least you did it. And he had me do it, like, fourteen different ways—I mean, loud, soft—just to see if there was a range. And it had nothing to do with the ultimate finished product. But that's where the taking a chance comes in, too. If you just dare to—concentrate on what you've been asked to do, no more, don't try to second guess, do just what you are asked to do at that point.

GH: Let me ask you this. When you were auditioning as kind of a matter of course, what kind of preparation did you do before you'd go out on an audition? Or did you prepare?

MORROW: Not really...I would think about who was out there—people that hadn't seen me before. Some minor research about the part. Are they looking for somebody who is big and loud and bubbly or are they looking for somebody who is kind of sensitive—and something into the character. My music very rarely changed. I would do pretty much the same things. I always had extras, just in case. I would have any kind of thing they might want.

GH: *Did you do physical warmups or vocal warmups?*

MORROW: Sure, I would do some vocal leads. Absolutely, do some vocal leads. And I wouldn't eat before.

GH: *Did you psych yourself, in any way?*

MORROW: Just with enthusiasm for walking out onto the stage and meeting new people. Or with old people—have the pleasure of sharing again. That sounds so noble...and in retrospect, do you suppose maybe I'm lying? Do you suppose maybe these things never happened? Or that they are happening in my head now? I don't know. I just know I love it! And I love it because I'm a born show-off! That's why I got into show business. I've been showing off since I was three years old. But I would never dislike anybody for not liking it. I don't dislike those people. Only once did I dislike a system—and that was a pre-view of my last show in New York. I got so angry at the system of judgement. Judgement! I didn't want to be judged that night, I just did not want to be judged because I was having one helluva time with the part—and I saw Hal Prince and all those people come and sit third row center. And I thought...you...rrrrr! And I hit that stage like a bolt of lightning and I heard a laugh come out of the back of the house because that was exactly the way they wanted the part played. I was sensational that night! But I couldn't duplicate it. I mean, I was very "bluugh!" for the rest of the run, which was four days. But, you've got to like those people, I think, and you've got to like what you are doing. If you have ANY DOUBTS, any doubt at all that you are in the right business, then—get out! I really think get out because nobody wants to see somebody who is not committed. I don't want to see a doctor who is not committed, I don't want to see a teacher who is not committed. I don't want to see anybody just passing time. As an audience, I don't want to see an actor up there get rewards for something that they are just doing to pass time. Auditioning is an opportunity to go beyond where you are right now. It's an opportunity to extend yourself—to go outside of yourself a little bit, to become a little bit bigger than life. It's very easy to sit at home and go to class, you know, and think and study and read books, you do a job here and there. But to actually put yourself out and talk to other people, take a chance. You might meet some nice people out there. I'm talking about those that are judging you, too. Filling in the book, filling in the blank pages—it helps to fill in those pages—with names. When I first went to New York, I went to an audition every day and I must have met twenty people after only three days—and the word got around. I went and got an agent right away, I got a pianist right away—people were all of a sudden in my corner. I had a social life. It was wonderful. It was just the most exciting thing. Auditioning meant to live!—to get out with the public. I mean, going to the grocery store isn't going to fill the bill. Going shopping with crowds of people isn't it. It's like going to your club where you are going to see other club members. You all have something in common. To me it was always an opportunity for something. An opportunity for your name to get around, an opportunity to meet a possible mate, even. An opportunity to meet a lunch partner, an opportunity to meet some other talented people that you might want to associate yourself with—like an accompanist. In fact, that's what I feel about jobs now, even jobs that sound crummy. And I remember I kept postponing my nightclub engagement and finally I said, "No, there's going to be something that I can gain from that. It's an opportunity. What's it going to be an opportunity for? It's an opportunity for me to go on a diet!" Ah, hah! So I used it as an opportunity to lose ten pounds—a nine days engagement, or something. You've got to. You've got to do this. That's what auditioning is: it's an opportunity to meet, to do, to extend, to feel, to work.

GH: To live?

MORROW: Sure.

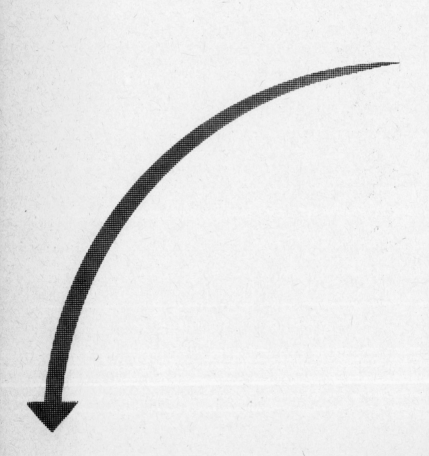

"You have to take a risk. . ."

Charles Nelson Reilly

AN ACTOR TALKS ABOUT AUDITIONING

REILLY: See, when I was in New York recently I went to the William Morris Agency and I passed a door that said "Audition Room" and just seeing that on the door brought back 1950 to 1961, you know, right between the eyes.

GH: *Were those your audition years?*

REILLY: Oh, sure. I never had the courage to audition. Isn't that funny? Auditions are so funny.

GH: *Do you remember your first audition, by any chance?*

REILLY: I'll tell you something—yes—the most important audition— the first audition was 1956. I auditioned for Jerry Herman, who at the time was a piano player in a bar, the Showplace, and he had written a revue, and he lived in a two room apartment in the Village, and I had an appointment to go. Now, at that time, 1956, I was seriously thinking of being a singer. I mean, a real singer. And I had no idea I was funny. But, anyway, I went and I sang and I said to him—and this was in all seriousness, talking about actors and auditioning, I said to him, "Now, I cannot have anyone look at me when I sing." Now, I mean, how many people are you going to be able to put in the theatre with that as a premise? So I said, "I have to turn toward the wall." So then I sang from BRIGADOON that song "There But For You Go I", which was very fake baritone, Earl Wrightson. Do you know what I mean? A few drinks and you could say it was Earl Wrightson. And if you were sober it was a crummy baritone. So I sang, "There But For You Go I" and he almost died he got so hysterical—but I didn't know because I couldn't see because, of course, my back was turned so I couldn't look at him. So, anyway, when it was over he said, "You are definitely in the show." I said, "Of course, with this voice." So, I went and we began a show and he said, you know later he said, "The baritone is Lester James," who had a beautiful voice—for real, and I was the comedian. But he was such a talented man that he realized that I was a comedian.

GH: And you didn't know it.

REILLY: And I didn't know it and I got the appointment through Phyllis Newman, who had a voice lesson after me at Keith Davis. And so she knew that this was a maniac in there trying to sing the flower song from CARMEN and that other one from FAUST. You know, I can't do it now because I have too many caps. And I used to do that and she said, "There's some maniac in the room ahead of me that would be terrific in a revue." So that's how that morning changed my life.

GH: And was that your first New York job—that revue?

REILLY: Of consequence. I used to be in children's theatre and I'd rather not go into that. You didn't have to audition. If you could walk they took you. Clare Tree Major. Remember that name? She had a children's theater. I was the only prince in "Snow White and Rose Red" that wore glasses. It was an historic first. But, yes, the Herman thing was a turning point and then...ah, another moment before that, when I was in summer stock with Richard Berger, who produced Starlight Theatre in Kansas City, I was a bass. And I was a legitimate bass. I got the job by being a bass. And I didn't even have lines or anything, you know, for the first couple of things. But Berger always used to look at me and he would say very quietly, "You know, you're not really a bass." Which I never have forgiven him for.

GH: Let me ask you this. When you go back to those early days when you were struggling so hard—did you have nerves and if the answer is "Yes" then what did you do with them?

REILLY: Well, you see, I was always a nervous performer. So it worked for the crap that I did. Like, my only audition song was "I'm In Love With A West Side Girl " which was a nervous boy. Well, Jerry Herman wrote it and that was the only song I ever used which was very funny. "I'm in love with a west side girl..." and I lived on the east side...And it had wonderful lines like, I was all set to...something or other...and I found out she came on the shuttle, you know, and all that kind of thing. And it was funny so I could always put the nerves into the work—so it didn't look like nerves for nerves' sake. It sort of helped it along all along. But I always knew that it would be all right so I didn't get too nervous at auditions.

GH: *You always knew it would be all right?*

REILLY: Yes, I knew that it would be all right. I knew that eventually I would get to where I had to go and...

GH: *How did you know that?*

REILLY: I don't know.

GH: *You mean, you just knew?*

REILLY: I knew it would be all right. I mean, you live in the roaches in a cheap room and you sell your blood but you have to know it's going to be all right. Do you know what I mean? You have to know— in New York, recently, like four or five years ago, I went to a wonderful party where I used to live on Sullivan Street and I met an actress there. Lois Kibbee was a very fine actress but she was in her own way. Most people are in their own way. And she said, "I have to go home." The party was wonderful because it was such a warm Italian thing with the free spaghetti and it's terrific. We were drinking Black Russians. And she said, "I have to go home because I have a reading in the morning." I said, "Lois, how many readings have you had in the morning and how many jobs have you gotten?" "Not too many." Why don't you stay until you're the last one to leave the party, don't worry about your hair, and go in tomorrow with a little of the party instead of the reading." See, that's the main problem. They always make an adjustment for the consequential thing of getting the job. It's "got to get the job." So, instead of coming in like they come into the Safeway and say, "Where's your liver? Where's the dog food?" they come in, and because it's consequential, they change. Like, in the theatre, they go, "Half hour." Now, half hour to me means a half an hour to change to something else and you can't change. Oh, by the way, Lois got the job which lasted four years—the lead in a television daytime soap opera and right now she's in another one.

GH: You mean, after staying at the party?

REILLY: After staying at the party—she got the part. That's true. She's now moved to a penthouse in her fifth or sixth year as Queen of the Soaps and has written two books. The Christine Jorgensen book and the Joan Bennett book. I mean, that doesn't mean if you have spaghetti you can become Eugene O'Neill but I mean there's some connection.

GH: Let me ask you about commercials. Have you been on situations where they go in and just ask you to start winging something for a commercial?

REILLY: Yes. That's hard, that's hard.

GH: What happens there?

REILLY: See, what I did, I never was a good ad-libber but I did three years of Excedrin commercials. And in the three years I became loose as an actor. It takes a long time to do that. You mean improvise.

GH: Yes. What did you do?

REILLY: I really don't know. It was just very difficult the first year.

GH: Did you create those yourself or were you given a format?

REILLY: We created them ourselves. And then the last year we wrote them...because there were so many, to edit them was taking forever. Like, we would do a half-hour spot that they would edit down to a minute. You know, they were wonderful.

GH: *Would you sit around a microphone?*

REILLY: Yes, twenty minutes. And everything is an Excedrin headache. I mean, you'd write the thing down during the day and you'd just come in...that's a hard thing to discuss, improvisation, isn't it?

GH: *Yes. Because a lot of actors are asked to go into a situation like, "Now you're the husband and wife and you are coming to look at the new home. What do you say?" Boom! And they're on, as an audition, you know?*

REILLY: Yes, that's hard. And I think the most talented ones survive. I mean, that couldn't be harder...I don't know how to do that. You just do it, you just talk. You can't try to aim it to be comedic, you have to try to just deal with the partner, moment to moment.

GH: *Does taking a chance have something to do with it?*

REILLY: Yes. Risk is a big word. Risk is a big word in all of that stuff. Like Herbert Bergoff says, "Angel, darling, the best vay to audition vot you have to do is, you do anything to get the part," which is pretty good. Then another story you can put in—Gerry Jedd, who's dead now, was a great actress. She died maybe about eight years ago. She was a great actress and she was in New York getting in her own way, and she had a friend that sold orange drinks at the Alvin Theatre. And the orange drink salesman at the Alvin Theatre told her that they were reading for Gittel, for London, and he said, "I know the stage manager and you can get an appointment." So she read and she got the part. She later played the part with Peter Finch in London and won over Lynn Fontanne in THE VISIT and Gertrude Berg in A MAJORITY OF ONE and Margaret Leighton in something—SEPA—RATE TABLES I think, as the best actress. She got the part and she, Gerry Jedd, went to her agent, and she said, "They are reading for Gittel." and the agent said, "Yes, and you are not right that's why I didn't send you." And she said, "No, I got the part. You have to call about the money." So you see there's no rules, that's what's difficult. You go with yourself, I guess. That doesn't make too much sense.

GH: *Yes, it does.*

REILLY: You see, a lot of young actors are always looking for some-body in a blue suit that's going to do it for them. Now, the most important audition I did was for HOW TO SUCCEED...They wanted a dance lead, you see, like Harry in BRIGADOON or—in those days the musicals always had the second or third man who was the dance lead. So they had tried everybody in New York and they couldn't find a dancer who was really funny, as well. So Bobby Morse was my friend and he said to Abe Burrows, "I know somebody who'd be perfect." and he said, "Charles Nelson Reilly." and Abe Burrows said, "Who is that?" So they arranged an audition for me at the Mark Hellinger Theatre and the main thing was: could I dance? So, at the time I was an understudy to Dick Van Dyke and I had danced the "Happy Face" number with the two girls. And the "Happy Face" number is about seven minutes and it's a dance number—Gower Champion, up and down stairs, and if you make a mistake you kick a teen-ager and knock her down in front of 3,000 people. And there again you have to face the audience, you can't put your face to the wall, which I did in the beginning of my career. So, I called up both girls—Sharon was one and oh, another lovely kid, and they both had commer-cials and the two understudies were out. So, the only thing I could do for Bob Fosse and Hugh Lambert—there were two choreographers, was to do the "Happy Face" routine, which was the only routine I knew, without the two girls. Now, I had tried for four girls—the two understudies to the two girls and the two originals. And all of them I couldn't find. So I had to go in and dance this dance without the two girls but as if the two girls were there. Now when I went in I saw that both Fosse and Hugh Lambert had towels around their necks. So, I got a towel and put it around my neck. Like, if you're a dancer look out because here I come and my dance shoes, Capezio, which I wore in BYE, BYE, BIRDIE and then I danced the "Happy Face" number, all the time explaining while I was doing it what the other two girls were doing. And also it was in the Mark Hellinger Theatre where Mary Martin was playing THE SOUND OF MUSIC. So the set was up for THE SOUND OF MUSIC. So every once in a while I stopped while I did, "The hills are alive...(singing).." as if the walls were permeated with Mary Martin. So then I had three missing women, you see. So, the audition was sensational...and then Frank Loesser came right on the stage and said, "You have the part. At last I know how to write it. And at last I know what kind of music to write." and I said, "Well, whatever you write..." I've forgotten what I said, "I can't promise you anything." But I knew when I was doing it that it was a sensational thing. So, the point is: you have to make do with what you've got. So if there's a set on the stage, then use it. In other words, what could have been a mistake in going without the two partners—in my turn it enhanced it. And if I had the two girls there it would have stunk but without the girls...in other words, I took advantage of everything and so it was right.

GH: *Had you prepared any of this?*

REILLY: No, I had been rehearsing eight months in dance routines— that I knew backwards and forwards but I couldn't do it without the girls. And I counted out loud, too, which was funny. Turn, one, two, face. Because I had to count out loud. But with the orchestra, when you are doing the part, you don't hear that.

GH: *We were talking about risk and that has something to do...*

REILLY: You have to take a risk, yes. See, most people when they audition will come out with the same song they've used before. Now, it hasn't gotten them anything but they are still going to use that same song. You know what I mean? I guess now it's...what is it now? I left off when it was "Who Can I Turn To?"—or something like that. Anyhow, you also have to, if you are reading for a part, get the material ahead of time and to study up on it. You know?

GH: *Do you find ways of doing that?*

REILLY: I would just ask or have the agent ask, or something. But the most important thing is—it has to become a routine that's natural rather than an intrusion that's a job opportunity. It's the 'job opportunity' that makes everybody shatter, I think. Like, when I teach— you saw the thing—the two boys were lovely, that did BLUE DENIM. You know? Before class they are out practicing it in the parking lot. And you look at them and you see them standing a certain way, their hands in the pockets, and they are terrific. Right away they got an A. They're great. Now, from the parking lot to the stage—you see, they have to walk a half a block, something happens to them because now it's for real. And I do it myself. Like, everyone says, "You are very good in rehearsal." The camera rehearsal, before we shoot the scene.

But then, everybody, except Spencer Tracy...you just know that this is the consequence time and you make that slight buck-up adjustment.

GH: Let me ask you this which might, in a strange way, be helpful. Can you remember your worst audition?

REILLY: I remember, yes, Jerry Stiller and I...(Now, today it would be expensive to get us). You get Jerry Stiller and I auditioning for Tamara Geva for some play at the York Playhouse where we were to be clowns. Now, I don't know what it was but we were a team like Bobchinscky and Dobchinsky, or something, but we were clowns and we worked as a team and we prepared and I remember that my glasses got broken and he was bleeding. Because the two of us together are too much energy. And I remember we were just ushered out like, "Thank you so much." It was terrible, awful. It's funny but I guess I blocked that whole thing out. Oh, something else...You've got to know that the people out there need you just as much as you need them. They are looking for the right person.

GH: Most actors don't know that.

REILLY: Yes. I mean, they are friends. They are looking. And it's the way you walk out. You just walk out and say, "Hello." You've got to just be able to say, "Hello, I'm so and so." which is very difficult. Now, yesterday I woke up early...I was whisked to the studio while the producers had a private screening just for me. And I didn't face the wall. I walked right in and it was to show me *The Diana Rigg Show.* "Hello, darling!" So, in other words, they had done all of this—she had done the series, they had done the whole thing so that one Monday morning a former usher, who used to face the wall and sold his blood, could come in all by himself to see if it was all right that he might possibly be part of it. So, there was just me in the room and the agent and just as it started I laughed and I thought of the line, which you've got to use in the book—when Marilyn Monroe vomited at the audition for understudy in *All About Eve*—she had an audition and she vomited and she was waiting by the lobby and George Saunders came to pick her up and he said, "C'mon my dear." He said, "We'll try television." and she said, "Oh, are there auditions in television?" and he said, "That's all television is, my dear. A series of auditions." So, I thought of that and I laughed right out loud because they were auditioning this great actress, who had a whole front page of *The New York Times* last Sunday and she was wonderful. But it goes on forever. So, whatever adjustment you can make to help yourself now, works for you for the rest of your life. I don't know dance auditions—singer auditions. Singers should learn the new songs. They get caught up with the old habits. And they don't grow because as soon as they pick up the old song, with the old song comes all the old habits, all the old problems and all the memories connected to that song, which usually led them to defeat. But still they take out the song. Do you know what I mean? And they should learn a new song.

GH: Do you keep current with your song? You have one song.

REILLY: I have one song. I left in a blaze of glory.

GH: Charlie, it seems to me that the really key thing that you said there—and,you know, people have different ways of finding that out—is that you knew.

REILLY: Yes, you've got to know. And that's free. I mean, you have to think it's going to be all right. You have to know. Now, I had bad teeth—they were all falling out. My hair was coming out. I was a mess. Phyllis Diller started at 40. Did you know that? She started at 40, in San Francisco, she went to a night club and she saw a woman get up and said, "I could do better than that." And she started at 40. So, the age has nothing to do with it. There's another thing. I do a lot of commercials with Marian Mercer. You know. Radio. And what I find about radio people is that they will go, "Well, what voice do you want?" And that's not what radio is. What it is is—it's a life and somehow the microphone gets in the way. So, Marian Mercer has no voices except one yet with the one she has everything. And that's what people have to think about when they audition. If you can try to go in with just yourself, yourself is everything. Do you know what I mean? You've got to find that. But most people don't service the material because they are too busy with, "Would you want Voice 9?" And Marian doesn't have any of that. Do you know what I mean? So, I guess you can sum up with what Herbert Bergoff says, "You do anything to get the part." You can sit down on the stage or stand up. I auditioned—it was a very important audition, funny it's coming back to me now. It was the Phoenix Theatre Company. And the stage was set for ONCE UPON A MATTRESS and I used the whole thing and I auditioned with the opening speech, which is terrific for men, from THE GLASS MENAGERIE, and you don't do anything—Mr. Williams already did it and you just have to talk—speak. You know, you just have to tell them about "my father fell in love with long distance"—you know. And "the play is memory" and everything. And, as I did that I used the set as if it was my kitchen or my living room—where I live with my mother and my sister. So if you use the things around you, even if it's ONCE UPON A MATTRESS, you can make it work...because the guy ahead of you didn't use it and the guy after you won't use it. So it's not an intrusion. An enhancement, if you have the courage to use it. Do you see what I mean? Because the other guys didn't. And I got the job and I decided, since I already did 22 Off-Broadway shows, and that was Off-Broadway, I would go to Broadway. And, of course, the rest is history! Darlings!

GORDON HUNT
(Director and Casting Director)

Mr. Hunt is one of the West Coast's leading Casting Directors, serving in that capacity for the Mark Taper Forum for the last five years. As such, he has cast over 100 plays and musicals including the premiere production of the Pulitzer Prize/Tony Award winning production of THE SHADOW BOX. He has also served as West Coast Casting Director for many Broadway shows including ANNIE, THE ACT, PAL JOEY and PIPPIN.

As a director, Mr. Hunt's work has ranged from New York...where he directed musicals and plays for Music Theatre of Lincoln Center, Equity Library Theatre, The New Dramatists Committee and all the leading summer stock theatres...to the Mark Taper Forum and Mark Taper Lab, where he has directed world premiere performances of six plays. He recently staged Leonard Bernstein's MASS with the Kansas City Philharmonic.

His directing assignments have also taken him to Australia once to do the award winning 1776 and again to direct SAME TIME NEXT YEAR.

He teaches an advanced acting class and serves as a director of the Los Angeles Civic Light Opera Workshop.

Notes

Notes

Notes

Notes

Notes

Notes

Notes

Notes

Notes

Notes

Notes